The Tourist Tra

Brian Moynahan was born in 1941, and educated at
Sherborne and Corpus Christi College, Cambridge where
he was a Foundation Scholar. As a foreign correspondent,
largely for the *Sunday Times*, he has covered events in more
than 50 countries. His interest in the travel industry dates
from his wedding, when he and his bride travelled to
Malaysia to find that their honeymoon hotel consisted of a
concrete mixer and a wet hole in the ground. Over the
years, he has been shot up in luxury hotels in the Caribbean
and Middle East, robbed in Puerto Rico, ripped off in Paris
and Saigon, and brings a weight of experience to his theme.
His previous book, *Airport International* (Pan and
Macmillan), was a best-selling exposé of the international
airline industry and was translated into four languages. A
Senior Editor on the Sunday Times Magazine, he lives in
London with his wife and two children.

Also by Brian Moynahan
in Pan Books

Airport International

Brian Moynahan

THE TOURIST TRAP

The hidden horrors of the holiday business
and how to avoid them

Pan Original
Pan Books London and Sydney

First published under the title Fool's Paradise 1983 by Pan Books Ltd,
Cavaye Place, London SW10 9PG
New edition entitled The Tourist Trap 1985
© Brian Moynahan 1983, 1985
ISBN 0 330 28881 4
Printed and bound in Great Britain by
Collins, Glasgow

for William, Katie and Helmut

Contents

Introduction

It will not seem it to the man at Luton Airport with the bucket and spade and the children and the delayed departure to the Spanish sun, but he is the core of an industry of phenomenal growth that is expected to be second only to defence by the end of the century. Tourism already employs more than world oil and steel combined, though based simply on the 'four S', Sun, Sand, Sea and Sex.

It does so in hundreds of trades. Some are relatively new, the villa salesmen, car hire agents, foreign currency clerks, charter yacht skippers, ski instructors. Some are traditional, the waiters, chefs, pickpockets, tarts of both sexes, pavement artists and chambermaids. All live off the anxious man at Luton.

In 1981, 310 million people took a holiday abroad. They spent $95 billion, excluding air fares. That in itself accounted for more than six per cent of world trade. Add holidays taken at home and the figures quadruple. On the whim of a tourist's destination, concrete covers a coastline or a country goes into decline.

This is a megabusiness. Yet, since it is made up of millions of individual experiences, it does not have the flavour of an industry. 'Nothing is more personal in business than the relation between a hotel and its guests,' says the manager of the London Ritz.

Quite so. It was my own relations with that excellent hotel chain, Inter-Continental, that alerted me to the unique appeal of the travel industry. Despite the vastness, it operates, as far as the traveller is concerned, on the smallest scale with unpredictable results. A trip can be truly the high point or the disaster of a lifetime. No other business can provide that.

I was staying at the Embajador Inter-Continental in

Santo Domingo during some local disturbances that had resulted in American intervention. I was inadvertantly involved in a bizarre wedding between a local streetwalker and an expatriate banker, a temporary resident of the hotel.

During the reception, paratroopers of the 82nd Airborne Division exchanged shots with US Marines stationed in the swimming pool cabanas and the bunkers of the hotel mini-golf course. Both sides mistook each other for rebels.

From there, I went to the Amman Inter-Continental, to be trapped in the Black September fighting. The assistant night manager billed me before I was evacuated on a Red Cross bus. He charged full rate for room and meals. Much of the room had been destroyed and the meals were a bowl of rice a day. I told him that I laughed at his bill.

'And I laugh at your bus,' he said.

'Why? There's nothing funny about it. It's just a bus.'

'The bill also, sir, is just a bill. But without it there will be no bus.'

'I am going on the bus. I have been shot at for eight days.'

'So has everyone else, sir. They are not going on the bus.'

'King Hussein has arranged that bus to take us out of here. The king is great.'

'The king is great but he is not paying your bill.'

He motioned to an Arab Legion sergeant who stood next to him at the hotel's shattered entrance. The sergeant's face was pitted with cordite and hostility.

'You pay, or no bus,' he said. 'Stay Amman. Bad.'

'Very bad. That is why the king has given us the bus. The king is great.'

'Fuck the king.' He paused. The Legion was said to be devoted to its diminutive and plucky monarch. This treasonable talk showed a passionate attachment to the bill. 'Fuck the bus. You want go Beirut, you pay.'

I did. In Beirut, I stayed at the Phoenicia Inter-Continental, an excellent hotel that was soon to go the way of its sister in Amman, only more so. Christian gunmen ate pâté and truffles in the basement. A Muslim rocket cut off the water supply and they lived on the hotel's supplies of alcohol, which may have contributed to their defeat. When the Muslim gunmen took the Phoenicia, they filled a bath with complimentary eau de cologne sachets and used it to wash the grease off shells.

Later, the Ayatollah did for the cellars of the Tehran Inter-Continental. Manager Hartwig Schnuppe looked on with tears in his eyes, from emotion and the fumes, as revolutionary guards poured $315,000 worth of fine wines and spirits down the drain, victim of Iran's anti-alcoholic religious fervour.

This is one of the biggest and best-run hotel chains, sold in 1981 to Grand Metropolitan for £340 million. But travel is always full of incident. Anything that is rapidly expanding and that deals with people away from home is certain to be that.

The growth is extraordinary. Tourism is worth a billion dollars a year or more in twenty-two countries. It is the major foreign currency earner in countries like Spain, Greece, Morocco and Ireland. In Britain, it has overtaken insurance as the major source of invisible exports. It benefits British airlines by £900 million a year, shops like Harrods by more than a billion pounds, hotel keepers by £750 million, restaurants by £350 million, cinemas, theatres and casinos by £270 million, and coach and taxi owners by £250 million.

It affects the balance of payments of major industrial countries. The thirty million foreign tourists who visited France in 1980 brought ten billion francs more with them than French tourists took out. On the other hand, West Germans travelled more than any other nationality, leaving the Americans, French, Canadians and British trailing in their wake in that order. The $8.5 billion they spent put pressure on the mark.

The effects on capital cities like London can be considerable. Overseas visitors bring £2.1 billion a year to London, spend nearly £1.5 million a week on London Transport and create 220,000 jobs.

Some cities, like Benidorm, have been built entirely for tourists and those who service them. A fishing village in 1956, with a guest house and a couple of holiday villas, by 1981 it had a quarter of a million beds and could take five million visitors a year. It had thrown up an estimated forty-five millionaires. The early ones speculated in land that has risen from an average of £8 to £120,000 an acre. Next came the hoteliers, the fortunes going to those who bought and sold hotels rather than simply ran them, for the profit margins on running package hotels are razor thin. Builders, chain restaurant owners, a big pedalo operator, food wholesalers and lawyers specializing in land deals and evading planning permission added to the list.

This tourist gold-mine has also pumped raw sewage off its beaches at the rate of quarter of a million gallons a day and had a seven-man fire department to protect its millions of visitors.

No matter. It is growth that matters to the industry. Plans to turn a West African state into a vast holiday camp called Tarzania have reluctantly been shelved. Other fantasy worlds, costing up to $1 billion, have been created. Set firmly in the past or the future, nothing reminds the tourist of today. Thus, Disneyland in California offers King Arthur's Carousel and Frontierland, with Mark Twain's steamboat and Tom Sawyer's raft, or Tomorrowland, with Space Mountain and Mission to Mars.

Holidays grow apace with the industry. In 1961, ninety-seven per cent of British workers had two weeks or less paid holidays. By 1981, only one in a hundred had a fortnight and most had a month or more. At the same time, spending by holidaymakers abroad had increased from £150 million a year to £1,750 million.

They were no longer spending it on individual trips to the old resorts in France, Switzerland and Germany. Most were going on package tours to the Mediterranean, which tourism is said to have changed more than the Greeks,

Phoenicians, Romans and Napoleon combined. Physically, if not culturally, that is undoubtedly true. Since 1923, when hotels stayed open for the newfangled summer season for the first time, more than half the coast of the northern Mediterranean has been developed.

By 1981, almost as many British holidaymakers were flying to Spanish hotels as drove to the South West to stay in a caravan or guest house. The ten-night break in Devon and Cornwall in July was about to be overtaken by the August fortnight on a Spanish Costa.

The business looks set for further expansion. The World Tourism Organization reports that it remains dynamic in recession. People are willing to make sacrifices, even of food, for their annual dose of the four Ss. Holidays ranked as the expenditure people were least willing to reduce. Where twenty-eight per cent would cut back on clothing, and fourteen per cent would reduce their spending on food, only six per cent were willing to spend less on holidays.

At its best, the industry offers superb value for money. A fortnight can be had in a foreign resort, with rooms, meals and air travel, for the cost of a suit. It has opened up the world. Anyone with the price of a secondhand Mini can tour New Guinea, wallow in luxury in Tahiti or climb Mount Aconcagua, and come home with some change. It has given much pleasure, employment and profit.

It has also ruined beauty spots from Corfu to Copocabana. It is turning the Mediterranean into a dead sea. Hundreds of thousands of peasants have become landless building workers and waiters. (This is normally reckoned a bad thing, though the ex-peasants themselves may be delighted.) It has seriously corrupted moral values in places suddenly opened to tourism, like Fiji and the Philippines. It often does little for the morals of the tourists, either. The divorce rate for the British on the Costa del Sol is four times that in Britain. The specialist gambling resorts, Las Vegas or Monte Carlo, can lead to ruin.

And, of course, that traditional partner of travel, the

rip-off, is also a great growth industry. Bill padding in Paris after Easter has become so common that it is considered to be simply a sort of tourist tax. As the tourist season approaches, chefs practise cooking pork to look like veal. Gallery and shop owners order 'antiqued' prints, furniture and curios. Pickpockets hone their skills: in one department in the South of France, the Var, which includes St Tropez, an average of 250 thefts were being reported every twenty-four hours in the summer of 1981.

The individual traveller will be startled by many facets of the industry he and the four Ss support. An apparently straightforward affair like traveller's cheques has an unexpected bonanza worth several hundred million pounds a year to those who issue them. A cruise ship could seem safely isolated from the raffishness and trickery of land. Far from it.

Even the basics, eating, drinking and sleeping, turn out to be far from simple on careful examination.

1 THE BUSINESS

Travel agents

The first links in the chain that tugs the tourist on holiday are the travel agent and the tour operator. At best, they are pioneers of experience and flair. Thomas Cook created mass foreign travel with the help of the newfangled railways. Sir Arnold Lunn turned the habit of strapping boards to the feet, and falling down snow-covered Swiss cow pastures, from an eccentricity into the multi-billion pound skiing industry.

At their worst, their interest in commission is overriding. Travel agents live off commissions. The more a traveller is charged, the more commission his travel agent will make. The interests of the travel agent and the public are therefore diametrically opposed, and far from being the tourist's best friend, the travel agent is often his worst enemy.

When British Airways announced that air fares on many routes would be halved, travel agents denounced this as 'diabolical' and 'appalling'. That is hardly the customer's point of view. Because of the commission system, travel agents are usually opposed to fare cutting. They are reluctant to discuss and explain group discounts or advance purchase tickets, which may cost them half their commission. They frequently overcharge on scheduled flights by applying the standard fare when the customer might qualify for one of the many discount fares available. They also tend to recommend the airlines, package holiday operators, car hire firms and shipping lines that pay them the highest commission.

Evidence of overcharging is rife. I contacted ten travel agents, all members of the Association of British Travel Agents, for a return air ticket to Nice. Only one quoted the lowest available fare. Another sample of ten were little better with a request for Malaga, an airport awash with British tourists throughout the holiday season. Two got it right.

This appalling record is not confined to flights. *Holiday Which?* wrote: 'Anonymous visits to nearly 200 travel agents left us more than disappointed with the help and advice they gave our holidaymakers.

'When asked, for example, the quickest and/or cheapest ferry to the North coast of Spain, only a quarter of the agents gave the correct answer, and only eight out of ninety-eight gave the total cost correctly.'

When asked the price of the cheapest package safari holiday to Kenya and northern Tanzania, fewer than half the travel agents answered correctly and they also gave wrong information about the necessary vaccinations and visas.

Travel agents have been found to give outrageously bad advice or wrong information.* *Holiday Which?* had an anonymous inspector who asked one agent to recommend a hotel on Corfu. He came up with one on the island of Kos, 500 miles away. Others, asked for advice on the Bahamas, quoted a fare 'direct to Barbados' or recommended the island of St Lucia. Both these are in the West Indies, many hundred miles from the Bahamas.

Another agent told the inspector: 'the Bahamas are like a powder keg; the Government does not encourage tourism'. Several said that the wet month of October would be a good month to go.

Asked for advice about crossing the Adriatic from Italy to Corfu, two agents said that it was impossible and two others said that the best way would be to drive all the way round the Greek mainland and get a ferry from there. Another suggested taking a ferry from Naples to Piraeus in Greece. In fact, several ferry operators run between Brindisi and Corfu.

Even agents who knew the correct way did not know

* *The Times*, 4 September 1980.

how the ferries ran. Some said there was one a day, others five. Five agents said that visas were needed for the Bahamas, and one said that a smallpox vaccination was obligatory. Not so.

More than two-thirds of the agents, asked about the resort of Kanoni on Corfu, did not mention that it was highly developed and overlooked the airport and suffered a great deal of noise. 'A nice, quiet, out-of-the-way place,' said one. The conclusion was that, although six million people a year book with agents, good ones are thin on the ground.

It is true that fare structures have become very complex, with as many as twenty different rates being charged in the same aircraft between London and Los Angeles, for example. But there are not twenty different rates between London and Nice, or on a ferry from Brindisi to the Greek Islands.

'Of course, they do understand the complexities. But it's in their interest to ignore them,' says fares expert Martin Page. 'Eight per cent commission on a standard £200 fare is £16 in the agent's pocket. Eight per cent of a Supersaver Off-season Friday night £65 fare, which the customer doesn't ever know he is entitled to get, is £5.20. The standard fare is charged. It's wrong, but its legal.'

Travel agents may be on a 'preferred' or higher rate of commission from a particular package tour operator, whose holidays they will plug. A bonus scheme may put them on a higher rate if they sell a certain number of holidays, which they will try hard to do, regardless of how they will suit individual customers. Bonuses pay a further one to five per cent on top of the flat ten per cent commissions.

A travel agent's commission list makes interesting reading: British Rail pay him seven per cent; cruise lines pay from seven to ten per cent; P & O give 7 per cent for summer cruises, eight per cent on fly-cruises and 8½ per cent on winter cruises; Cunard and Chandris pay ten per cent, which makes them more attractive to the agent, if not to the public. Some foreign cruise lines will pay up to fourteen per cent commission to get passengers aboard ships with poor reputations.

Theatre tickets normally carry 7½ per cent, and some from big companies like Keith Prowse, add on as much as fifteen per cent. The major airlines like British Airways, which are members of the IATA cartel, pay 7½ or eight per cent on domestic tickets and nine per cent on international tickets. Charter and smaller airlines pay from ten to 12½ per cent.

Package holiday operators pay the same and so do coach firms. An agent normally gets a ten per cent commission for a hotel booking, which involves one phone call to the local sales office. In turn this will be charged at up to five times the amount for sending a telex to the hotel.

Maps sold by travel agents are very expensive. This is because they get from twenty-five to thirty-five per cent commission for selling them. The principle is also true of traveller's cheques, which the agent is likely to recommend at least partly because it benefits him.

Any travel agent can now provide traveller's cheques. This can mean an average extra profit of £3.50 a booking. With car ferry bookings, where motorists going on holiday carry a lot of funds for petrol, meals and hotels *en route*, compared to a package tourist, the profit can be as high as £10 a booking. Thomas Cook, which issues over £1.5 billion a year in traveller's cheques, normally pays travel agents half a per cent commission but this can increase to one per cent if an agent sells £125,000 worth of cheques a year. There is nothing disinterested about a travel agent recommending traveller's cheques.

Rent-a-Wreck

Another of the travel agent's many vested interests is in directing a customer to the hire car company that pays him the biggest commissions. These vary from twenty per cent to fifty per cent on reaching incentive targets. Typically, Avis, Hertz and Europcar offer twenty per cent, Godfrey Davis, Kenning and Thrifty, fifteen per cent. The travel agent is likely to favour a 'twenty per center', as he will call it.

These may not represent the best buy for the traveller. Indeed a survey* of nine European countries showed that the 'fifteen per centers' are the cheapest. Rates were examined in France, Germany, Italy, Switzerland, Holland, Belgium, Spain, Sweden and Britain. Godfrey Davis and Budget were cheaper than Hertz and Avis in every case on a one-day, 100 kilometre basis.

They were often much cheaper. Thus, in the UK, Budget charged £9.25 for a small car and Hertz charged £14.04. In Switzerland, Godfrey Davis charged £14.28 and Avis £22.02.

There are substantial differences between countries which are rarely pointed out by agents. A Ford Escort can cost £50 a week more in Switzerland than in France, which could make it worthwhile to hire in France and drive to Switzerland. The competitiveness of companies also varies, as the Hertz against Avis battle shows. The 'World's Number One' is cheaper in Denmark and Italy. The two firms tie in Belgium and Holland. The 'We Try Harder' people win in France, Switzerland and Germany.

It is interesting that the Avis discount rate is only five per cent in the US. This is because car hire is generally competitive and cheap there. However, there are insurance snags, particularly in that new Mecca for European tourists, Florida.

Angry travellers have complained that they were unwittingly providing their own insurance cover for hire cars. The law in Florida allows rental car companies to make the renter's personal liability and personal injury protection insurance primarily responsible if he causes an accident.

* Executive Travel and Leisure, 1979.

Not all rental companies in Florida refuse primary coverage. The Big Three – Hertz, Avis and National – offer primary liability coverage, as do Greyhound, Merlin, Budget/Sears and American International. But most smaller companies have taken advantage of Florida law and thus have lowered their own insurance costs by letting their customers take the risk.

The man fighting to get the law changed, Miami attorney Donald Pevsner, is cordially disliked by the rental car business world-wide. The compliment is returned. Mr Pevsner has as little time for the industry, Big Three included, as it has for him. 'There are rip-offs rampant beyond belief,' he says.

He describes one contract: 'If the customer reads the fine print, he wouldn't sign it. But customers don't read fine print. If the extra-cost Collision Damage Waiver fee is not paid, the customer is assuming liability for the car's entire value. Allowing anyone under twenty-one to drive the car voids the insurance totally. The customer is liable not only to the total damage to the car, but also towage and storage and £6 a day 'loss of use'.

'All insurance is voided if the customer does not file a written report of an accident within twenty-four hours of its occurrence. The rental firm can refuse to reimburse the customer if he fixes the car on the road from his own pocket. The rental firm provides only secondary liability insurance. The final catch-all clause seizes the customer if the others did not. The insurance is voided if any motor vehicle statute is violated. Say drifting over a double line for a second, or speeding five mph over the limit.'

This is a contract of a small agency. But Pevsner also attacks the giants. He considers the Collision Damage Waivers of Hertz, Avis and National to be grossly expensive. 'In the US, CDW runs at $2 a day for a waiver on the first $250 of damage. It's slightly more in Europe. The company can thus get $730 a year for $250 worth of collision damage. CDW must be the world's worst protection buy in actuarial terms, and a tremendous money-maker for the companies.'

Pevsner considers that 'car-rental contracts are a virtual "snake-pit" of traps for unwary and unsuspecting renters, usually pressured to just "Sign here and drive off" '.*

The big firms can be expensive, but at least the car will be in good condition. Smaller outfits may palm off unsound cars, rebuilds from insurance write-offs, ex-fleet and police vehicles that have already had the heart driven out of them. There are some agencies in the US that make an honest living renting out battered cars, advertising them as Rent-a-Wreck.

Beware of Greeks driving cars

The general legal leniency extended to tourists does not include driving. In some countries, foreign drivers are more severely dealt with than locals. High bail limits are set in Spain following accidents. Car insurance should include provision for bail bonds, since a driver who cannot raise bail is likely to be detained before the case is heard. In the Middle East, notably Saudi Arabia, compensation is often demanded if a local is killed in an accident, even though he was at fault. Thus, a British driver was held for eight

---

* Those who reckon a car too much trouble can always try an animal. Similar trickery can apply, however. 'When hiring a camel, the traveller should note its brand and general appearance,' states the Harvard Travellers' Club, 'in order to be quite sure afterwards that he sets out with the same beast he hired, or thought he did. Rheumy-eyed camels, or those which slaver over-much, camels which on rising are seen to tumble slightly in the hind legs, are to be looked on with suspicion.' There is one advantage over the car. If the camel does drop down, it can be eaten. That way the traveller gets some of his money back. The Club recommends the meat from the hump and ribs.

months before £7,000 was paid to the family of a man who had driven into his broken-down truck.

Agents should make sure that clients have valid insurance if they are driving abroad. Tourists are particularly liable to accidents. According to Europ Assistance, France is the danger area. Almost half the accidents involving British drivers abroad take place in France, particularly in the Pas de Calais, routes N42 and N43, Lille, Bordeaux, Toulouse, Perpignan and Brittany.

There are four main reasons. Driving on the right is a problem, particularly when turning left. The priority to the right rule is misunderstood. Tired drivers crash rushing to catch a ferry. Overtaking in a right-hand drive car is difficult.

It is inevitable that the incidence should be high in France, since it attracts the most GB plates. Europ Assistance found that twelve per cent of crashes occur in Spain and Portugal, where Barcelona, the Costa Brava, San Sebastian and the Algarve rate high. Overspeeding on bad roads is the chief cause.

Germany accounts for ten per cent, largely in Munich and the South. Most crashes happen after drivers leave autobahns for ordinary roads. Italy's eight per cent, primarily in Tuscany, is accounted for by the heat, tiredness and unpredictable pedestrians. Switzerland and the Austrian Tyrol both have seven per cent and the same chilling reason: heavy braking on mountain roads leading to brake failure.

Greece is dangerous, since the Greeks are amongst the worst drivers in the world. They run up twice as many deaths as any other Western European country. In 1979, there were 195 deaths per 100,000 cars. Ireland was next with 95, Belgium had 91, France 90, the Netherlands 64, and the much-maligned Italians 58. The British did well at 46, though the Americans registered an excellent 37.

The Greek epidemic is so bad that an international medical conference discussed it, and decided that the undisciplined and individualistic Greek character was to blame. 'It is undeniable that Greek drivers are extremely temperamental,' was the conclusion. 'They have the mistaken impression that everyone is out to challenge and demean them and therefore must be defeated, which leads to a vicious circle of illegality and recklessness.'

Adequate insurance cover for luggage in cars is particularly important in Italy where thieves make a good living stealing from cars with foreign number plates. They do not steal only from parked cars. There are traffic light gangs. One member slashes a tyre when a tourist's car draws up at the lights. The driver gets out to investigate. The others wait for him to go to summon help, and then loot the car. Sometimes, they do not wait. A Leeds couple had a tyre slashed at traffic lights in Milan. As the husband jacked the car up, his jacket with his traveller's cheques and cash was lifted from the front seat.

Insurance – what's it worth to the tourist?

Stolen money can ruin a trip, and illness abroad can be worse. Under-insured Europeans have been faced with having to sell their houses to pay American medical bills. Adequate insurance is necessary, but it can come expensive.

When it comes to travel insurance, travel agents often get commissions as high as 37½ per cent paid by travel insurance firms. This means that the tourist is being seriously overcharged for his insurance. It also gives travel agents an incentive to load customers with unnecessary policies. Many winter sports brochures already include insurance in the price, for example, so a further policy is a waste of money.

Travel insurance, besides often being expensive, is also confusing. Some insurance companies repay on the basis of the total possible life of an article. With the life of a suitcase reckoned at eight years, the company will only pay half its value if it is lost after four years. Other companies pay the new replacement value.

Many policies are subject to the nasty principle of 'average'. Say there is cover under the 'Loss of Luggage' section of £200. The luggage is actually worth £600. If it is all lost, you get £200. But if half of it is lost (meaning £300 out of £600), the insurance company, according to the principle of 'average', will only pay out half the sum insured, or £100.*

Insurance taken out before a flight or holiday does not cover industrial disputes, although strikes aimed at causing maximum inconvenience to tourists are now commonplace in Spain, France and Portugal as well as Britain. 'You could go to a solicitor, you could tackle the French air traffic controllers, you could go to the Almighty,' said Airline Users' Committee Director General, James Lawrie. 'But there's not the slightest chance of compensation.'

Some form of travel insurance is worthwhile, particularly for those in the forty-five to sixty-five age group. In 1979, four per cent of travel insurance policy holders made a claim, a high proportion by insurance standards. Most claims, forty-six per cent, were for cancellation. Illness was the main cause, with seventy-two per cent of claims coming from forty-five to sixty-five year olds. This group also made most claims for medical and emergency reasons, which accounted for thirty-three per cent of the total. The very high cost of bringing the dead home was reflected here; although only eight per cent of the 'claimants' for emergency expenses were deceased travellers being repa-

---

* And it will only pay that if the tourist behaved 'sensibly'. Commercial Union had a client who left a watch and wallet on a deckchair when he went for a swim. They were stolen. The company deemed this foolish behaviour and refused to pay. The following year, the same man, mindful of that experience, attached his watch to the collar of his Alsatian dog. He attached the dog to his deckchair. The dog got free and ran into the water after his master, ruining the watch in the sea. This time, Commercial Union paid.

triated, they accounted for forty-nine per cent of the expenses in this category. Loss or damage of personal effects and cash made up twenty-one per cent of the total.

Special medical insurance for holidays is expensive. The agents receive as much as a third of the premium in commission. The fact that the insurance companies can afford such inflated commissions shows the high level of profit.

This insurance is important, since medical bills can be alarming. A simple broken leg can cost £750 to treat in Paris* and £1,100 in Switzerland. If broken on a ski slope, it can cost an additional £400 in helicopter and ski ambulance or 'blood wagon' charges to get the victim to hospital.

Treatment for a heart attack in Germany averages £1,700, in Switzerland £2,900 and in the US often exceeds £10,000. Mass European tourism to the US started in 1980 and by March of that year the inevitable stories had started of underinsured holidaymakers facing ruin with American hospital bills. Four couples, one with a heart-attack bill of £17,500, were forced to sell their homes to pay medical expenses.

It is expensive to get home on a stretcher, a common enough event for skiers. Airlines charge three times the full fare in Europe and four times that in the Middle East, and they will not carry people who need treatment in the air or extra equipment. The seriously ill or injured must therefore charter an air ambulance, normally a converted executive jet.

The average price of air ambulance repatriation to London from Paris is £2,800. From Malaga, on the Spanish Costa del Sol, it is £3,750, from Corfu £4,800, from Moscow £5,800, from North Africa £6,000. From West Africa, the cost is £23,500 and from India £34,210.

It can be vital to be repatriated by air. In 1980, 81,000

---

* Form E 111 can be used by citizens of Common Market countries for refunds of some medical expenses entailed in other EEC countries.

West Germans fell sick on holiday abroad. More than fifty died on the Costa del Sol, including Günther Rüschenbeck. A fit thirty-nine-year-old, he started each morning with a swim. One August day, he dived into a wave that caught him and slammed him onto the beach, knocking him unconscious.

He was dragged from the sea and taken to hospital. A doctor confirmed that he had crushed three vertebrae and was paralysed from the shoulders up. The German consul advised his sister to get him out of Spain and into a German hospital as soon as possible. His insurance company considered the cost of a special flight too high. News from the Spanish hospital got worse. Rüschenbeck had caught a serious infection following an operation. His sister went to the German Ministry of Health to try to arrange a flight.

After ten days of bureaucratic wrangling, she approached a mercy flight organization in Stuttgart, whose motto is: 'First rescue, and then argue about money.' In the event, the flight cost DM 14,000 or some £3,400. The patient was flown to a specialist clinic in Karlsruhe.

He died a few days later. The specialist said: 'If he had got here a little earlier, he would have lived.'

Around 1,500 tourists with acute conditions are flown back to Germany in air ambulances each year. 'Hotels and night clubs are flung up overnight.' says a doctor. 'But seldom a hospital. It's a scandal and medical insurance is the only way round it.'

Each August, hospitals in and near the Mediterranean resorts fill to overflowing, with patients sleeping on the floors. Harrassed doctors, working without the benefit of case histories, make errors of diagnosis.

Ibiza, for example, has a resident population of 60,000 and three hospitals. The island gets 450,000 tourists a year, plus 50,000 foreigners who are summer residents. Medical facilities are scarcely adequate in the winter. In the summer, they are overrun.

A tourist in Ischia with a severed Achilles tendon was

kept waiting for four hours in hospital, only to be sent away when she failed to come up with £120 in cash to pay for initial treatment. The doctor only agreed to treat her when she produced a Eurocheque.

A tourist on Grand Canary cut himself slightly whilst swimming. Two days later, he had shivering fits and pains in his left calf. The hospital in San Augustin said that it was not equipped for this and transferred him to Las Palmas. The duty doctor at the Nostra Señora del Pino hospital considered that he should go to the Clinic St Palomas. The clinic said that they could not help him and the ambulance brought him back to San Augustin.

After six hours, he was left in the Clinica Santa Catalina. He lay there for thirty hours without medical care, and died. The dead tourist's sister was at once faced by a Spanish undertaker, who 'waved his list of charges under my nose and offered me a cremation for 70,000 pesetas.' That is some £390.*

Spanish undertakers make much money from dead tourists, either cremating them or charging for preparing body and coffin for the trip home. Julio Alfaro Martin of Malaga is the king of the undertakers on the Costa del Sol. 'Alfaro knows when a tourist has died an hour before us,' say the foreign consuls. With around 200 tourists a year dying on his patch, Alfaro needs to get there first, for the trade is worth some £250,000 a year.

If places like the Canary Islands are casual about tourists' health, they can also be indifferent to their safe arrival and departure. The then British Trade Secretary, John Biffen, warned Spain of the effect that air disasters could have

---

* *Stern* Magazine, 9 July 1981. The German magazine advised its readers to visit former British colonies if going outside Europe. 'Where the English have been, you find good roads and good hospitals.' If ill in underdeveloped countries like Nepal or Somalia, the magazine told tourists to 'get home — at any price'.

on the tourist trade in the aftermath of a Dan Air crash in Tenerife in 1980.

The holiday flight was the worst disaster in British aviation history. The Spanish accident report blamed the British crew for flying off course and hitting a mountain whilst flying an unpublished holding pattern for Los Rodeos airport. Mr Biffen commented that: 'The report seriously understates those inadequacies of the Spanish air traffic control organization which contributed to the crash.'

The attempt to shift blame away from local authorities is all too common in tourism. Mr Biffen warned: 'I have no doubt that British travellers and tourist organizations will be making their own judgements, and in a sense their own representations, to the Spanish authorities about what this kind of accident does for tourist business between our two countries.' In the meantime, it underlines the need for adequate insurance.

There are other dangers abroad which cannot be insured against. Civil wars and *coups d'état* have affected several holiday countries. They do not make for happy vacations. Tourists were rescued from Cyprus in the aftermath of the Turkish invasion by aircraft carrier. An airlift was arranged to get guests out of Gambian hotels during a bloody attempted coup in 1981. But the nine tourists who were reported missing in Zimbabwe in July 1982 show that there can be real political dangers in tourism.

But loss of life is rare. The United Nations has a definition of tourists that has helped maintain immunity for them.* A tourist, the UN says, is a temporary visitor stay-

---

* It was not always so. The first recorded self-catering tour of Spain was in 1620. It was not an unqualified success for the pioneer tourist, William Lithgow, who had to buy his own food and cook it himself in his lodgings. He was arrested as a spy in Malaga. His money, 560 ducats, enough to buy a Titian, was taken by the Spanish. He was then tortured with water, strangulation and the rack. Eventually freed through

ing at least twenty-four hours but less than one year in a country other than his own place of residence, with the purpose of leisure, recreation, holiday, health, study, business, family affairs, convention or congress. It does not include the armed services, diplomats,* resident students, those employed in a foreign country or permanent residents.

Tourism is the safest and most effective way of defecting from a Communist country. Half the 819 Poles who travelled on official tours to the 1982 World Cup in Spain defected.† Some did not bother to watch the football. As one coach entered Italy en route, a passenger asked the

---

the English consul, he returned to Britain. When the promised compensation for his ruined holiday did not appear, the mettlesome tourist insulted the Spanish Ambassador. The Ambassador hit Lithgow, who struck him back. He got another two years in prison, in London this time.

* Diplomats are the happiest of travellers since they enjoy, and frequently abuse, immunity that extends from murder to parking fines. Under the 1961 Vienna Convention on Diplomatic Relations, the traditional immunity of the Ambassador, dating back to the Renaissance, was extended to cover all embassy staff and their baggage. The 'diplomatic bag' can be anything from a letter to a ten-ton crate as long as it has the right seal on it. Items found in diplomatic bags include a live man, $13.5 million worth of heroin and 60,000 rounds of ammunition. The man was a drugged Israeli, Mordecai ben Masuud, whom Egyptian agents had strapped inside a case in Rome which they were sending by air to Cairo. The heroin was the work of a Uruguayan Ambasssador and the ammo was Iraqi. As an example of personal immunity, an Algerian diplomat had to be released at Schipohl Airport in Amsterdam. Amongst what he modestly described as 'articles for self-defence' were eight kilos of explosives, five hand grenades and twenty-one letter bombs.

† Reuters, 23 July 1982.

tour guide, 'Can I defect now?' Six others left the coach in Marseilles. Only eighteen of the thirty-seven passengers returned to Poland.

This was despite the fact that all those allowed on the tours had been carefully screened. As for the disappointed, the magazine *Polityka* reported a telephone call to the State travel firm Orbis, in which a client was asking about trips abroad. The clerk reeled off a list of possible but defection-difficult destinations: 'Czechoslovakia, Soviet Union, Bulgaria, Romania, Mongolia, Cuba . . .' 'Wait a minute,' interrupted the optimistic client, 'where is the stop-over on the Cuba trip?'

Package tour operators

Tourists may learn to live without travel agents. They may survive without travel insurance. They will not get by without package tour operators. No individual could arrange his own holiday at anything near the prices offered by the holiday companies. Someone buying his own hotel accommodation in, and scheduled flight to Majorca can expect to pay at least two and a half times the cost of a package tour to the same hotel. Some packages offer fourteen days full board in a hotel plus return flight for less than the price an individual would pay simply for a one-way scheduled air ticket.

In principle, if not always in practice, tour operators are indeed a tourist's best friend. This is because they buy in bulk from hotels and airlines to make up their package, and then sell at a tiny gross profit.

The first air-inclusive tour service was flown by Horizon Holidays to Calvi, Corsica in 1950.* By 1963, inclusive

* The pioneer of the 'All-in-holiday' was the Workers Travel Association, which in May 1922 sent a party to a Château in Normandy for £5 for one week and £8 for two, with everything included. The tour's guide arrived at Victoria to say he would not be accompanying the group due to pressure of work. He promised them a good bacon and egg breakfast on the way, and packed them off on the night ferry. There was no breakfast. The advertised bus did not await the pioneers to take them from a railway station near Rouen to the Château. They walked across lanes and fields with their luggage. They asked a farmer for directions to the Château and he set his bull on them. The Château, once found, proved very beautiful but they were escorted to stables at the back. Most had opted to pay 10 shillings a week extra for 'luxurious private rooms' rather than

or package tours were running at 630,000. That figure was 2,482,000 in 1971 and in 1981 the British bought more than five million package holidays.

The industry was pioneered by the British, and British holidaymakers have good reason to be grateful to it. Since its start, it has had a reputation as an industry of profitless growth. Prices have been kept very low. Most tour operators need to sell as many as ninety per cent of their holidays to break even. By contrast, a scheduled airline needs to sell sixty per cent of its seats, a hotel fifty per cent of its beds and a railway forty per cent of its seats to stay in the black.

The breakdown of the cost of a typical £200, fourteen-day holiday to Majorca shows how little money there is in it for the operator. The air transport accounts for 39½ per cent of the cost, hotel and transfer buses 40 per cent, commission to agents 10 per cent. That leaves just 10½ per cent for overheads and profit. After overheads, that leaves a profit of around £4 or two per cent.*

The package holiday business is extremely volatile. The smallest change in the number of customers makes a difference to profits. On a typical £200 holiday, where the tour operator has budgeted on the aircraft being 95 per cent full during the season, he will make a profit of £400,000. If the load factor of the aircraft slides to ninety per cent, he loses £80,000. If it creeps up to 96.4 per cent, something seldom achieved, he will be £836,000 in clover.

'You have to go for a mass market where the profit is

'comfortable dormitories'. Wooden partitions in the stables marked off the private rooms from the dormitory. Promised 'exquisite French cooking', they were led to a basement kitchen and given black bread and bean soup. Sound familiar?

* That is on a charter flight holiday. Most big companies reckon to make a 17½ per cent gross profit on upmarket, scheduled air flight holidays.

so small,' says a tour operator. 'People complain that we pack them into airports and aircraft and hotels like cattle. Well, we're only charging them cattle prices.'

There is a little more money in it than that. The operator can improve things by selling direct to the public, and saving the travel agent's commission. He can impose height of season surcharges and fuel surcharges. By getting the deposit, and payment in full, from the public as early as possible, the operator earns interest. He also gets commission from selling cancellation and travel insurance.

This high volume, low profit business makes over-booking attractive. Almost all travel agents and operators overbook. This is normally at one over for every twenty, giving twenty-one bookings for every twenty rooms, but sometimes at one in ten. It is based on the likelihood of cancellations: the operator keeps the deposit on the cancellation and already has another person booked to take the space.

Airlines also overbook, relying on 'no shows' to keep them out of trouble. So do hotels, often at one in ten. They could all use a waiting-list to avoid the trouble, but they do not. They seldom admit to overbooking either. If the expected cancellations do not materialise, the operator will try to get through by making people, particularly families, share rooms. Hoteliers may also oversell their rooms to operators. Bulgaria and Spain have the worst records for overbooking.

Currency surcharges also affect costs. A falling pound in the summer of 1981 boosted the cost of a two-week package from £800 to £905. A big operator can, however, use the forward currency market to iron out the bumps in exchange rates.

Even so profit margins sometimes prove too thin, and operators collapse. The biggest failure came at 11.59 p.m. on 15 August, 1974 when the huge Court Line stopped trading. All flights by Clarksons, Horizon, 4S, 4S Sports and Airfare were cancelled. More than 40,000 holidaymakers were stranded abroad. Clarkson's had grown very rapidly under the direction of Tom Gullick, who had helped pioneer the low mark-up, high turnover philosophy of package tourism.

There have been plenty of other bankruptcies. The big group Horizon had run into difficulties earlier in 1974. Passengers on a round-the-world voyage have had their ship sold under them in Singapore. Others on a coach trip from London to Katmandu lost the coach in Beirut.* A group on a tour from London to Egypt were perhaps more fortunate: they never left London because their aircraft had been padlocked by a bailiff to a concrete slab. It can be a rocky business. Tour operators and travel agents have collapsed frequently enough for legislation to be introduced to protect the public. When Court Line failed in 1974, a rescue operation had to be mounted to bring back 40,000 British holidaymakers stranded abroad. Other major failures have included Sun Villas, Erna Low Travel Services, Horizon, and Clarksons, part of Court Line.

A myriad of smaller firms have got into difficulties. Sir Rupert Mackeson's cultural tours firm, Master Classes, was investigated by police after the baronet transferred

---

* Coach trips are ordeals with cut-price companies. Cowboy operators use old machines and sometimes a single driver on a journey as far as London to Athens. Wheels fall off and drivers fall asleep.

As an example, take the obstacle course completed by Brian Marfleet and his family in August 1981. They travelled by coach from London to Malaga. En route, a Moroccan passenger threatened to kill an elderly Dutch woman. The family, which included a girl of nine, was surrounded by transvestites and prostitutes during an overnight stop in the red light district of Barcelona. The driver resigned after arguing with frightened passengers, who were screaming, spitting and fighting amongst each other.

As for the coach, it burst a tyre, hit a car in Valencia and broke down in the Sierra Nevada. Mrs Marfleet said on getting back to London: 'All we need now is another holdiay to get over it.'

himself to Rhodesia-Zimbabwe. In the summer of 1981, holidaymakers on Aegean Flotillas were not allowed to set sail in their hired yachts because of alleged unpaid bills, and remained steaming with rage in harbour. Palmland Travel, Cruise-Drive Tours, Tri-star Travel are amongst the collapses.

Police are looking in Singapore for a Hong Kong Chinese student who went missing from his one-room office in London's Shaftesbury Avenue with the cash he had taken for 350 return air fares to Hong Kong. He had overlooked issuing the tickets. A Brazilian, operating from an accommodation address in Trafalgar Square, did likewise with the money for a charter jet to Rio.

Cowboys

Guarantee schemes by the major tour operators and the Association of British Travel Agents mean that there is little risk in dealing with major firms. ABTA agents and the major operators subscribe to funds which are used to reimburse members of the public if a firm goes out of business. Introduced in the wake of the Court Line collapse of 1974, the schemes only cover member companies.

The cowboy survives on the fringes. All he needs is a source of discount tickets from the airlines, an accommodation address and some classified advertisements in the press. At best, he can offer the public startling bargains.

There are as many as twenty constantly fluctuating fares across the North Atlantic. The same row of seats on a Transatlantic flight could find a businessman who has paid £230 for a standard economy ticket, a grandparent visiting relatives on a £150 ticket bought three months in advance, a student on a £130 bookable same day ticket and another on a £120 standby ticket, a holidaymaker on a package tour where the flight represents £95 of the package, a travel agent on a £35 trade discount ticket, an Australian on a round-the-world ticket where this sector represents

£70. There are 325 separate pairs of agreements for air fares between the twenty-six European countries, with European prices consequently over-protective and over-expensive.

Big agents, conscious of overheads and commission rates, will often fail to come up with the cheapest fare. The cowboy depends for his survival on offering the lowest prices and will strive to keep the cost to a minimum. With an airline's connivance, he may break IATA regulations. The International Air Transport Association is the airline cartel responsible for price-fixing on many routes. It regularly fines its own members for breaking its regulations. An airline with surplus seats may sell these off to a fringe agent well below the official fare.

A common practice within Europe is to take advantage of ITX, the cheap Inclusive Tour fares. To qualify for this, the passenger should be on a holiday with accommodation pre-paid in advance. The agent gets round this by issuing the passenger with an accommodation voucher. This may be to a non-existent hotel or holiday flat and will certainly not be useable. But this bit of rule-bending can save the passenger upwards of £125 on a flight from London to Rome or Athens.

Passengers are unlikely to be prosecuted for this. It is not their fault that the airlines have fares of such complexity that passengers paying the 'normal' full economy rate are often put in a special 'executive' cabin of their own, away from people on cheaper fly-drives, winter breaks, package tours, block charters and so forth. But there is a danger that the passengers with rule-bending tickets may not be allowed to board the flight.

The cowboy operator may also abscond with the takings. The Mafia and organized crime have exploited ticketing, particularly in the US where the illegal rewards exceed $50 million a year. The Mafia infiltrates a failing travel agent, promising the owner cash if he turns a blind eye to his ticket stocks. The criminals take away blank tickets relying on the six weeks that it takes for the average ticket to be checked out by IATA's ticketing headquarters in Montreal.

Properly routed tickets are made out and sold at a discount to the public. The criminals do not pay the airline, relying on the six week lead time.

Cowboys are attractive because they can offer real bargains. That is fine if the airline, anxious to fill its seats, knows what is going on and turns a blind eye. But if the tickets are stolen, or contravene rules that the airline wishes to impose strictly, they may be worthless.

Promises, promises

In 1981, Intasun was fined £750 for recklessly making a false statement in a brochure. Reigate policeman Donald Bell and his wife spent £700 on a holiday to the Lanterna hotel in Yugoslavia. The Intasun brochure said that the hotel was 'in a quieter area of Porec. The resort centre is about 200 yards away'. Porec is in fact eight miles distant.

Also in 1981, Intasun (North) and Intasun (South) were each fined £1,000 for false statements. The brochures promised a 'poolside bar' and 'children's pool' at Il Gattopardo Hotel in Sicily. Neither existed, and nor was there much in the way of 'after dark entertainment'.

Some companies take unusual steps to be realistic. The 1981 Sovereign winter sun brochure has an honesty page entitled: 'What it's really like.' Earlier pages in the brochure described Cairo as 'an Arabian Nights' adventure of tangled alleyways, teeming bazaars and dreaming minarets.' The honesty page said it 'has traffic conditions like the centre of London in a permanent rush hour' and 'is large, sprawling, dusty and noisy'. Acapulco, 'the glossiest of tropical resorts' at the beginning, becomes 'about as authentically Mexican as a polystyrene taco' at the end.

Travel agents and tour operators themselves use the Agents' Hotel Gazeteer as a guide. Designed for the retail trade, it gives details of 3,861 hotels in Europe.* The Hotel Europa Park in Salou on the Costa Brava is described as 'an attractively designed modern hotel in a pleasant setting a little away from the main part of the resort' in an Intasun brochure.

The Gazeteer describes it thus: 'Crude for its category, resembling an overgrown Wimpy bar and situated in a bleak though central location, severed from the newer centre.' Thus agents should be well aware of the hotel they are sending clients to.†

Even horrider holidays?
The most common recent complaints against tour operators, however, have not been for collapse and stranding but for poor quality holidays.

The most horrid package holiday on record is French. A Frenchman went on a package to Colombia. The hotel

* CHG Travel Publications, 30 Grove Road, Beaconsfield, Bucks.
† The Advertising Standards Authority criticizes holiday firms for foreign hotels which do not come up to the standards claimed by brochures. Horizon Travel was top of the list in 1981. Also criticized were Ellerman Sunflight Holidays, the British Airways subsidiary Enterprise, and Thomson Holidays. The authority investigated complaints about thirteen holiday companies in April 1981, and found that the complaints were not justified in only two cases.

  The most criticized was a brochure by Horizon Travel for the Sani Beach hotel at Halkidiki in Greece. Despite the glowing descriptions in the brochure, the hotel had self-service rather than waiter-served meals. There were no radios in the bungalows, no ladies' hairdresser, no pool-side bar, no pedaloes for hire on the beach, no riding.

  Thomson Holidays were criticized for charges for tennis courts and mini-golf. Other companies against whom complaints were upheld included Butlins, Cruise Centre of Redhill, Modernline Travel, Swan Hellenic, TWA, Puerto Rico Tourist Office and Inghams Travel.
  Daily Mail 10 June 1981.

in the small Caribbean port was overbooked. The holi-daymaker was roaming the streets, looking for a bed and breakfast place, when he was arrested for vagrancy. Un-willing to bribe the police, he blamed the hotel to the magistrate who was hearing the vagrancy charge. The magistrate was the hotelier's brother, and he sentenced the tourist to eight days imprisonment for slander. By the time of his release, his return flight had left. He had insufficient funds to buy a scheduled ticket. He went to the post office to send a telegram to his home in Montpellier, asking for some money. He was re-arrested before he could send it. This time he was charged with illegal immigration. It was explained that having missed his return flight, he could no longer be classified as a tourist. He now needed a work permit and he did not have one. He was fined $500 for this offence and a further $500 for slander when he again blamed the hotel for overbooking him. His luggage was confiscated in lieu of the fines. Down to the clothes he stood in, he hitch-hiked to Bogota where the Consulate arranged for his repatriation.

No British story appears to equal that, but there have been plenty of horrors. The MacLeod family from Ilkley went on a two-week package to Majorca in 1980. The hotel was overbooked, so the parents were put in the same bedroom as their young children. It rained. The children fell ill. There were expensive medical bills. The family were split up on the delayed flight home.

The MacLeod's aircraft eventually touched down and the holiday seemed over. This is the point which abused British tourists often become sentimental. As they leave the terminal, they kneel and kiss the ground. 'Thank God we're home.'*

---

* A group returned from the two star Elba International Hotel on Elba – 'it was sheer hell, cockroaches in the food, fleas in the bedrooms, mould in the kitchens and unchanged linen on the beds,' said one. 'Now we know how Napoleon felt when he was exiled there.'

Mr MacLeod was about to leave the Green customs channel at Leeds-Bradfield Airport when a customs man stopped him. The MacLeods had forgotten that they had bought a bottle of Bacardi rum to help them survive the hotel, before getting their full duty free allowance at Palma Airport. Mr MacLeod was warned that he had one bottle too many. He had had enough. He picked it up and broke it on another bottle. A small amount of liquor sprayed on to the customs man.

Mr MacLeod was fined for assaulting a Customs officer, attempting evasion of duty and destroying two bottles of spirits, and ordered to pay compensation for the officer's uniform.

The 'main meal' at a 4-star hotel in Sicily was made up of a bowl of soup, one rissole and a dish of fruit. One woman lost ten pounds during an eight-day stay at the Hotel Kennedy at Sant Alessio, a weight reduction a health farm would have been proud of.

A Costa Brava holiday home was advertised by Club 32 Holidays of Romford as a 'seaside villa', 'the romantic holiday you have always dreamed of and will always remember'. Remember, yes. Dream of, not quite. The villa turned out to be a squalid room above a disco near the bus station on the main street of the Spanish resort of Estartit.

Another Spanish villa was described as 'set in its own grounds about two minutes from the beach with meals prepared by expert cooks'. The only furniture was a rickety chair, a table and a bed without pillows or sheets. The 'expert cooks' were in a café fifteen minutes away. As for reaching the beach in two minutes, 'only a superhuman athlete could have done it', said consumer protection officer, Ian Forsyth. 'It was three quarters of a mile away.'

Some tour operators have curious ideas of what constitutes a holiday. Americans can pay £2,200 for a 12,000 mile journey to Antarctica, where they spend a night in a white-out, travel in sub-zero temperatures and lean into seventy-mile-an-hour winds.

Quester Tours and Travels in New York specialize in £1,000 trips to the Amazon. 'We forbid anyone to wander alone,' says Quester's Michael Parkin. 'They must always have a guide with a machete and a knowledge of the country. It's easy to get lost. There's the danger of malaria, snakes and insects, and you could get bitten by a cayman. That's where the fun lies.' Indeed.*

A three-week tour of New Guinea costs £2,500 and includes a nineteen-day stay with aborigines in mud huts. 'You get to eat roots and insects with them, and share their lifestyles totally,' says Thomas Cook's senior vice-president for world-wide travel, Ari Drbal. 'It's better than sitting at a desk.'

For £750, there is a Mountain Travel tour to the top of Mount Aconcagua, South America's highest peak. Ropes and tents are included, but not the air fare, and clients must take their own sleeping bags and rucksacks.

Robinson Crusoe holidays are an operator's dream. The tourists are neither fed nor sheltered and are in no position to complain. They are dumped on a near-barren island in the Bahamas. They pay £40 a day to live off shellfish and sea snails, which they catch themselves, whilst keeping a weather eye open for sharks, eels and stingrays. Heather Milnes, who went on the first tour, said: 'You had to watch out for scorpions and there wasn't much shade, but it was a real test of endurance.'

Bread can be delivered by launch – for an extra £2 a day. Clients are only allowed to take one change of clothes, rainwear, sleeping bag, swimsuit, torch, pocket knife, plastic sheet, bucket and matches.

The firm See Britain offered a tour of public lavatories.

---

* But that old romantic holiday, the African safari with a white hunter, is all but extinct. After fifty years, countless movies, and Ernest Hemingway, the East African Professional Hunters Association was disbanded in 1977. Tourists use cameras now. Ivory poachers use the guns.

For 25p, tourists saw the best Victorian and Edwardian lavatories in the City and West End of London with a guide, who discussed the style of the interiors, the architecture, the hours of opening and the history.*

The number of complaints against operators has been rising sharply. Complaints made to the Association of British Travel Agents, ABTA, more than doubled over a two-year period. Gordon Barrie, the Director General of Fair Trading, had to call on ABTA to bring ten tour operators into line who were stipulating unreasonable booking conditions in defiance of their own code of practice.

Barrie objected to conditions which sought to exclude the operators from liability for delay, disappointment, damage, injury or death. They were also intended to let the companies improve last-minute surcharges.

Some operators consider their customers naïve. Thus Saga Holidays state 'the prices in this brochure are protected by Saga against any currency fluctuations whatsoever. No matter what happens to the pound, the prices here are the prices you will pay.' Yet paragraph 10 of the Booking Conditions on the back of the brochure says: 'We must, however, reserve the right to amend prices, dates, travel arrangements or accommodation if we feel it necessary.'

Other firms think the public easily cowed. Blue Sky wrote in their Booking Conditions: 'the right is reserved to vary reasonably all itineraries, travel arrangements and

---

* Tourist sights have changed since the early 1900s. The most popular tour of Paris in 1903 took in the sewers ('The sewers of Paris!' ran the blurb. 'The words alone carry an aura of romance and adventure!'), the morgue, a slaughterhouse and a tobacco factory. The favourite was the morgue: 'People go there to look at the corpses, as in other quarters they go to see the fashions and the orange trees in flower.'

hotel accommodation, at the absolute discretion of the company'.

In the holiday field, even the best and biggest companies occasionally go wrong. Thomson Holidays, the market leader, has been fined for recklessly stating in a brochure that a hotel in Greece had facilities which it did not.

Complaints are not taken seriously enough by tour operators and travel agents. *Holiday Which?* found that, of 120 members with serious complaints about holidays, eighty-five per cent had no satisfaction even though they complained whilst still on holiday and followed this up with a letter on their return. Sixty per cent said they felt that the tour operator was either avoiding responsibility or was not taking their complaint seriously.*

Agents and operators may be slouches when it comes to complaints from the public. But they are as fast off the mark as the next man when it is their own comfort that is upset.

A group of top British travel agents went to Mexico in 1975. They got all the usual ingredients of a package disaster. Three couples stormed off to Florida when the wives got upset stomachs. Those still in Mexico complained of 'unfinished, squalid accommodation', changed itineraries and missing excursion tours.

Prominent ABTA members demanded their money back. One said that the hotel annexe was still full of builders who 'used the corridor outside the bedroom as a urinal'. He took legal action for compensation.

It is a nice irony that the tour was organized by the Mexican tourist authorities.

Travel agents are used to getting the red carpet treatment

---

* In fairness, most people thrive on their holidays. The business would not have expanded if they did not. An NOP survey for the Office of Fair Trading in 1980 found that nearly two-thirds of those who took package holidays were 'very satisfied'. Twenty-five per cent were 'quite satisfied' and only three per cent were 'not at all satisfied'.

on trips abroad, particularly the British, German and Americans with their mass markets spending a combined £35 billion a year on foreign holidays. When the 6,000 delegates of the American Society of Travel Agents hit Madrid for their annual junket, there was not a spare bed or hospitality suite in town. The Hotel Palace reported its busiest week in its sixty-five years.

Anxious to impress these men who control the world's biggest tourist market, the British wooed them with two parties a day. At cocktail parties they were ushered in by the Yeoman Jailer of the Tower of London, in full regalia, and the resident Governor of the Tower and the Keeper of the Jewel House kept their glasses primed.

The Mexico fiasco was thus totally unexpected.

'It was a hell of a shock, old boy,' said an ABTA man. 'I mean, the hotels in shambles, the sightseeing buses late, the wife down with the runs, Mexican navvies pissing in the corridors. I'm not used to being treated like that.'

Unfortunately, a lot of his customers are. They should note what the professionals did: complain bitterly and sue.

Tour operators check out hotels well before they include them in a brochure.

'There are two things you have to get right,' says hotelier Paul Benvenuto. 'Cleanliness and food. That's what most complaints are about. So you make sure there are enough chambermaids. As for food, the golden rule is that it mustn't complicate people's stomachs. They are away for fourteen days in the heat, so you need a bland, international menu. Steak, chicken, fish and chips, and lots of salad.

'Then there's one thing you just hope your luck holds on. Politics. Almost every big package tour destination on the Med has had its nasties. The Turks invaded Cyprus. The Greeks had the Colonels and the Italians have the Red Brigades. The Spanish have the Basques. The Portuguese had a revolution. Corsica has got separatists and King Hassan has got problems in Morocco.

'With politics, you pray nothing happens until the end

of March. If it happens after that, it doesn't much matter. If people have booked they'll come anyway and most people have booked by then. The crucial period is January to March. Any trouble then can wipe out your summer season.'

Money

The credit card game

The credit card is a great boon to the traveller. A small piece of plastic will buy him an airline ticket in Brazil, a hotel room in Crete, a bottle of duty free in Alaska. He can use it to buy a gallon of petrol or to charter Concorde. An American used his card at the London Boat Show to buy a yacht for £140,000.

Credit cards result from an insult in a restaurant in 1950. Frank McNamara, a multi-millionaire who seldom deigned to carry cash, was dining out in New York. At the end of the meal, the maitre d' refused to give him credit and threatened to call the police.

McNamara was thrown on the mercy of his guests who, being less mighty than himself, still carried cash. He was determined not to get caught again, but he was not going to start carrying cash either.

So he introduced the general credit card, previously only issued by petrol companies. He founded Diners Club, named for that restaurant incident, and issued his friends with credit cards. It was essentially a status symbol for the very rich who preferred a piece of plastic to money.

Status is still part of credit cards. The American Express advertising slogan shows this: 'the card says more about you than cash ever can'.

But, far from being a rich man's toy, they are now so widespread that more than 100 million are in use. In some parts of the world, notably America, it is difficult to travel without one. Many hotels and car-hire firms refuse to handle cash and will only deal with holders of credit cards.

It is safer than having cash around, it cuts down on staff fraud, it makes for easier accounting and it reduces the human side of business. A receptionist no longer has to perceive a customer's respectability and weigh up his honesty. She takes his card and runs it through a machine and the risk is gone. If he's a 'midnight runner' and decamps, the credit card company pays. Where car-hire and hotel receptionists were never left on the desk alone until they had at least a year's experience, a card-only concern will let a vacationing student run the desk after two days instruction.

The spread of plastic in Britain has been swift and of great importance to the travel industry. Starting from scratch, Barclaycard built up to 105,000 UK outlets in a few years. A large proportion is travel and entertainment, including 9,675 garages, 5,709 restaurants and night clubs, 4,300 travel agents, 4,258 hotels and motels, 621 British Rail stations, 539 tour operators, 321 airlines and 70 shipping lines.

The number of cards is also mushrooming. British Airways now accepts Access, Air Canada En Route, American Express, Amoco Torch, Bankamericard, Banco Bilbao, Bancunion, Barclaycard, Barclaycaart, Carte Blanche, Carte Bleue, Chargex, Diners Club, En Route, Eurocard, Master Charge, Standard Bank of South Africa, Sottomayor, Sumitomo and Visa.

There are two types of card. With the credit card proper, the company charge the customer monthly interest as well as taking a small percentage of the sale from the retailer. The big British cards, Access and Barclaycard, work like this. The interest the customer pays often exceeds twenty-three per cent a year.

With a charge card, like American Express, the customer must settle his account each month but is charged no interest. The card company gets its money from the retailer.* In effect, it 'factors' its members' bills. It buys them

* It also gets an annual membership fee from its members. These are around £10 to £15 a year. It may not seem much for the service, particularly since the members settle most

from the merchant at a discount and then charges the card member the full amount. The card company normally charges the merchant between three and five per cent of the bill. This drops to around one per cent for very large concerns, big stars like Harrods or a major airline like British Airways.

When cards are used abroad, the charges bear no relation to the exchange rate that existed on the day the purchase was made. Most card companies charge at the exchange rate on the day they receive and settle the bill. They also choose their own exchange rates.

These differ. On one particular (pre-Mitterrand) day in Britain, where Lloyds was offering 8.49 francs to the pound, Barclays was at 8.52 and National Westminster was 8.54. In the US, the official rate was 4.619 francs to the dollar. American Express was 4.627, Diner's Club 4.648.

It is a rapidly growing market and a profitable one. Credit card transactions in Britain almost doubled between 1977 and 1979, to £2.4 billion. Worldwide, cardholders in the Visa group, including Barclaycard, are spending $32,000,000,000 a year by card. It is a high profit section of a high profit industry. Barclaycard's return on capital resources was 28.9 per cent when examined by the Monopolies Commission. Barclay's Bank, no slouch at the usury game itself, was returning 25.7 per cent.

Access and Barclaycard make their money through charging their cardholders interest and through deducting a commission from traders. Interest rates vary, but in 1980 were 2.25 per cent a month, or over 30 per cent a year. Access charges traders who accept the card an average discount of 2.61 per cent Barclaycard charges an average

---

bills seven weeks after signing them. In effect, that is seven weeks free credit. But American Express, for example, has over 11 million members. Those annual fees add up fast.

of 2.8 per cent.* The amount depends on the volume of business. A small restaurant might have to pay a five per cent discount, where a big hotel pays two per cent and an airline like British Airways pays one per cent.

American Express charge no interest to their cardholders since they require immediate payment. An annual membership fee is charged, bringing them in £6 million a year in Britain. More is extracted from traders than by Access and Barclaycard. The average American Express discount is just under 4 per cent: with £408 million being spent through their cards in Britain in 1979, the discount brought in a further £15 million or so.

In essence, credit cards are a new form of money virtually outside government control. They are so important a part of life for some that psychologists categorize people according to the number and type of credit card they carry.

Dr Herbert Hoffman† studied the subject. He found that holders of only one card are easy-going individuals who are ready to be flexible and casual in outlook. Those with four to six cards are well-organized types who need to feel in control of their lives. Those who refuse to carry any cards at all are conservative and outspoken, ready to uphold traditional values and respected for it by those who know them.

* Barclaycard's discount rates vary. Thus, petrol sales are discounted 3 per cent, clothing from 1 per cent for Marks and Spencers to 5 per cent for small boutiques; department stores from 1½ to 3 per cent; hotels and motels 2 to 5 per cent; travel 1 to 2 per cent; travel agents 1 per cent; restaurants and night clubs 2 to 5 per cent. For comparison, American Express charge restaurants from 4 to 5 per cent; car hire 4 to 5.5 per cent; travel agents 3 per cent; travel 3 per cent; hotels 3.3 to 5 per cent. If you hire an aircraft on your card, the airline loses 5 per cent in discount.
† Director of the Hillside Psychological Guidance Center in New York.

People who collect as many cards as possible, with department stores as well as general cards, are cautiously trying to protect themselves from unforeseen disaster. They like to gain emotional comfort by surrounding themselves with the familiar.

Dr Hoffman finds that how cards are used is as indicative as their number. A person who uses a card whenever he can is 'efficient, with a well-earned reputation for getting things done'. If he spends only on special occasions, on holidays or luxuries, he is fun-loving and impulsive and leads a well-balanced life without worrying about his problems. Prestige cards, the sort you have to pay an annual fee for, are for people who 'entertain lavishly and wear way-out clothes', says the doctor. 'They have a need to impress people and wish to stand out in a crowd.'

In Britain there are 25 million in circulation, including cheque guarantee cards. Only three per cent of personal spending is done with plastic. The average income of American Express's half-million sterling card holders is £15,200 a year.* The only cardholders earning less than £7,000 a year are retired people. The bulk earn between £10,000 and £20,000 though sixteen per cent earn over £20,000.

Access and Barclaycard are not so financially blue-blooded. Barclaycard, for example, approved eighty six per cent of all applicants. Where American Express holders are almost exclusively from the rich AB social group, only forty three per cent of Access cardholders are AB. Thirty per cent are C1, which includes clerks and office workers, and twenty per cent are C2, skilled workers. Six per cent are D, and one per cent E.

---

* As of the beginning of 1981. Holders had done well in the pay stakes. At the end of 1979, the Monopolies Commission had found an average cardholder salary of £12,500, with twenty five per cent over £15,000 and twelve per cent over £20,000. Ninety per cent of cardholders held managerial or professional jobs.

The biggest card-carrying age group are the twenty five to thirty four year-olds who account for twenty six per cent. The old do not trust plastic: over 65s constitute only nine per cent of the market.

A full half of all cardholders in Britain live in London and the South East. 'The regional splits in Britain are extraordinary,' says American Express's Andrew Rondell. 'The South East accepts plastic in a big way. So do the Scots. West Countrymen and Midlanders are so-so. But Yorkshiremen, Lancastrians and Welshmen seem to hate the stuff.'

Only five per cent of British cardholders live in Wales, and three per cent live in the North. Barclaycard is the most popular card with 39 per cent of the market, followed by Access with 35.7 per cent, American Express with 17.1 per cent and Diners with 5.2.

The companies are fussy about who they enroll. American Express turn down forty per cent of applicants. All references are followed up, particularly banks and employers. It is very unlikely that anyone without a bank account would be accepted. Employers are asked if the applicant is doing what he says he does and earning what he says he does. The self-employed are checked through their accountants.

The credit analysts who vet applications are looking for an idea of stability and collateral. They want to be sure they will get their money back if anything goes wrong. 'A tenant in a furnished flat could be a problem for debt collecting,' says an analyst. 'Owner-occupiers are best.'

It is important to get the right cardholders because the commitment is open-ended from the card company's point of view. A card has been used to buy a £208,000 ring from a London jeweller and to settle a £120,000 hotel bill in Park Lane. An American Express Gold Card holder has an automatic bank credit line of £5,000, a £100 a day cheque cashing facility and the ability to draw $1,000 in traveller's cheques round the world.

'It could be rather drastic if things went wrong,' says

the analyst. The companies reckon to limit defaulters to one per cent of cardholders.

Yet cardholders still take a risk for their money.

A customer may develop 'carditis'.* This means that he goes on a signing spree, and cannot meet the debt. It has been known for people to go round the world on a credit card without having any money in the bank to pay for it, but it is not common. The companies check carefully into an applicant's financial history before issuing a card.†

---

* There are organizations for those suffering from 'carditis'. Consumer Credit Counselling Service is typical of the agencies dealing with credit card abuse in the US. Another is called Spend-a-holics. New York's Debtors Anonymous is modelled on the mutual self-help programmes used for alcoholics and gamblers. A typical client earns £7,000 a year, is thirty with a family of four and owes about £4,000 to nine separate creditors.

The counsellors usually shave £125 a month off the client's budget. Family food bills are cut by an average of twenty per cent if children are not allowed to go shopping and cannot wheedle extras from their parents. The client must agree to give up his credit cards, which are cut up in front of him. 'There are tears at that,' says Consumer Credit Counselling's president Stan Benson. 'The cards are like old friends.'

The client pays a lump sum each month, which the agency distributes to the creditors. Consumer Credit Counselling pays back more than £3 million a year to creditors. Alternatively, the client could go bankrupt. However, sixty-one per cent of bankrupts turn out to be recidivists, soon in debt again, and bankruptcies are listed on credit records for fourteen years.

† Sometimes not carefully enough. London Bankruptcy Court was told in July 1982 of a nineteen-year-old who had used his Barclaycard and Access to embark on a travel spree. The lad, who was unemployed and had previously been bound over for dishonesty, went on a five-month holiday to Israel. He stayed at the Tel Aviv Hilton and then flew to the US to stay at the Miami Hilton. 'I had a jolly good time,' he said gratefully.

They also limit the amount that can be spent on travel. There is a maximum beyond which an air ticket cannot be sold without special authorization from the company. The limits vary: Access is £200, Barclaycard is a more generous £250, Chargex a miserly $300, Diners Club $500, American Express and Carte Blanche $750. Most of the smaller cards have a limit of $500.

An airline clerk has a list giving maximum credit, and the phone number for approval above that amount and for the blacklist check. This is for cards which are over their limit, and a sharp-eyed airline girl or travel agent will collect £25 reward from the card company for picking one up.

To authorize an Access or Interbank Eurocard, the clerk telephones a number or makes a check automatically through a computer terminal. Point-of-sale terminals in big department stores, airlines and major hotels are connected to the credit authorization computer. The sales clerk enters the cost of the item and the card number, and the computer either authorizes the sale or refuses it.

Sometimes, this is done on a flat limit. The more sophisticated companies have individual credit ratings for each customer, based on the experience of his past spending habits and promptness in payment.

It is normally the computer that, impersonally, allows a sale to go through or stops it. An account supervisor may deal with an authorization personally.

'You get a feel for each account,' says one. 'With some of them, the pattern of payments seems odd. Someone will just use his card for petrol and the odd meal, and then there is a run of bills from boutiques, jewellers, flower-shops, theatres, hotels. You think, hello, this customer has just fallen in love or has just started an affair.

'That sets the alarm bells ringing. You get out his application form and you check. You see that he's married and has children. It could all be a second honeymoon, but that's not likely. So you take special care. A bachelor falling in love can be expensive but he can probably afford it. A married man's affair can develop into a serious case of "carditis".

'You bear all that in mind. You can still get it wrong. I had this "gallon". We call them gallons if all they ever buy is petrol. He seemed steady. Then he started getting a few heavy items, a stereo set and a video recorder. He paid up promptly. Then there was other heavy stuff, jewellery, cameras and an air ticket. It got authorized because we didn't think of him as a "gallon" any more.

'I sometimes wonder where he is now. Maybe Miami. The British seem to go to America now when they've had a spree on a card. It used to be Spain.'

This is rare because the companies have a good idea of who their customers are before they will issue a card. Since the card can only be used in an approved outlet, it is much more difficult for a front outfit to 'launder' credit cards than traveller's cheques.

The major headache is stolen cards.

'People don't bother to counterfeit credit cards,' says Jim McGrath, head of American Express security, formerly with the FBI. 'Its much easier to steal them. One simple ploy is to take a customer's card and hand him back one that is expired or has been stolen long enough to have become too hot to be worthwhile. Waiters and prostitutes do this a lot. It works because very few people take a good look at their card when it comes back. Or the card may not be given back at all, particularly if the customer is a bit drunk – as many people in massage parlours and restaurants are.'

Prices in the developed market for stolen cards in Britain run between £10 and £150, in the US from $40 to $300.

The most valuable cards are those stolen from rich people, particularly tourists staying in top class hotels. This is because the computer will automatically approve high credit for the card where the thief uses it to buy merchandise.

Some Americans habitually turn over $200,000 a month on a card. Arabs can also be big spenders with irregular spending habits which tend to reassure the computer if a burst of purchases is recorded. A card like this could fetch £400 for the pickpocket or hotel thief who steals it and sells it on to a major South American gang.

Other valuable cards are those stolen from the post. These have a long period of validity and have not been signed, so they are easy to use. The alarm may not be raised for some time. Cards with easy signatures fetch a small premium.

'The cheapest card would come from a mugged Chinese,' says a security man. 'If someone has been hit over the head, then the alarm is already out. And if he's Chinese, your average South American could look a bit foolish claiming to be Mr Ah Wong.'

South Americans are the top 'card artists' in Britain and the Continent. They are organized into Argentinian, Colombian and Chilean gangs. They are provided with identity documents and good lawyers, and are paid a 'prison pension' based on their previous earnings if the lawyer is unable to get them acquitted.

A 'card artist' will never use a 'hot' card for more than three days. It will start appearing on bulletins by then and a sharp-eyed shop assistant can make £100 reward from the card company for spotting it.

A professional will reckon to get at least £10,000 in purchases in a good run on a card and more probably £15,000. He will try to do it in as few stores as possible to reduce risks, making four or five 'hits' in an afternoon. He will buy goods that he can easily fence: jewellery, cameras, stereo equipment, fur coats. Oxford Street, Knightsbridge and Kensington High Street are the top three London areas for stolen cards, with Bond Street fourth.

'A typical haul on a card stolen from a top hotel would be a couple of diamond rings, three Nikon cameras, two Rolex watches, two gold cigarette lighters, a couple of video recorders, an emerald brooch and a fur wrap,' says a security man.

'Incidentally, they always go for Rolex and Nikon. Must be the advertising. Say, £9,500 the lot.

'But one or two are very smart. An Iranian's card was pickpocketed in his hotel before lunch. The card artist was finished with it by three. He had just two hits: a Persian prayer rug in one antique shop, and a Georgian silver salver in the other. That was £46,000.'

Amateurs are relatively simple to catch.

'They'll buy something silly like clothes,' says McGrath. 'They'll ask for their suits, no alterations, just wrap them up, they are in a hurry. Or they'll ask what the credit limit on the card is. Our card says how long the owner has had the card. It will say "member since 1960" and there's some kid of twenty-two trying to use it. So you know it's stolen.

'The professionals can be very good. We can always tell if the rightful owner is using the card. We put in all those dumb-sounding questions on the application form. Like what was your mother's maiden name. If our credit controller is talking to a store, and she wants to check that it really is the customer, all she has to do is ask that. No thief knows the maiden name of his victim's mother.

'But we can't check out every purchase like that, only ones where there is already suspicion. We have to rely on bulletins of stolen cards and rewards. At any time, we have a Top Ten cards that are really hot and we give a $250 reward to anyone who notices one.'

The card companies call the bulletin of stolen cards the 'stoplist'. Most outlets receive a stoplist weekly, but in active areas like Oxford Street or New York's 42nd Street, it is daily. A minimum of $25 is paid for every card that is picked up. American Express have a Special Award of $100 for 'Code 10' stolen cards that are particularly active.

Shop assistants, hotel receptionists and others who take cards have a set drill if they are suspicious. 'Whatever the amount,' say American Express instructions, 'call us for authorization and ask for Code 10. We will handle your call discreetly without making the card member aware of your suspicion. Your alertness could earn you an award if your suspicion is correct.'

Code 10 means that the computer will at once be interrogated to see if the queried purchase fits the cardholder's regular patterns. The cardholder can also be asked personal questions from his application form.

If the card has been altered, with the specimen signature changed, the reward goes up to $200, along with a gourmet dinner for two worth up to $60.

Cardholders can be defrauded by the card service establishment. There have been cases of tourist shops in Holland and restaurants in Greece simply writing in a 'one' in front of the figure to be paid. In the US and Spain, restaurants and shops have been opened specifically to cheat card-carrying tourists. Once they have passed the card company inspection, they put each customer's card through the franking machine several times, thus obtaining a number of duplicates of the bill on each card. They send these off to the card company, collect the considerable amount 'owing' to them, and disappear before the bills get back to the customer.

Waiters note the name and number on card counterfoils. They can then order merchandise or airline tickets by telephone on a 'clean' card. The plastic has not been stolen, simply the name and number.

It is very important to keep the original card member's copy of the charge. An American couple in Europe charged an $8 pair of slippers. When the bill arrived from the card company, it was for $78. The card company said no correction was possible unless the couple had saved their copy of the charge, which they had not.

Saving the customer copy is the only protection against this sting.

Credit cards have even been used to attempt to finance a revolution. A group of militant blacks in Pittsburgh bought thirty stolen cards and used them to buy goods to convert into cash. Before they were arrested, they had bought and sold hundreds of cameras, electric frying pans and film projectors. They had also rented Hertz and Avis cars which they drove to car accessory shops, selling the tyres and batteries.

In New York, two bartenders in midtown Manhattan made $165,000 in a year. They bought stolen credit cards, using them to get airline tickets which they sold to customers at the bar for their holidays. A New York group had a $1,000 credit card package, selling one American Express and one Master Charge card, two petrol company cards and a driving licence, all in the same name.

Most valuable of all are Q-cards, which are issued to a company rather than an individual. A Q-card bearer needs no identification and has high credit, so that the cards sell for £2,000 and up. Some restaurants and shops will 'charge' a card thief for supplying non-existent goods or food, splitting the amount involved with the thief.

The record for stolen credit cards is believed to belong to a guest arrested at the Hospitality Motor Inn in Pittsburgh. His wallet was splitting under the strain of cards that included Diners, American Express, Carte Blanche, Gulf Oil, Playboy Club, two BankAmericards and a Charge Association of Cincinnati. The airline tickets he had bought on one of these stolen cards totalled $9,500.

The traveller's cheque bonanza

Thirteen billion pounds worth of traveller's cheques were issued in 1981. Their advantage to the traveller is that, in principle, they are as good as cash and he gets his money back if they are lost or stolen.

The practical disadvantages are that many people will not accept them, or charge a premium if they do. The banks, or whoever issues the cheques, charge one per cent for the service – which may not sound much, but means travellers shelled out £130 million in 1981. And some banks are slow when it comes to refunds.

Traveller's cheques are excellent business for the banks, and they market and advertise them aggressively. The profit from the one per cent issuing charge is pleasant. The cream comes from having the use of the money paid for a cheque until the cheque is cashed. A traveller buys a £100 cheque in, say, May. He does not spend it until August. The bank has four months free use of the traveller's money. With twenty per cent interest rates, it makes £6.66 easy profit.

The money held by a bank between issuing a cheque and redeeming it for cash is known as 'outstandings' or 'the float' in the trade. American Express 'average outstandings' reached $2,300,000,000 in 1979. The float has only declined once, by six per cent at the height of the Depression in 1932.

'It's magic,' says a banker. 'You have a float of over $2 billion to invest at a high interest rate, loaned to you free by the travelling public.'

The trade call the period between a customer buying a cheque and redeeming it by spending it the 'float time'. It averages thirty-five to forty days with strong regional variations. Americans leave cheques idle for shorter periods than Europeans. The British 'float time' is over forty-five days. In the Middle East, it averages over sixty days.

American Express know of cheques originally bought in 1948 that have still not been cashed, giving them over thirty years free use of the money. 'Good until used – no time limit' American Express says encouragingly on its counterfoils. No wonder.

If the 'float' is the name of the game, it is not surprising that banks do not like handling cheques they have not issued. The profit is in issuing them, and most of them migrate with the world's tourists.

They are issued by big banks in Western industrial towns, in Britain, Germany, Scandinavia, Australia, South Africa, Japan, the East Coast and the Mid-West of the US. They are then cashed in local banks in the Mediterranean,

Florida, North Africa, Mexico. Since the real profit has already been made at the point of issue, the banks in the sun feel they are getting a raw deal. There is a lot of paperwork for little reward.

So, increasingly, they impose a handling charge. If the transaction involves currency changing, as it normally will, then the traveller gets fewer pesetas for his pounds than if he was changing cash. The rate of exchange is loaded against the traveller's cheque.

The rate of exchange for traveller's cheques varies more between banks in a particular resort than the rate for cash. Even in Europe, some banks as well as many hotels, restaurants and shops refuse to take traveller's cheques at all.

This is particularly true during times of currency fluctuation and crisis. When sterling was suffering a rapid decline in value in 1975, many British travellers were unable to exchange traveller's cheques for several weeks, even at poor rates of exchange. Those with cash had fewer problems. Americans found the same problem in Europe in 1979.

The reluctance is because, whereas a foreign bank can convert cash immediately, it takes time to clear a traveller's cheque and the exchange rate may have deteriorated in the meantime.*

A traveller could insure his own cash with any large insurance company for less than the one per cent charged by the traveller's cheque issuers. He would probably find more places willing to accept his cash, and at a better exchange rate than traveller's cheques.

* The first traveller's cheque was invented by Marcellus
  Fleming Berry of American Express. It was for $50 and it
  was cashed on 15 August 1891 at a Leipzig Hotel by
  William Fargo, a member of the Wells Fargo stagecoach firm
  which merged into American Express.
    There were no problems with exchange rates in 1891. The
  cheque was firmly marked: 'Good for US $50 or £10 4s. 1d.
  or 256 francs 25 centimes or 206 marks 25 pfennigs or 256
  lira 25 cents.'

The industry argues that traveller's cheques mean security and on-the-spot refunds that save both holiday and peace of mind if there is a theft or loss.

This is untrue of the traveller's cheques issued by many Continental banks. They commonly refuse to make any refunds until a year after the disappearance is reported. And, if any cheques are fraudulently converted during that time, then it is the customer and not the bank who loses. In õther words, the traveller's cheque is merely delayed insurance against loss, not theft. Some Italian banks have been known to refuse any refund whatever, whether there was fraudulent conversion or not.

Matters are substantially better with British-issued traveller's cheques. A full refund will be paid provided that the cheques were not countersigned before the loss or theft; that proof of purchase can be produced; that there is no suspicion of fraud; and that the loss has been promptly reported to the bank and the local police.

But an instant on-the-spot refund is by no means guaranteed. Lloyds has no provisions for instant refunds and, until the Lloyds branch which issued the cheques receives notification of the loss, the customer is responsible for any fraudulent conversion that takes place in the meantime. That is only waived if Lloyds can establish that the foreign bank which accepted the stolen cheque was negligent.

The Midland also has no on-the-spot refunds. The process normally takes one working week, which is little help to the traveller on a short holiday. The customer, however, is protected as long as he informs the bank as quickly as possible. The Midland stands the loss in the meantime.

The National Westminster offers a better deal, at least to account holders. They get full refunds from NatWest branches abroad or its corresponding banks as soon as they have received a telex from the UK issuing branch confirming the customer's bona fides. Non-account holders wait longer.

Barclays offer all purchasers an on-the-spot refund in

full as soon as the issuing branch has received a report of the loss and confirmed that a refund is in order.

Perhaps because they are in closer competition with Americans, Cook's mince fewer words when it comes to refunds. 'From the moment of loss, the customer is never liable. We refund without question as part of our policy of creating goodwill for our company,' they say. Apart from large sums that could arouse suspicions, on-the-spot refunds are made 'in the time it takes to send a telex from any Cook branch or agent in the world'.

Well, it can take a long time to send a telex, but travellers should note the difference in attitude between Lloyds and Cook's. On-the-spot refunds are standard with the big American issuers, like American Express, Citicorp and Bank of America.

American Express, one of the promptest payers, reckon that four out of five refunds are authorized on the same day that the claim is made. The major cause of delay is the customer's failure to keep the serial numbers of the cheques together with details of those spent. The paper with the serial numbers should always be kept separately from the cheques, or both will disappear together.

'Some banks are simply taking the public for a ride,' says an insurance broker. 'At one per cent plus the float, people are paying way over the odds for the pure insurance. What they should be buying is peace of mind, the certainty that they will get a refund at once and without having to travel a few hundred miles to collect it.

'I know of cases where people were told to get refunds for money stolen in Sicily from Rome, and one where a traveller, penniless after being robbed in Peru, was advised to find his way to Brazil for repayment.'

In the right circumstances, traveller's cheques are almost as attractive to thieves as cash. Dollar cheques are most popular because of their ready acceptability round the world, and fetch up to ninety per cent of face value. Stolen sterling cheques sell for around 80p in the pound in big British tourist destinations like France and Spain. In contrast, rarities like Thomas Cook's rupee cheques are seldom touched because they are difficult to negotiate. The rate for stolen sterling cheques falls to 50p per pound in more exotic places such as Senegal.

Cook's reckon that three customers in 1,000 lose their cheques, which involves an annual £3 million in refunds. American Express customers seem not so careful, with an estimated one in 200 making claims. The Company's New York offices has thirty-five staff coping with 3,000 calls a day in an average of thirteen languages, and 250 support staff process claims.

With toll-free calls coming in from Malibu and Manchester, it is an expensive business. American Express reckons to pay out $60 million a year in refunds to 190,000 people. It puts its losses from fraud, counterfeits and theft at 0.13 per cent of sales.

It spends $5 million a year on security. Its staff of 140 makes it one of the largest investigating forces in the world, with nineteen offices in the US and Europe, including London, and others in Hong Kong, Mexico City and Toronto.

Case studies for 5,050 selected refund claims in 1978 showed that forty-seven per cent resulted from theft. The most common cause by far, accounting for ten per cent of all claims, was sneak theft from hotel rooms. Theft from cars came next, followed by unarmed street theft by pickpockets and purse snatchers. Theft from the home is rarer, and travellers would be pleased to know that even in New York only one per cent of losses were the result of armed robbery.

Simple loss accounted for forty-two per cent of claims. The remaining eleven per cent includes the many people who leave their cheques at home when they go on holiday. The company will make a refund at the holiday resort as long as the customer promises to return the original cheques when he gets back.

Other refunds include cheques eaten by a giraffe in a safari park, carried off by a seagull, chewed by a horse, and deliberately destroyed to see if the refunding system worked.

'There are thefts in all the big tourist areas,' says Jim McGrath. 'Italy has always been a big situation, hotel thefts, pickpockets, purse snatching, car breaking. There have been tourists there for a long time so the locals have had plenty of experience – like Miami Beach.

'The Far East is picking up as the tourists increase, particularly the Philippines and Thailand. The really high refund-claiming cities are Bangkok and Amsterdam. In Bangkok, it's theft. In Amsterdam, it's fraud. People are making refund claims who either never bought cheques in the first place, or who cashed them themselves or sold them to a buddy.'

Hotel thieves usually strike when the traveller is still in the hotel, as he will take his traveller's cheques with him if he goes out. A common trick in big resorts is to go round the swimming pool picking up room keys from tables and sun chairs whilst the owners are in the pool. Buffet meals in hotel restaurants are another target. Whilst the guests queue for their food, the keys disappear from their tables.

Leaving notes for friends, or hotel signs to 'Please make up this room', are advertisements that the room is empty. Spanish hotel thieves specialize in stealing when guests are in their rooms. They claim to be hotel repairmen. They choose a room where they have seen from outside that the guest is on the balcony, or heard from the corridor that the shower is on. They knock on the door, claim to be fixing the electricity or plumbing, and help themselves when the guest goes back to the balcony or shower.

The 'Chambermaid Special' has a long tradition. A few cheques are stolen from the middle of a block of cheques. The owner may never realize that they have gone. Prostitutes also use this trick.

Hiding valuables makes little difference. Thieves know

where to look. Records show that most traveller's cheques are stolen from suitcases, followed in order by piles of dirty clothes, sponge bags, under mattresses and inside pairs of shoes. The dishonest know only too well where the honest put things.

The traveller's cheque issuers are liable to four main types of deception: customer fraud, the theft of cheques from customers, the theft of cheques in transit or from banks, and counterfeit.

Tourists also defraud insurance companies with non-existent thefts. In 1982 a German tourist claimed that his 18-foot speedboat had been stolen in the Italian Lakes. Police found it in his garage at home.

'Our first line of defence is nose,' says McGrath. 'Our refund people get a feeling for people who are wrong. Mainly you find they bluster. They demand service, they say they want speed, they bang the table. An honest person who's had his cheques lost or stolen isn't like that. He'll be apologetic. He'll feel embarrassed and guilty that he lost them in the first place. He's going to be very meek with us, and wants a shoulder to cry on. Any aggressive behaviour is automatically suspect.

'Even if we make a refund, the numbers of the missing cheques are fed into the computer in New York. As the cheques come in, they are picked up and checked for signature and identification, a passport or driving licence number. So we can prove that Amsterdam hippies, who are notorious, were cashing the cheques themselves.'

When a cheque is stolen, the signature is the main safeguard. The customer signs the cheque where he buys it. The original signature should be matched by the counter-signature when it is cashed.

'It's the original 1891 system, but it's still the best,' says McGrath. 'The cashier looks at the top signature and the bottom one, and if they look the same, he cashes it. It works for Japanese signatures just as well as European. People ask why we don't use finger prints. Its a lot harder to teach cashiers about prints than signatures, and no more effective.

'The trouble is that we've done too good a job persuading people that they will get their money back. Some people will cash anything as a result.'

Stolen cheques have been cashed with entirely different names on them, as well as different spellings. Cheques with obviously oriental names on them have been cashed by Europeans and vice-versa.

'We've had specimens cut from newspaper and magazine advertisements that have been honoured,' says McGrath. 'A guy in Karachi collected a dozen promotional specimens from dustbins when we had a direct mail campaign in Pakistan. He cashed each one for $50. Not bad, $600 from a few dustbins.'

Although the cheque companies are not obliged to pay up when names and signatures do not tally, it is big-scale 'laundering' operations that worry them. Here the cheques are signed by professional forgers for a small fee and cashed through a front company, normally a restaurant or jewellery store. The forged signatures will be good enough for the cheque company to be forced to pay up unless the 'laundering' can be proved in other ways.

Cheques will often be transferred from the country in which they were stolen to a big 'laundry'. The first halting place for the many cheques stolen in Italy, after they have been bought at twenty or thirty per cent of face value by a gang from the petty thieves who actually stole them, is Marseilles. Here forgers work in shifts countersigning them. They are then 'cashed' by restaurants and shops owned by the gangs in Spain, which claim from the cheque companies. Italian cheques are prone to surface in Madrid and Benidorm, just as cheques stolen in London often appear in Rome and Majorca.

Things are a little tougher for the freelance thief, who has no tame outlet to cash the cheques for him. He has to countersign in front of a cashier. The most skilful do this freehand. One, who was eventually arrested, was searched for a weapon. He produced a gold Cross pen: 'This is my gun.'

Others laboriously trace out a signature in pencil. They then go over the pencil lines with a felt tip pen in front of the cashier. 'The cutest just pretend to be drunk,' says McGrath. 'You get a lot of real drunks signing their own cheques in abominable scrawls when they are on holiday. Its easy for a thief to pull the same stunt.'

The signature problem does not arise when blank cheques are stolen. The thieves can sign them as they like. Thefts of 'clean' cheques are increasing and they are now a popular target in bank hold-ups. In 1979, $2.4 million was stolen in a single raid on an Ottawa post office.

'But its a headache for them to get rid of them in bulk,' says McGrath. 'We had $1 million worth stolen from a post office in South Africa. A Swiss bank teller noticed someone who was in a great hurry to cash a large amount. You can be in a tearing hurry to cash a few hundred dollars. But not $20,000. You don't leave the car on a double yellow line or have a taxi with the meter running when you're changing thousands. The man was arrested.

'We get most of the cheques back that are stolen in bulk. We bulletinize the system. We put out the numbers to all the banks, and the cashiers know there will be good rewards if they spot a hot cheque. We can't do that with every cheque that gets lifted from a hotel room. The list would be too long.'

Counterfeiting flourishes. In 1979, American Express seized $4.5 million worth of counterfeits. The main areas are North East Canada, the US, Italy, the Benelux countries and Latin America. The company identified thirteen new counterfeits. One printing press in Tiajuana accounted for $1.7 million.

Some successful 'printers' do not counterfeit cheques at all. They simply invent the bank. The traveller's cheque industry is growing at fifteen per cent a year, and more banks are issuing their own cheques. These banks are often unheard of in the foreign resorts where the cheques are cashed.

So the printer thinks up the name of a bank, pays an art student a small amount to design a suitable cheque, and has a print shop make up some plates and run them off. The total investment is unlikely to exceed £2,000.

Cheques of the 'First National Bank of London' have been cashed by unsuspecting Malaysians in Kuala Lumpur. Fake Australian banks have figured prominently in London. One Australian 'printer' made several thousand pounds in the Earls Court area of London before moving on to Majorca. His bank was the Western Australia Cattle Grazer's Bank. Never mind that he left the 'i' out of Grazier. The design included a kangaroo, a koala bear *and* an aborigine and had clearly had a lot of work put into it.

Another character was sentenced at the Old Bailey after inventing his own bank and printing his own cheques with Letraset. He called it 'Coutts and Hoares', dropping the Coutts when he ran out of Cs on his Letraset sheets. He claimed to be a member of the Bath Club, the Athenaeum, the National Liberal Club, the Garrick and Wentworth Golf Club. After being given the last rites when a lung was removed, he got out of hospital and into the most expensive nursing home in Sussex. He was finally caught at the Savoy.

There is nobody to indemnify a hotel or restaurant that cashes a cheque on a non-existent bank. Indeed banks have themselves been taken. This is making it more difficult to cash cheques from lesser-known banks and further reduces the value of traveller's cheques.

Though the banks may not like it, the traveller's cheque business may soon start to wane. Personal cheques with a banker's card are already accepted in many European countries, and credit cards have revolutionized the ease of travel.

2 FUNDAMENTALS

Eating

Feeding and watering the tourist is a mighty industry. Its worldwide turnover exceeds $15 billion, and it enables great armies of tourists to make their holiday campaigns to lands impossibly remote a generation ago. The 100 million who descend on the Mediterranean each year outnumber the combatants in the Second World War. The British in Spain exceed those of the British Expeditionary Force by 20 to one, and more Australians visit the Far East than fought at Gallipoli and Anzio combined.

The rewards from all this to the caterer can be enormous.

But the spectacular growth in the Mediterranean resorts and the big tourist capitals like London and Paris has strained supplies to the point where a country like Spain, whose thirty-seven million population plays host to more than that number of visitors each year, has changed from a seafood exporter to a major importer. The demand for fashionable dishes has pushed up the cost of some ingredients beyond recognition.

Food faking

Salmon was once so lowly that Scottish ghillies insisted in their contracts that they would not have to eat it more than five days a week. Veal was cheaper than chicken before the war. Scampi was the staple of peasants and fishermen. Oysters were the food of the poor, wolfed down at street stalls.

They are now essential dishes in any self-respecting restaurant or hotel. This is reflected in the prices, to the point where restaurateurs and chefs use elaborate methods to fake the ingredients. None will admit to food faking, of course. It always happens in someone else's place. But everyone in the trade knows the details and a special slang has emerged.*

In Britain, lobster fakers are known as 'monkfish men' after the cheap fish they use to replace expensive lobster. In France, faking is known as 'truquage'. The pig, widely used as a substitute for more costly meat, is affectionately known as 'cher ange', the dear angel of profit.

It is possible to have a totally bogus menu, in which none of the main ingredients are what they are said to be. A restaurateur who fakes widely can more than double his profits. Further, it enables him to offer items on his menu that are vital to the restaurant's status, but which are unavailable to him because of short supply and over-demand.

A skilled faker can work his way through many of the classic dishes on a menu. All he needs is a little ingenuity and a gullible public.

It is often thought that France, as the home of fine food, is innocent of sharp practice. This touching belief is misplaced. Their skill gives French chefs a head start with faking. Snails, for example, count as fish in culinary terms. In legal terms, French snails can be a near complete fraud.

As early as 1907, fake escargots were being made in France by a machine which filled shells with twisted calves' lungs, heavily garlicked. A more common practice is to serve cheap Chinese slugs in snail shells. Frozen Chinese slugs are difficult to distinguish from snails once they are garlicked, and they cost a fourth as much. It is estimated

* It is not new. The first International Congress for the Repression of Fraud in Foodstuffs was held in 1908. It examined a typical case, a 'Roquefort' cheese that was a mixture of cheap cheeses and in which the familiar greeny-blue marks of Roquefort were made with copper. However, the scale of faking today is inflated by the growth in holidays and leisure and is unprecedented.

that three times as many slugs as snails are sold in French restaurants.

Bisque d'Homard should be a soup made of lobster. It is often made of fish stock, herbs, cheap white wine, tomatoes and cream. The tomatoes give an authentic pink colouring to the white fish base that is used instead of lobster. A little tinned lobster may be added. To get the characteristic strong taste and smell of shell, old lobster shells are boiled up with fish heads to make the stock.

A few real prawns are put into a fake Bisque de crevettes. This 'prawn soup' is a thick poultry soup with raw sea-weed that has been put through a mixing machine. It is then sieved and coloured with a little tomato sauce to make a handsome profit, particularly for Chinese restaurants.

Salmon mousse is another temptingly expensive starter. A convincing mousse can be made with a base of tinned tuna fish and some artificial colouring at one fifth of the cost of the real thing.

Caviar can be cod's roe or lumpfish roe with colouring. Expensive truffles are frequently faked. A common practice is to use black mushrooms, or dyed, salted and boiled potato. A slight scent is given by a little tinned extract of truffle. A slab of commercial pâté de foie at £1 on a menu becomes pâté de fois gras truffe and is worth £3.

Price makes truffles open to fraud of all sorts. They sold wholesale for $175 a pound in 1981 at Perigord, France, the centre of truffle sales. Shops sold them at $350 a pound, with restaurant mark-ups taking the price to the public up to $650 a pound. For that, the diner should be getting the *Tuber melanosporum*, hunted out by pigs from beneath the ground near oak tree roots. The high season for hunting is in February and March.

The finest Perigord truffles, known as *premiere cuisson*, are sterilized once and sold quickly because they lose their weight. Perigord truffle production in 1977 was eighteen tons – but the area managed both to meet heavy French demand and to export 27 tons. This is because the bulk of 'Perigord' truffles are not collected there at all, but in the Quercy region of France, and in Italy and Spain. The *Tuber aestivum*, a tasteless summer truffle, is sometimes substituted for the real thing. So are parts of broken truffles, sterilized twice so that they keep their weight.

Charcuterie is easily transformed. It is difficult to tell whether a 'game' pâté is made from pheasant and hare or chicken and rabbit if there is a strong taste of alcohol, herbs and spices. Galantine de veau can be made from pork whitened in lukewarm water at half the cost of veal.

Occasionally, it is the manufacturers who get up to the tricks. Canned lobster has been found to consist entirely of squid, octopus and cuttlefish. Strict government regulation of the food processing industry makes this a rarity in Europe, if not in the Far East and notably in Thailand.

Restaurateurs are as prone to fake or misdescribe main courses as starters. Sauces provide useful disguise to the flavour and profits are considerable.

Veal is the unscrupulous restaurateur's best friend. It is lean and tender and popular. Customers know it to be expensive. It can be served with a variety of supposedly costly and expensive sauces. Since it has little taste of its own, the restaurateur can charge veal prices whilst actually using something much cheaper.

Chicken and pork are the common substitutes. British restaurateurs sometimes call pork 'veal with a curly tail'. Rabbit is also used in France and Italy in made dishes such as blanquette de veau. This insipid, tasteless and often faked dish with a white sauce is nevertheless very popular.

Veal escaloppes are beaten out flat before cooking to break up the fibres and make the meat more tender. The beating out process is convenient if chicken is used because it disguises the shape and texture of the meat. A real escaloppe is cut on the bias, which prevents it from shrinking and bending during cooking. In a top class restaurant, it will be cut from the leg and will be quite flat after cooking.

Fake veal can be spotted with a dish like Wiener-schnitzel, where the escaloppe is cooked in egg and bread-crumbs and not masked by a sauce. The edges will curl. Cut into it and examine the grain. Chicken will come away in long flakes, but veal is much firmer.

The texture of pork is similar to veal. It is difficult to detect especially when a sauce is used in a classic faker's dish such as Veal Marsala. Sweet sherry with a teaspoon of brown sugar is used instead of the more expensive Marsala, and the taste is strong enough to disguise the origins of the 'veal'. Ironically, before the war when fac-tory farming of chickens was unheard of, restaurants would pass off veal as chicken.

In a bizarre case, the Horses and Ponies Protection So-ciety has claimed that London restaurants are serving roast donkey as veal. The Secretary for the Protection of Horses says that donkeys and mules are used in Italy for salami.

Beef often turns out to be horsemeat. 'This is a criminal practice that must be stopped,' says John Locke, director general of the Bacon and Meat Manufacturers' Associ-ation. In one case, the owner of a Chinese take-away in Tulse Hill, London was prosecuted after he had been seen buying large quantities of horsemeat from a pet food stall in Penge. Peter Ablett, an environmental health officer in Hertfordshire, estimated that enough horsemeat and con-demned meat for 110 million meals was sold in 1980 as beef in Britain.

The profits on horsemeat are considerable. It could be bought for 35p a pound but, described as beef, it sold for 58p. Donkeys were imported from Ireland and Australia. Meat from animals which died on farms, often diseased and with a high level of veterinary drugs, is bought for 10p to 15p a pound and sold at beef prices. The knacker's yards which deal with this meat also make regular calls to vets, buying dead household pets like cats and dogs. Bruce Coover, the environmental health officer for Hammersmith in London, says: 'We reckon that two per cent of beef comes from knackers' yards or is not beef at all.'

EEC regulations encourage the trade. 'EEC restrictions on Argentine beef coincided with a glut of knackers' meat because of a reduction in the amount used for pet food,' says Coover. 'The result was a boom in knackers' meat sold as beef. There is also a twenty per cent import levy on beef from the US and Australia that is fit for human consumption. If you import unfit meat, you evade the levy, and you double your profit if you can then sell it as fit meat.'

Coover says: 'You cannot stop restaurants from buying this meat. Few of them do it deliberately. It's sold to them by companies collecting from knackers' yards from Cumberland to Pembrokeshire. But cheap restaurants, and some expensive ones, will buy meat on the verge between pet food and fit for human consumption, the stuff that just slides through.'

The hamburger is most at risk. Thousands of tons of horse and kangaroo meat have been exported as prime Australian beef to hamburger manufacturers. Buffalo and donkeys have also entered a scandal that has caused serious damage to the Australian beef trade. In one instance, 36,000 pounds of 'horseburgers' were sent to San Diego, Phoenix and Texas from Australia. The involvement of the American Mafia is being examined by a Royal Commission set up in October 1981 in Australia. The disappearance of one Andrew Komarnicki, a Queensland kangaroo meat dealer, is thought to be linked with the affair.

Operation Meathook, coordinated by the Association of Environmental Health Officers, discovered that hundreds of tons of kangaroo and donkey flesh are used in hamburgers in Britain. One seventy-ton load of kangaroo meat was sent for processing into hamburgers in Bedford before the trade was stopped.

The big hamburger chain Wimpy narrowly avoided buying horsemeat passed off as beef. 'I was ashen faced and horrified,' said managing director Ian Petrie. Another Wimpy executive said of the 1981 case: 'If this stuff had been sold it would have killed us stone dead.'

'You cannot tell horse from donkey, or kangaroo from wallaby, and it's not easy to tell them from beef,' says Bruce Coover. 'As a rule of thumb, a restaurateur will run his fingers through a sample hamburger. If it's gooey like putty, with a slight smell like linseed oil, it's horse. Analysis takes time, and some cuts of horsemeat and donkeymeat are virtually indistinguishable from beef.'

Tests involve injecting rabbits with horseflesh to produce antibodies. Blood samples are taken for use on suspicious meat in hamburger plants. The antibodies stick to horseflesh but not to beef.

The fakers are clever, however. The Shropshire Trading Standards department says: 'In seeing if there is enough meat and meat protein, the analyst makes a calculation based on the amount of nitrogen present. So the manufacturers put nitrogen in to disguise this and put in "meat extenders" like bone protein and water.' Urea is put into ham to add nitrogen, and the department found a 'chicken product' made from chicken necks and stripped carcases.

Wild boar is popular on Continental menus. It commands both high prices and respect, and it can be made from pork. Noisettes de marcassin, the expensive young boar, is easily made from fillet of pork, as is jambonneau, the knuckle of boar. Venison is another prestigious game dish which can be made from pork, marinated horsemeat, kangaroo, impala and gazelle.

Coq au vin is misdescribed more often than not. The cock is replaced by battery chicken, which is boiled to a pulp in order to make the meat indistinguishable and to hide the fraud. It should be in a rich juice of wine and the cock's blood. A battery chicken produces little blood and so pig's blood is added. This tends to curdle.

There may be still stranger things in the sea than ever came out of it, but this is not due to lack of effort by the fakers.* They have, for example, invented a lobster that is a fish, and a prawn that is manufactured like a croquette potato.

Lobster is expensive and has snob appeal, an irresistible combination. Monkfish is widely used as a substitute. Lobster Mornay should be lobster in a sauce flavoured with brandy, cream and cheese. It is easy to fake with white fish, particularly monkfish, because the cheese disguises the fish. Monkfish does not separate into flakes when cooked and mixed in a sauce. Like chopped lobster meat, it keeps the shape in which it was originally cut. The chef will use enough cheese and brandy to ensure that the dried up and re-used shell is the only clue to the fraud. If a small amount of tinned lobster is used, the resulting and convincing hot lobster dish will also satisfy trades descriptions legislation.

There are two clues. A dry and brittle shell, or one that is a washed pink instead of bright red, indicates that it has been used before. It is also suspect if a restaurant does not offer lobster mayonnaise or a similar cold lobster dish where the meat is visible. It is more difficult to use monkfish cold than submerged under hot Parmesan cheese.

---

* Sometimes, though alas not often, the reverse of food faking takes place. Here rare items of value are sold as common ingredients at low prices. In 1981, thousands of kilos of Russian caviar were sold to the West as smoked herring. Several hundred Russians, including Caspian Sea fishermen and Department of External Trade officials were imprisoned. A member of the mighty Soviet Central Committee, Alexander Akimovitch Ichkov, was fired from his post. The principle was simple. The conspirators put caviar in boxes of three to five kilos marked 'Smoked Herring'. This was sold as such to the delighted customers in Western Europe and Japan, who were happy to pay a herring price direct to Moscow and an unofficial extra payment for caviar into Swiss banks. Senior Russian officials who could travel benefited from the money in Switzerland, and paid off fellow conspirators in Russia, albeit at a poor rate of exchange.

In France eel and devil fish are used as lobster substitutes, most commonly in Lobster à l'Americaine. The best restaurants try to get the ingredients for their lobster bisque at the expense of those who order lobster as a main course.

Scampi is widely faked with monkfish and other fish. Southern Mediterranean recipes, French and Italian, such as scampi Provencale, are the easiest to doctor. These dishes are rich in garlic, herbs and tomato. As with veal dishes from this region, the main ingredient becomes a mere vehicle for the sauce in unscrupulous hands.

Restaurateurs also use up fish from the previous day in 'scampi' dishes. Scampi are best cooked plainly in batter and then served with a sauce into which the fish is dipped. The customer can then both taste and see what he is eating. The tartare sauce should have a mayonnaise base with chopped chives added to it. Chopped gherkins are used to disguise leftover fish, and the whole sauce is swamped with vinegar.

There are other ploys which do not involve outright faking, but which are used to disguise poor or ageing ingredients. Making new dishes from leftovers on returned plates is called 'repasse' by waiters and 'Arloque', after Harlequin, by proprietors. These 'phoenix' dishes are common with chicken vol-au-vent, beef Stroganoff and veal Venitienne. The big French regional dishes, like bouillabaisse, choucroute and cassoulet, were originally designed to get rid of leftovers. They are used as a profitable dumping ground for every bit of sausage, meat, fish or vegetable that comes back on dirty plates in some form or other.

Pungent sauces are important aids to disguise. Some restaurants have what they call a 'sauce á tout faire', a pot into which are slopped the leftovers of osso buco, cooking grease, wine dregs and gravy. The pot is called the 'dustbin' since it is where the slops turn up. Modern cuisine, with light sauces and simple display, is more difficult to fake.

Strong and piquant sauces are used to revive tongue that is past its prime. Fresh kidneys are first dipped in vinegar and then flambéed in front of the customer. Old ones are covered in mustard and put in the oven.

Taste is hidden with pepper, herbs and flambées – what the French call the 'arts of *poivrage*, *herbage* and *flambage*'. Bad meat is sold covered with pepper and grilled over an open fire to further disguise the taste. The liberal use of herbs transforms mutton into lamb. Using a pastis such as Pernod or Ricard in a flambée gets rid of the smell of ammonia that clings to old meat. Cooking stove alcohol is added to ensure a good flame.

Tired meat is freshened up. It is washed in running water to get rid of the maggots and mouldiness. Coal dust is rubbed into it, and it is cooked over a low heat for an hour and a half before being washed in fresh water again to soak off the coal dust.

Fish is made to look new by washing it in bicarbonate of soda, scrubbing it and putting glycerine in the eyes and rabbit or pig blood in the gills. Chefs lick old tired bits of truffle with their tongues, an old trick to make them shine.

Chemical aids transform the appearance of stale or cheap food. Total-Fix spray 'prolongs freshness and keeps an appetizing look'. Meats and pâtés get a lively pink colour from the reddening salt Selrose or the nitrate colourant Colorado. There are specialist colourants for salami and luncheon meat and one that makes horsemeat resemble beef.

'Home-made' dishes include quenelles, bouchées a la Reine, and apple pie. These may be mass-produced by factories using powdered milk, and bread regularly collected from restaurants. Fish is described as '*du golfe*' or '*du ligne*'. This should mean that it is locally caught, though it comes from Senegal and has spent a couple of weeks on ice.

All such ploys are known as 'stretching the menu' in the trade. A 'stretched' menu can start with terrine du chef that still has tin marks on it, go on to truite de la rivière from a Swedish trout farm and end with a tarte maison from the neighbourhood supermarket.

Tell-tale tests of a good restaurant

It seems a daunting task to be able to tell whether a restaurant is honest or whether it is busily ripping off its customers. The trade itself relies on the difficulties outsiders have in judging it. 'The food guides can send inspectors until they are blue in the face,' says the proprietor of a bistro in a fashionable resort. 'They don't catch the little things that add up to how good a business is. Neither does the public.'

In fact, there are criteria for judging restaurants which the customer can follow as easily as the trade. The rules are well established. When a rival sets up, a restaurateur will visit it with a specific set of inquiries in mind. He will check on faking, draw arcane conclusions from the lettuce content of prawn cocktail, pay special attention to the crème brulée, whether he eats it or not.

It is a question of learning the give-away signs.

The first check is whether the restaurant is practising what the French call '*mise en place*'. This means getting everything ready well in advance, and it is common with restaurants that deal mainly with tourists. Although it makes sense to lay the table settings in the afternoon for the evening, and at night for the next day, it is bad if the sauces, the salad dressing, the flowers, the roasts, the sweets have already been prepared. Everything becomes stale, and sauces like hollandaise and tartare are notoriously swift to go off. It is easy to tell a '*mise en place*' restaurant. The place is orderly. There is none of that edge of chaos feeling that marks the good restaurant.

There is too much emphasis on display, known as '*cuisine de la vue*'. The sweet trolleys are lined up, the sauce boats neatly laid out, the roast is visible keeping warm, the cold meats have been temptingly displayed on a great platter, the hors d'ouevre is ready prepared on a trolley.

Such a restaurant will also go in for '*le nappé*', the French expression for squeezing the maximum impact out of tablecloths, napkins, cutlery, table lamps, gilt mirrors and whatever else keeps the mind off the food. Elaborate place settings, with napkins folded into exotic shapes, 'theme' décor, waiters dressed as fishermen, toreadors or Yeomen of the Guard, waitresses dressed as Austrian peasant girls, Elizabethan wenches or Spanish senoritas,* all this spells poor food.

'A restaurant ought to look like a restaurant,' says a Torremolinos bar owner. 'Not like a fishing village or an Alpine resort or a stately home. And food is meant to be eaten, not laid out to look tempting on trolleys or in the window.'

The art of making food more attractive looking than it tastes is part of the '*cuisine de la vue*'. Everything that can be is cut into shapes. The carrots are shaped, the melons, the piped potato, the pie dishes, the cheeses. The lemon wedges are cut with little curly tails. Every surface of the sweets gleams with cream.

A restaurant that specializes in an obvious '*cuisine de la vue*' is likely to cater for functions and groups as well as for individual tourists. The chefs are chiefly concerned to meet the ratio of ingredients to cost laid down by the owner or food and beverage manager. They will often cut back by ten per cent on package groups, conferences and other mass meals because the customers will not notice.

---

* The world's most exotic menu is at the Safari Restaurant in the Saarland. It offers shoulder of lion in red wine sauce, leg of tiger with sauté potatoes and red cabbage, and Cape Antelope with game chips and redcurrant jelly.
  The restaurant is popular enough for owner Adi Zimmer to claim that Europe's zoos and circuses cannot keep up with his demand for meat. A Saarbrücken wholesaler now flies in frozen buffalo, tiger, bison, bear and lion.
  Herr Zimmer says: 'It is difficult to explain what a lion tastes like. But one thing is certain. None has ever been sent back.'

Waiters are given instructions to take specially allotted large portions to the tour or conference organizer (or, with a wedding, to the parents of bride and groom). Thus those responsible for paying assume that their fellows have done as well as they have.

Still in general terms, a restaurateur will always check whether a rival changes his menu regularly, or whether he goes on repeating it ad infinitum (more accurately for the customer, ad nauseam, for good chefs are often temperamental and do not take kindly to being stuck with the same dishes). He will also note when the rival gets to market. The best are there between four and five in the morning, the worst between seven and eight when only suspect rubbish is left.

A quick glance at the kitchens will show if there are poor cooking oils, such as corn oil, reused butter, butter sauces which are rejuvenated with starch, reheated dishes without the fat removed. There will be flour everywhere, in the sauce bearnaise, the white sauce, bulking out the omelettes.

Admittedly, the traveller is at a disadvantage here. He will not be able to tell how often the menu is changed unless he has been there before. He cannot check what time *le patron* goes to the market: the bags under the eyes may be the result of late nights rather than early mornings. It is difficult to get a look at the kitchens.

The ground rules for meat and fish are more easily observed. There is a simple test to see if a restaurant buys good meat. Its menu will include the classic beef dishes, roast beef, steak tartare, Chateaubriand and steak au poivre. These depend on the quality of the meat. The sauces served with them are either subtly flavoured, like sauce bearnaise, or served in small quantities, like horse-radish.

Restaurants which buy inferior meat will avoid these dishes generally, since it is easy to tell the poor quality. The roast beef will have to be served with a lot of gravy to disguise the taste. The dish is automatically suspect if the gravy is added in the kitchen and not at the table. Curled edges show that the beef has been reheated. This is done because cold beef can be cut into thinner slices than a hot roast, thus saving money.

Neither the beef nor steak will run blood when a fork is pressed into them. This is because the grain is damaged in cheap frozen meat. The freezing also gives the meat a slightly grey colour and a dry taste. A restaurant that only offers beef casseroles and pasta dishes with beef mince will be using cheap beef.

To the restaurateur's delight, tenderness is now more in vogue than taste. Young meat is the most tender. Because it needs less hanging time, it is cheaper. There is a big restaurant and hotel market for 'baby beef', bright red meat with little fat, tender but with little taste.

'It's as bland as cotton wool,' says a butcher. 'But a lot of restaurants are going for it. It may never be good, but it won't get any complaints for being tough. That's all people worry about today. It's got to be soft and the right colour.'

The baby beef market has been helped by the fashion for ordering meat rare or underdone. This was originally an American habit. The rodeo impressario Tex Austin was asked how he wanted his steak by the *maitre d'hotel* at the Savoy in the 1920s. 'Get a bullock, wound it slightly and drive it in,' he said. This has spread to most European tourists.

Lamb has a beautiful and distinctive taste which a good chef will not conceal with rich sauces if it is fresh meat. It is ruined by sauces with alcohol. There is a strong chance that any complicated creation made with 'fresh' lamb is actually mutton or New Zealand lamb, though at a different price.

Lamb freezes well and though not as good as fresh meat, frozen lamb is less easy to spot than frozen beef. The flavour is not so delicate, nor is it as tender. It is perfectly tasty in casseroles and oriental dishes where the lamb is marinated in liquid mixed with various spices, but it is not easy to use it to produce satisfactory grills or roasts. Lamb cutlets, for example, should be slightly charred on the outside and slightly pink near the bone. A uniform colour to a chop or cutlet is a sure sign of Kiwi or Argentine ancestry.

The English have never acquired the taste for underdone lamb and the significant absence of a pink centre is often lost on them. The French are seldom fooled and the best English lamb is easier to find in Paris than in London. Spanish lamb can be excellent but, like most Italian lamb, it is frequently mutton.

Pork is an excellent test of a chef, since it is improved by herb stuffings and sauces. They counteract the richness and greasiness of the meat, but need careful preparation. High prices should never be charged for pork dishes. It is relatively cheap and with intensive farming should stay that way.

Seafood starters throw much light on a restaurant. Prawn cocktail is a good test. It is on most menus and numerous liberties can be taken with it. Most prawns are frozen for a little time to get them to market in good condition. They should, however, be frozen for a minimum time to thaw out juicy and succulent.

Deep frozen prawns, and the cultivated Japanese and Scandinavian variety, are small and tasteless. There is an easy trick to see if they have been frozen too long. Dishes made with them will have a rim of water washing round the edges of the mayonnaise. This is because it is impossible to thaw out a deep frozen prawn completely and it continues to exude water.

The liberal use of tabasco or paprika is also a sign that inferior prawns are being used. Real mayonnaise has an unmistakable taste of olive oil. If this is missing, it indicates a commercial mayonnaise with corn oil.

A poor restaurant will also economise by filling the bottom of the dish with shredded lettuce or cabbage. It is baldly stated of a leading commercial prawn salad that it is 'cabbage based and while the pink paprika and tomato based sauce strongly hints at prawn cocktail, there are fewer prawns than would normally be acceptable'.

Potted shrimps made by the chef are the sign of a good restaurant. The shrimps are covered with melted butter, flavoured with bay leaves and allowed to cool. The covering butter is delicate and not quite set hard. If the portion is turned out on the plate it should look rather messy.

Commercially produced shrimps come in small, hard, circular portions in which the butter is set like a rock and there are no bits of bay leaf. Water will also run onto the lettuce leaf on which they are served.

Ask for oysters to be opened and served on the deep shell, not the flat one. The classic way of opening oysters is onto the flat shell and if they have been pre-opened they will be done this way. A restaurant that is unable to produce oysters on the deep shell when asked to is using pre-opened ones.

With whitebait, each small fish should be separate, crisp outside and soft within. This can only be achieved by getting the fish completely dry, coating them with a little flour, and frying in very hot oil. Frozen whitebait are difficult to dry before frying. The fish stick together in a tell-tale lump, the sign of a sloppy restaurant.

Where whitebait are eaten whole, the bones are best removed from sprats. This is a fiddly and time-consuming business, and the presence of sprats on a menu speaks well for the chef. So does a shrimp sauce, which is also difficult to prepare so that an average place will stick to prawn sauces. Cheap fish like herring and fresh mackerel on a menu also indicate a restaurant that is prepared to take trouble to satisfy customers who know what seafood is about.

Fresh salmon has a kind of milky curd between the flakes. It is clearly visible in the cooked fish. Its absence means that the salmon is either frozen or has been kept for several days. A frozen salmon that has been slowly thawed before cooking is tasty enough, but it should not be as expensive as fresh fish and it should not be on the menu as such.

Trout can either be the most delicate of fish, or the most bland, depending on their freshness and the skill of the chef. They are imported frozen from Japan and Scandinavia. These can be distinguished by their tendency to dryness. A fresh trout has a succulence to its flesh and a moisture lacking in frozen fish.

Turbot and halibut, together with the often-faked Dover sole, are the aristocrats of white fish. They are usually served in slices, or steaks, and need a good sauce to bring out their full flavour. Some French restaurants can still produce classic Victorian dishes like turbot with oyster sauce and halibut with shrimp sauce. The time and skill needed to make these sauces is the proof of a first-rate restaurant.

Travel has made fish like mullet and skate more popular. It is a good omen if a menu includes skate with black butter, raie au beurre noisette. 'Black' butter is actually browned to the point just before it burns. It needs split-second timing and confidence if it is not to be ruined.

The edge is the crucial test of smoked fish, be it trout, mackerel or salmon. Old smoked fish is dry. It will curl at the edges rather than lie smug and succulent on the plate. The strong taste of malt vinegar in commercial horse-radish sauce makes it unsuitable for smoked fish. A good restaurant will make its own rather than doctoring a factory product with cream.

Coquilles St Jacques is a revealing and fashionable dish. Fresh scallops are large and have bright red 'tongues'. They are very expensive. A poor restaurant will use tiny, frozen scallops which are cheap and tough. The ratio of mashed potato to fish will be high.

Restaurateurs reckon crème brulée to be the most significant sweet. It is a thick custard which should be made the day before use so that it sets properly and can be chilled. On the day it is to be eaten, a caramel top is put on using a salamander or a very hot grill.

The top should be an even, golden, brown, shiny and crisp, able to be cracked like ice with a swift blow from a teaspoon. It only remains like this for about twelve hours after it has been made. Then the top starts to melt and the custard to separate. It is expensive to make, and many restaurants will keep it for a few days if it is not eaten at once.

Old crème brulée is distinguished by the melting top, which cannot be cracked, and by the deposit of fluid which collects at the bottom of the custard. To avoid this, one trick is to put the caramel top on only after the pudding has been ordered. When this happens, the custard beneath will be hot from the grill and unpleasant.

Menu fixing

The big chain and hotel restaurants depend on high turnover, copy writing and canny pricing. The perfect tourist*

---

* A perfect example of the more well-heeled tourist is Peter Cipolla, a New York restaurant and bar owner who took out his girlfriend Jean Schaedle for his fortieth birthday. The celebration cost him $5,004.20, or £2,924. The tip alone came to $878, or £512. It was the world's most expensive meal for two.

Cipolla ate at New York's Palace Restaurant, the most expensive in the US. It was not what he ate that got him the record, however. The Palace had a fixed price menu of $75 so food for two came to only $150. It was the drink that did it.

The couple started with three bottles of Cristal Champagne (1971) at $225, and went on to a single bottle of Cheval Blanc (1945) at $595 and four bottles of Bollinger Blanc de Noirs (1969) at $400. Two bottles of Richebourg Domaine de la Romanée-Conti (1962) then set them back $550 and four bottles of Dom Pérignon (1969) cost $300.

For good measure, they wound up with an 1880 Cognac, Gaston Briand Le Paradis, for $1,600.

They dined from 7.30 p.m. to 1 a.m., starting with lobster with truffles, fish pâté with goose liver, lobster bisque, at this end of the market, be he in Benidorm or Bermuda, will order a grapefruit cocktail, grilled gammon with egg and pineapple ring, and baked egg custard.

These items are often triple starred on the chef's menu, pinned up in the kitchen. Waiters try to push them, because they carry the biggest mark-ups and make the most profit. A grapefruit cocktail selling for 50p costs 11p in ingredients, leaving 380 per cent profit. Grilled gammon gives 230 per cent profit. 'With inflation bounding away, sweets and dishes of this type will save the day for the caterers,' says a menu specialist.

Menu specialists are used by the chain restaurants to work out the costs and profit of each dish to the nearest penny. A cost breakdown of a £2.50 grilled gammon shows: gammon slice, 8 oz, 42p; standard egg, 6p; canned pineapple ring 4p; 3 oz frozen peas 6p; frozen chips 5 oz, 8p; half tomato 3p; parsley butter, ½ oz, 2p; cooking oil, 1 fluid oz, 4p; seasoning, 1p. The food cost is 76p, leaving £1.74 for overheads and profit.

---

mussel soup, swordfish, crayfish and oysters, and angel's hair spaghetti. Rack of lamb and squab made up the entrées. For pudding, they nibbled at frozen soufflés with strawberries, petits fours, apple tarts with brandy, chocolate mousse cake, chocolate truffles and cheese.

Said Cipolla: 'It was well worth it, a good experience. The food was excellent and the booze terrific. The only thing you take with you in life is what you have in your belly. Besides, Frank Valenza, who owns the Palace, is getting divorced and could use the money.'

Jean Schaedle was less impressed. 'There was nothing wrong with the food. It was reasonably good but not the best I've had.' How about the wine? 'All very strong-tasting. I wasn't too crazy about them.'

Surely there must have been something outstanding for five thousand and four dollars?

'The soup with something like oysters in it. I think it's called oyster bisque.'

Other high profit items are prawn cocktails, fried fillet of plaice and rainbow trout, home-made steak and kidney pie, and lemon meringue pie. Fried onion rings and cauliflower are the best vegetables from the restaurant's point of view.

There are relatively low mark-ups, of around 100 per cent, with fruit juices, scampi, sole and steak. The best value for the customer is a T-bone steak, where the average mark-up is sixty-two per cent. On the cheeseboard, Stilton is the best value, although the restaurant will be delighted if the customer chooses Danish Blue or Cheddar, and better pleased still if he then has tea instead of coffee.

Like supermarkets, restaurant chains also have 'loss leaders'. The idea is imported from the US, where it is called 'over-abundance theory'. One chain gives anyone ordering chocolate or coconut cake a huge wedge of gateau weighing nearly two pounds. The fact that few people can eat this amount at the end of a meal is irrelevant. They divide it out amongst others at their table, or put it in a 'doggie bag'. But they see it as great value and, because it is at the end of the meal, they remember it.

The serve-yourself salad bars are the same. 'Nobody will spend the whole meal eating salad. They know they could, though, and they are grateful,' says a catering graduate. 'It's the same with monster, twenty-eight-ounce steak portions. People can see they are tremendous value, but they are too big to tackle. So they'll go for the twenty-ounce steak, thinking that must be good value, too. It isn't. The twenty-ounce will be the real profit maker.'

'You don't get fed by the chef in any of the big restaurant chains,' says a disillusioned chef. 'It's the menu profit planner who is in charge, and he is probably an accountant.'

Menu writers are also important. New dishes are not created by chefs. They are invented by copy writers for their image rather than their taste, and are called 'nonsense dishes'.

'The most common nonsense dishes are named after

83

French royal mistresses,' says food expert Diana Pugh. 'Frenchified restaurants call things after Madame Pompadour or Diana de Poitiers. It has nothing to do with cooking and it is a sign of poor food and high prices.

'Italian restaurants do the same thing with place names. You get Eggs Sorrento and Veal Palermo and Chicken Venezia. Restaurants that want to appear international, particularly in the big Mediterranean resorts and conference cities, use the French names of countries. You get hors d'oeuvres à la Danoise, beef à l'Anglais, seafood à l'Espagnole, ham à l'Americaine. It doesn't actually mean a thing.*

'The big international hotel chains often invent what are supposed to be local dishes. The copy writers try to get in as much royalty, nobility and double entendres as they can. You'll have Nell Gwynn's Veal Escalope – Charles II's favourite, rolled and stuffed with breadcrumbs and artichoke hearts – that sort of thing.'

Faster food

The fast food industry does not have any pretensions to practising the subtleties of restaurant cons. Organization is the secret of this vast operation. The product itself is well planned. Every chicken sold at a Kentucky Fried Chicken outlet round the world is almost identical. It has a life expectancy of exactly sixty days. It spends its days in a space six inches by six inches, at a temperature that

* Perhaps the most ingenious menus are Russian. They include mouth-watering dishes that are not available due to food shortages. Some have never been available. Thus one Moscow restaurant has eighty-five dishes on its monster menu. Of these, only forty-three have inked-in prices indicating that they have ever been on. On a typical day, the restaurant could serve just three dishes out of the eighty-five: Zazuski, chicken Kiev and chicken tabac. The menu ran from apricot ice to zabaglione, but there were no puddings actually available at all.

starts at 32.2 degrees centigrade and is reduced as it grows, in light of exactly 0.05 foot candle power, so that it can make out its food in the dimness but entertains no idea of exercise.

It is there to eat, from a conveyor trough that is always full. It will eat 7.8 lbs of food. At sixty days it is killed in a batch of 5,000. It passes along a conveyor belt, where its feathers, intestines, head and feet are cut off and ground into meal for the new generation of chicks. It emerges at the end in four-ounce portions, each with precisely 220 calories and 32 grammes of protein.

The same precision goes into the fast food store that feeds the tourist. Fast food is big.* McDonald's opened its 6,000th restaurant in 1980 and turned over more than $5.5 billion. An outfit based on hamburgers and chips is now bigger than most industrial firms. There are burger wars. Fighting off the challenge of the Big Mac, Wimpy spent well over £1 million building the world's largest Wimpy in Piccadilly Circus.

Profits can be startling. A top burger joint can go through two tonnes of beef in a week, together with four tonnes of chips, a quarter tonne of chicken and 1,500 gallons of coffee, orange juice and Cola. The profit on that little lot would be around £6,000 per week. Some McDonalds take over £1,000 per hour. Ian Petrie, managing director of Wimpy, maintains that trading profits of seventeen per cent of turnover are feasible.

Growth is remarkable. Wimpy were recording twenty-five per cent growth levels in 1980 and 1981 despite the recession. West Germans, who were eating 5,000 hamburgers a day in 1970 were getting through 650,000 a day by 1980. McDonalds had cornered three quarters of the

---

* But not new. Street vendors sold chickpea soup and bread in Rome. Piemen sold their wares to such as Simple Simon in medieval England. Victorian stalls selling oysters, at 3d for twelve, whelks, pork and fish became fish and chip shops, the first fast food shops as such.

new business, opening a new outlet every twelve days including a giant one in Hamburg.* In the US, ninety-six per cent of all children can recognize the chain's Ronald McDonald figure, ranking it second to Santa Claus and well in advance of the President.

The first fast food billionaire is Ray Kroc, the former ambulance driver, piano player, musical director and bankrupt property speculator who started McDonalds. He was selling malted drink mixers in California in 1955 when he came across the brothers Dick and Mac McDonald, who attributed the great success of their hamburgers to the consistency of the ingredients.

In return for one half per cent of the takings, they agreed that Kroc could market 'McDonald' hamburgers. Kroc bought out that half per cent share five years later for $2.7 million.† He believed his success was due to QSC – quality, service and cleanliness. He broke from the image of the hamburger joint, the kid with Brylcreem hair playing rock. McDonalds had no pinball machines, juke boxes, cigarette machines or pay phones.

Kroc drummed home the holiness of QSC in the staff manual. Until forced to change by legislation, he refused to employ girls as waitresses lest 'they attract the wrong kind of boy'. His male staff have to wear polished black shoes, shave daily and, states the staff manual, 'they must have frequent baths, use a deodorant, and display sincerity, enthusiasm, confidence and a sense of humour'.

His licensees have to graduate from a ten-day course at Kroc's 'Hamburger University' in Illinois as Bachelors of

----

* The city has nothing to do with the product. The hamburger is thought to have been invented at the food stands of the 1904 St Louis World's Fair.

† There was a warlike aftermath to this, as there often is in the burger business. When they sold out, the McDonalds kept their original restaurant. Kroc forced them to change the name, to Mac's Place, and started a rival McDonalds opposite. 'I ran them out of business,' said Kroc.

Hamburgerology. They also have to hand out around £150,000. The 'World HQ' at Oak Brook, Illinois picks sites, buys or leases land, arranges construction and rents it with equipment to the licencees for 8.5 per cent of the gross and a three per cent annual franchise fee.

Fast food competition is ferocious. In Britain, the bigger chains include Spud-U-Like, Burgerland, Burger House, Pizza Express, Wimpy, Denny's, McDonalds, Trumps, Bake'n Bite, Julie's Pantry, Burger King and Pizzaland. They do not like each other one bit.

There are stories of staff stealing and even the ultimate heresy, recipe stealing. Thus this news item about the 'Golden Arches', as the trade calls McDonalds:

'There's a lot of fat in the fire at McDonalds where the chain's key menu-development specialist, Robert Pickett, has left the Golden Arches to become Marketing Services Director at Pizza Hut. McDonalds has charged Pickett in a Kansas Federal court with removing "trade secrets" and "confidential documents". There's one report that Pickett left with two crateloads on everything from data on the new Chicken McNugget programme to various regional taste figures'.*

Pickett's attorney denied all the allegations. But, to the fast food man, the idea of a spy in the Chicken McNugget is as thrilling as a traitor in the White House, and a lot more important.

Wimpy had the market to itself in Britain, a dozy, waitress-service affair, until the aggressive McDonalds' young men arrived in 1975. That woke up Wimpy's and led to the flood of imitators.

They have that door-to-door earnestness and vigour normally found in successful Morman missionaries and encyclopaedia salesmen. They believe, passionately, in their product although they will drop it to join the opposition at the wipe of a griddle.

Their great ambition is to run a 'thousand pound an

* Fast Food, November 1980.

hour machine'. That is an outlet that can turnover £1,000 in an hour, normally at lunchtime.

A machine it is, designed and refined for maximum speed and turnover. The cooking equipment will cost £200,000. A vegetable preparation machine will produce 650 lbs of chips per hour and also crisp, slice, dice or grate. It will grate 330 lbs of 'Parmesan' cheese an hour.

The fryers have microprocessor solid state control technology – in other words, a chip controls the chips. A built-in frying computer automatically adjusts the frying time to compensate for changes in the oil temperature. The chip baskets rise automatically when cooked to standard.

Meat and chicken is delivered in computer controlled portions directly from the factory farm. Hamburgers can be supplied 'deep frozen and pre-grilled in a pre-toasted sesame seed bun complete in its own heat 'n' serve box'. All the 'chef' has to do is put it in a microwave oven for fifteen seconds.

Every standard McDonald hamburger contains exactly 1.6 oz of beef, 0.222 inches thick, in a soft sesame seed bun 4½ inches thick. The top layer of the bun is sprayed with ketchup and pickles in a process known as 'precondimentation'.

Each Coke machine will dispense 1,000 drinks an hour. A glasswasher will do 1,000 glasses an hour, and dishwashers will cope with 700 plates in that time. But a thousand-pound-an-hour machine does not like glass or china, so it uses expanded polystyrene cups and containers from Fibracan. This way, there is no cleaning for cups and plates. Everything is dumped into dustbins after use.

No need for cutlery either. Knives and forks are supplied to customers grudgingly and by special request. Only what are known as 'finger foods' are served. That means food that can be wolfed down with the digits rather than fussed over with knife and fork. The Kentucky Fried Chicken is 'fingerlickin' good.' Its good for Kentucky Fried profits to have their customers licking their fingers, rather than having to wash up after them.

Fast food men look at France with awe. It is a market they thought would never fall to them, its history of fine food being too deep. But it has. Onlookers reckon the 'burger battle of the Champs Elysées', where a McDonald's unit is locked in combat with a Burger King in the heart of Paris, to be the most crucial contest of its kind in the world. 'Whoever wins Paris could conquer Europe,' they say.

That will only happen if the customers can be rushed through in an unGallic way. Speed is the essence of a thousand-pound-an-hour machine.

The restaurants are built to blend reassuring familiarity with rapid throughput.

The signs, seats, tables, counters, take-away boxes, staff uniforms, colours and background music in a big chain will be identical in Boston, Birmingham or Barcelona. 'You normally get someone in for the first time when he's away on holiday,' says a fast food man. 'Then you get him again when he goes home, because the restaurant is identical to the one he was in 1,000 miles away on holiday.'

The design is intended to push people through as fast as possible. There are no seats near the counters or takeaway areas. This would encourage people to loiter. With a new Wimpy costing £200,000 for décor and cooking equipment, loitering is out.

The counters are wide to cut queueing. McDonalds reckon on a maximum queue of five. A customer should be served within ninety seconds. More than that, and people turn away. To keep the queues short, they keep a float of cooked hamburgers waiting for customers, throwing them away into a bucket after eleven minutes if the customers do not materialise.

Deliberately uncomfortable and back-straining seats are also used to avoid problems of the sort found in hamburger restaurants in Spain, where the clients seem to think they can sit and start reading a book after they have finished the food.

Other devices are used to ensure that this appalling habit

does not spread. McDonalds has false windows, with potted plants and an air-jet playing on them, to give an idea of fresh air and movement.

Colour is important. The Hungry Fisherman chain sells fish and chips on slick American lines. Its decor is bright green and yellow. 'Its screamingly loud,' says a designer. 'But its meant to be. You couldn't eat a three course meal with these colours around you. But you aren't meant to.'

A lot of theory goes into the sales. The greater the quantity of food bought by the customer, the higher the perceived value, while the restaurant increases its sales volume. There is what the trade call the 'three cup trick'. Small, medium and large sized containers are offered for drinks, French fries and coleslaw, instead of just small and large.

According to the Sweetheart Division of Maryland Cup Corporation, the typical effect is to convert an existing sixty per cent small, forty per cent large sales pattern to twenty per cent small, sixty medium and twenty large. That means a real growth in the cash take against an only marginal increase in costs.

The same philosophy in what is known as the 'science' of menu presentation, is the 'topper'. This is a huge portion that tops the menu, persuading the customers to go for the merely large portion below it. Thus one chain sell a ¾lb triple hamburger as a 'topper'. This oversized burger puts the money-making double hamburger in the middle of the menu rather than at the top. Sales of the double-burger shot up.

There is no longer an approachable girl at a manual cash register. There's a 'cashier' or 'kooltron' fabric uniform, the style a bland 'Lyn' or 'Vicky' or 'Denise'. The machine itself is electronic, with 'full alphanumerical print-out and stock control, linked into a master/slave situation and with a data capture on-line capability'.

That is how a thousand pounder works. Only one thing worries the fast-food man, apart from their own in-fighting, as they watch their sales soar into the wild blue yonder. Occasionally, one will say: 'Remember what happened to the Espresso bar fad?'

People pushing

When it comes to service, restaurants have an added edge by way of manipulating tourists into raising their profits. The perfect customer arrives with seven guests, shows a lively interest in the menu and wine list, pays by credit card and also gives the waiter a cash tip as he leaves. 'Such a man,' says a waiter at the Ritz, 'is always going to get the best table, regardless of who else wants it. It doesn't matter if he's ugly and a nobody. To us he's someone special.'

For this customer has combined, from the waiter's point of view, self-interest and flattery to a high degree. A table of eight is the best from the staff's point of view. It is not so large that it will dominate the restaurant, thus making other diners feel isolated and unwanted. It guarantees the maximum tip for the minimum work; serving a table of eight requires little more effort than looking after one of six, but the tip will be one third higher. People paying by credit card almost invariably tip better than those paying by cash or cheque.

The waiter also feels flattered. Waiters spend much of their working lives flattering other people, and they appreciate some of it coming back. A customer who asks intelligent questions about the wine and food helps the waiter feel important. A special cash tip, no matter how small, in addition to the service charge, makes the waiter feel special.

There are equally people whom waiters do not like.

'Nobody likes couples too much,' says the *maitre d'hotel* of a smart Kensington restaurant. 'They take the same amount of time as a table of four, for half the tips, or less. The more people at a table, the more they will tip per head. They vie with each other. Even a single will tip fairly well; he's alone and wants to be loved.

'Couples are often mean. I'll turn down plenty of requests for twos every day and hold space for fours, sixes or eights. If you want to make a same-day reservation at a restaurant, say you want a table for three or four. Never two.'

All staff are united in loathing of drunks. Barmen shift them into the dining room as quickly as possible. 'You just say you will serve their next drink in the dining room,' says a barman. 'A drunk will go along with anything as long as there is a drink at the end of it.' The dining room staff hustle them through the meal, seeing them safely out of the door and into the black list of cheque-bouncers, heavy complainers and drunks that every restaurant keeps.

After that, each specialist has his peculiar likes and dislikes.

'I can't stand people who complain that a wine is corked,' says a wine waiter, a commonly echoed cry in the business. 'They don't know anything and they're simply out to impress. It's about the only thing they know that can go wrong with wine.

'It's very seldom that wine is actually corked. What is usually wrong is that the wine has not breathed for long enough. That is inevitable when it cannot be opened beforehand. All I do is remove the offending bottle, with an ingratiating "I'm sure Sir is right" and a mental "the little twit" and get another one. It will be exactly the same as the other, but I've seldom known people complain twice.

'The original bottle? I sell that to another table. Its pretty easy to steer a customer towards a particular bottle. You say: "Could I recommend the Haut Medoc with Sir's steak?" You know perfectly well he's not having steak, because you checked with the waiter, and he tells you he's having lamb. You say: "You're absolutely right, Sir. In that case, it must be the 1976 Latour," or whatever the twit at the far table sent back as corked.

'This way, the customer thinks he turned down the Haut

Medoc and settled for the Latour. He can't very well go back on his own choice, can he?'

Wine waiters dislike wine snobs who order an expensive burgundy or claret for immediate drinking. 'It's only being done to impress. If they really knew anything about wine, they would have ordered it beforehand so that it can be served in proper condition.' Very old clarets do have to be served quickly because they oxidize fast, but few restaurants stock them.

Complaints about temperature are usually treated by putting the bottle under the hot tap. This can be seen easily enough, because the label is slightly damp.

'But the sort of people who complain don't know enough to look for this,' says the wine waiter. 'It's a stupid complaint to make anyway over red wine, because any attempt to warm it up quickly will do more harm than good.

'It is far better to let it stand around and to drink it slowly until it comes to room temperature. Most restaurants are hot so it won't take long.' Drink is, incidentally, the reason why temperatures are kept high. Customers drink more. In the bar this is encouraged by thirst-inducing peanuts and almonds and olives with a high salt or brine content. 'Surely nobody really thinks we put out nuts and onions and olives for *free*?' asked a puzzled barman.

'Things don't happen by chance in restaurants,' says a waiter at a Spanish restaurant in Soho. 'We grade our customers. Some get the best table, and some the worst.'

The worst tables are those near the bar, the kitchens, the cloakrooms and the entrance. There is a constant traffic of guests and waiters. Service is interrupted. These tables are also inconspicuous. Its occupants attract few glances: smart restaurants reckon that people dine out as much to be looked at as for the food. Given the standards of cuisine in many restaurants, this is obviously true.

The most conspicuous tables are found half-way into the restaurant along the central aisle. This is where theatricals will be placed, and particularly good-looking women. That reflects status in the restaurant. 'TV stars or anyone else who's been on the box, politicians, models; you make a show out of anyone the other punters will recognize,' says a manager.

Care has to be taken not to give rivals adjacent best tables. *Maître d*'s are trained not to put two beautiful women next to each other. The manager at Rule's, a famous restaurant off the Strand, remembered with horror putting two parties of actors opposite each other. Everyone looked at one table as they passed ignoring the furious occupants of the other.

Window tables with a good view are prime positions. 'An alcove isn't a good position at all, unless the client wants privacy,' says a *maître d*'. 'But give it a raised floor, and people start fighting for an alcove. Suddenly, they think its grand.'

Tables against the wall are given to people who seem to be distant and who feel they can be superior by observing without being seen. Parties of four are used to 'open up' the unpopular tables in the centre of the restaurant where a couple would be conscious of being out in the open. A party is likely to talk non-stop and not notice its position.

Women like to sit with their backs to a wall so as to see more of what is going on. A good waiter will see that they are always shown to this seat. The Savoy stresses that a lady and gentleman, arriving separately and dining alone, are never put at adjacent tables.*

A restaurant keeps control of who sits where by a simple long-established ploy. Guests have not been able to choose their own table since César Ritz. The first manager of the Savoy, he introduced the practice of 'dressing' the restaurant in the 1890s.

The method was straightforward, but effective. All the best tables in the room were marked 'Reserved'. When a

---

* Whether this is for the protection of the lady or gentleman, the Savoy would not say.

party arrived whose elegance and sophistication would, he felt, enhance the restaurant, they were shown to one of these tables and the card was ostentatiously removed. Anyone whose appearance did not reach the required standard was told that all the best tables had gone.

The final touch

No review of eating out is, alas, complete without reference to bill-padding.

This is one of the oldest tricks in the restaurant business. It is a traditional sport in all major tourist centres. In Paris, open season is tacitly declared at Easter and runs to the end of September. Resident once in the City of Light, I was not cheated for four straight months in the winter. Come April, more than three-quarters of the meals and drinks I ordered in English were overcharged by an average of thirty per cent. The rate dropped to a quarter by ordering in French, but the mark-up remained the same.

This was true of restaurants right across the price range. The waiter 'forgot' to return twenty francs with the change at a smart café-restaurant close to Maxim's in the elegant rue Royale. A Trocadero brasserie which had charged me honestly during the winter went off its head in April. The same waiter overcharged me twice, admitting on the second occasion: 'I'm sorry, Sir, I didn't realize it was you. I'll change it at once.' Thoroughly flustered, he undercharged on a third visit.

Overcharging at a student-type bistro on the Left Bank was a cool forty per cent. Though I had ordered a fixed price menu, the waiter had added on soup, vegetables, cheese and bread. He removed them from the bill reluctantly, item by item.

In many restaurants, bill-padding has become a sort of tourist tax, indifferently applied to all foreigners as a matter of course.

There are many methods. The least subtle is to add drinks and courses. 'You have a large party who have ordered a lot of dishes and drinks,' says a waiter at a popular bistro near the Trocadero. 'They get good and merry. So you add a couple of courses and bottles of wine, making sure that they are ones ordered by the next table.

'If you are challenged, you apologize and explain how you got the tables mixed up. We call it "creeping". The items creep onto the bill from the next table. You'd be very careful with the Dutch, and you leave the Belgians alone. They don't feel embarrassed to go through the menu item by item. But it works with the Americans and the British. I sometimes get the feeling that the Japanese know what's going on. They just don't like to complain.'

Waiters are helped if they write out the bill. Trickery is more difficult in restaurants where the bill is printed out by a cash register. Waiters 'do the hieroglyphics', as they put it. The bill is scrawled to be illegible to all but the man who wrote it.

Some waiters benefit from having a professionally bad memory, charging for more expensive food and wine than was served. Service charges are a rich source of profit. Where service is already included on the menu price, it is added again at the end of the bill. If challenged, the waiter will claim that it is a VAT addition. Service is included in most Continental countries, almost invariably so in France. Cover charges are often not levied by a restaurant, but by a waiter in collusion with the cashier.

In Britain, many menus state that service is not included. The waiter writes in a fifteen per cent tip below the receipt line, so that it does not appear on the VAT section of the bill. This is rarely challenged. If it is, the waiter has a standard reply: 'Sorry, Sir, all our regulars ask us to add fifteen per cent automatically, and I made a mistake.'

The aim is to get a double service charge, unVATed and untaxed both times. The waiter adds £1.50 to a £10 bill, and the customer, unaware that he has already paid a service charge leaves another £1.50 tip. The waiter thus makes £3 cash. This will be split with the manager in a managed restaurant. These tricks are unlikely if the owner is on the premises. A restaurant with a resident patron is a good but not infallible defence.

Menus say that 'the wine prices include VAT'. On the bill, wines are added up with everything else and VAT is charged on the total bill. Wine is thus charged VAT twice. The second charge does not go to HM Customs and Excise, but into the pocket.

Waiters call the money they make from these tricks 'sparrow' or the 'dropsy'. The customers are called 'les pigeons', plump and ready to be plucked. The 'les' is used even in Britain through respect for the French who originated many of the ideas. In France, some bills are said to include 'the date, the barometric pressure and the weight of the patron in kilos'. Italy has a poor reputation and Spain, once a haven of honesty, is rapidly losing its.

'If you really want to pay only for what you get, use a pocket calculator,' says a cashier. 'Ignore the bill. It will probably add up, but you won't be able to read it and the prices and items will be inventions. Get the menu, take the prices of what you've had, total them. Add fifteen per cent service or VAT if necessary with the percentage key.

'You can do this very discreetly. In fact, it's most simply done before you even ask for the bill. Remember, the bill does not matter. It could be a Dickens novel for all its use, full of crafty fiction. Add up the total from the menu on your calculator. Check it with the total on the bill. If they don't tally, say that you are not paying it, unless they can prove your calculation wrong on a bill typed out or written legibly in block capitals.

'This avoids unpleasantness. It's the calculator that is doing the arguing, not you. And calculators don't make mistakes.*

* But cash registers do, or can be made to. The printout for a dinner I had in Chelsea had the correct prices – £3.85, £4.00, £1.60, £0.50, £5.50, £0.55 – but the machine had managed to add this up as £19.95. This gave the restaurant a neat rip-off of £3.95. The date of this machine fraud was 1 March 1982.

'But *don't* go through the bill with the waiter, particularly if it is not legible or if you are using a foreign language. He's done it all before, and he'll run rings round you. He'll pluck a service charge from the air, or a cover charge, or a butter charge, or a bread charge, or a vegetable charge. By the time a pro has finished with you, you'll be glad to pay and shut up. Don't argue on his ground. Argue from the menu. After all, from your point of view, that is all that you have to go on anyway.'

Drinking

Faking, twitting, and relabelling

Drink is more liable to false description and outright concoction than food. It is a more complex and international
business. The restaurateur should know exactly what he
is serving up on his plates, because he should have gone
to the market and bought it himself. If he delegates that
to his chef or to a buyer, he knows that will leave him
open to trouble. But he can order wine in good faith from
an honest shipper, and still be caught out because of sharp
practice by a foreign grower or middleman.

False spirits are a stock-in-trade with some discos and
nightclubs. Locally produced whisky is sold as Scotch at
inflated prices. This is found mainly in the Far East, with
relabelled Thai whisky, and South America where the Brazilian and Argentine product is upgraded. Italy, Spain and
Portugal also register cases of this.

But wine is the most affected. The wine trade has suffered a long series of scandals. It has got to the point
where a British wine shipper says: 'You don't need a good
nose or breeding to taste wine any more. You need a PhD
in chemistry.'

Quite so. For much wine sold in restaurants, hotels and
shops is not wine at all. It is totally artificial, untainted by
any hint of grape. One of the leading wine growers in Italy
was arrested for selling fake wine. He was literally a wine
manufacturer.

Gianfranco Ferrari had the process working with
streamlined efficiency, manufacturing wine in 1,000 gallon
batches at eight hours the batch. He sold it as Chianti,
Barbera, Soave, Verdicchio and Valpolicella. At one stage,
backed by a TV commercial campaign with the punch line

99

of 'Ferrari, the true wine', he was outselling any real wine in Italy. His product was on sale in reputable shops and supermarkets throughout the country, and was widely exported.

Artificial colouring was made from scum dredged from the bottom of banana boats. Dried ox-blood was used to clear the sediment. Sodium nitrate stabilized the brew and reduced the risk of exploding bottles. Figs, beans and dried apples as well as fish gelatine were sometimes mixed with molasses and synthetic alcohol to produce a tastier if more expensive concoction.

Oenologists were employed to use their special tasting skills to adjust the colour and flavour to match the type of wine being imitated. One recipe read: 'Crush the pulp and stone of dates, put in a container, mix in hot water. Clarify according to volume with lead acetate, add sugar to this mixture. Then add chloridic acid according to volume. Heat to sixty or seventy degrees C, let cool immediately and neutralize with potash.'

Ferrari sold 7,450,000 gallons of one type, making 45,335,462 bottles. Total synthetic production is believed to have touched 100 million quarts a year. The product tasted good and, ironically, was considered better for the body than wine by doctors. Hangovers were rare, for it had none of the headache-inducing congeners found in grape-based wine.

Ferrari's trial was as comic opera as his ingredients. The main exhibit for the prosecution was 770,000 gallons of his wine, stored in sealed vats. It was all removed during the trial and replaced with water coloured with red ink. Although this must have involved a fleet of trucks, the authorities did not notice.

Ferrari declared that: 'I may be the king of the wine fakers. But there are many others besides me, and not just in this courtroom.' Since he had 280 co-defendants alongside him in the courtroom in the Adriatic Coast city of Ascoli Picerno, Ferrari was making a remarkable claim.

It would seem justified. Another Italian who faked on

a massive scale was uncovered only because of his insatiable demand for glycerine, lactic acid, ammonium phosphate, ferro-cyanide and salt, which he bought by the lorry-load from the State monopoly. Even then, his system of collapsible vats and false-bottomed storage tanks kept the authorities at bay for a year.

This particular 'Chianti' was of excellent taste and body, as well it might, since it was much more difficult to produce than the real article.*

Italy is the world's largest wine producer, accounting for more than a fifth of total sales. The head of the Italian National Consumers Union, Vincenza Dona, says: 'Whether all of it is real wine is an open question.' The head of the wine producers' association of Faensa, an area hard hit by the notorious Romagna fakers, says: 'At night, they dump sugar and coloured water in underground tanks. A few days later, after fermentation, trucks appear and take the mixture away. Water into wine in seventy-two hours. The Italian miracle.'

Not that this is merely an Italian expertise. However, it is they who have been paid the ultimate compliment. Real Greek and Bulgarian wine is being treated and sold in France under Italian labels.

There are more ways to take the wine-bibbing traveller for an expensive ride than simple faking. There is 'twitting', the trade name for the common practice of sticking expensive-sounding labels on cheap wine. It is called this because it preys on 'twits' who are more impressed by a name than by the taste of the wine. There is 'upgrading' where the strength or quality of a wine is changed to move it into a higher-priced category.

---

* The making of real wine, by contrast, is simplicity itself. Put grapes in a tub, whack them around with a pestle, put the juice into a barrel with a tight bung, leave for ten days, and there will be wine. Sugar and yeast are there naturally, ferment together, and turn into alcohol.

Marketing men 'hype' a wine to suggest it has characteristics that in fact it lacks. Wine is 'got at', the expression for improving its taste by adulterating it with chemicals.

One firm, though innocent of outright faking, shows several of the ploys used to boost profits from real wine. It was French, for the French excel at this business. Its senior figure was M. Lionel Cruse, a socialite, urbane, sophisticated and very rich. An aristocrat, the doyen of the Bordeaux wine industry and head of the most famous wine house on the Quai des Chartrons, itself the Wall Street of wine.

M. Cruse's family have been selling on the strength of their name and label for generations. Very profitably, too: wine waiters the world over have pointed out 'Cruse' on their lists, a guarantee of good wine for the customer, and a good commission for the waiter.

But then M. Lionel, his brother M. Ivan and sixteen others, ranging from wine merchants to brokers and representing Bordeaux's finest, were arrested and charged with alleged fraud, adulteration of wine by chemicals, and false labelling. The firm was fined for a long list of offences.

More than 600,000 gallons of ordinary wine had been 'twitted' and sold as 'appellation controlée' or 'châteaux bottled'. These are government categories that should guarantee the quality of wine. The profits from this came to more than £1 million to help the Cruse lifestyle. Most of the 2.5 million bottles were sold in the US, Britain and Germany.

'Twitting' exists from Italy to Japan. It may involve 'cuisine', where various cheap wines are blended to produce a taste similar to the wine that is being imitated. It may merely involve sticking a false label, with a false vintage or country of origin on it, on to an unblended wine.

In either case, it is big business. In Italy, for example, the wine growing area of the Tronto valley has a maximum production of 1.6 million quintals of grapes. A quintal is 100 kilograms. Yet the area sells wine equivalent to ten million quintals of grapes a year. The Romagna area sells twice as much wine a year as it has grapes to produce.

At one time, the British were drinking four times as much 'Burgundy' as the French were shipping. The racket was based on a tank storage farm at Ipswich, regularly topped up by wine tankers sailing from French ports. By altering the mix pumped from different tanks, the farm turned out thousands of cases of 'Chateauneuf', 'Nuits St Georges' and 'Beaujolais'.

One product was elegantly advertised as 'Vin de l'annee 1963: Chateau de Corcelles, Beaujolais – Cuvée Speciale au Château de Corcelle – Mise en bouteille dans nos caves.' It was thus claimed to be a special vintage of Beaujolais bottled in the cellars of a chateau.

In fact, it was a mixture of cheap regional wines that had been sloshed together in an East Anglian port, and which was known to the trade as 'Chateau Ipswich'.* It was exposed, not by wine experts who make their living from the trade, but by *Sunday Times* journalists Colin Simpson and Nicholas Tomalin. Most wine scandals would go unchecked but for VAT men, policemen and non-specialist journalists.

In another case, Dutchman Bernard Kahn sold 176,000 litres of Anjou Rosé to two of Holland's largest supermarket chains, Albert Heyor and Dick den Broek. Kahn said: 'I have no idea if it came from Anjou.' The customers did not seem to know either.

Japanese shippers also play the label game.† They have

---

* Half of it was 'eleven five' or kiravi, a mixture of wines from the Languedoc of 11.5 degrees alcohol. The remainder was Vieux Papes, a slightly stronger branded wine made up of two regional wines.
† Wine scandals have a rich history. In the early 1930s, for example, Lord Ilchester's hall boy at Holland House in London was paid £40 a year, plus perks. These included the empty wine bottles and corks from the upstairs drawing room. The corks of vintage wine were stamped with their

taken to sticking on French-style labels with the names and pictures of non-existent French chateaux. For good measure, they say that these wines are 'Premier Grand Cru Classe'. This classification does not exist either.

Some of these wines sell in restaurants for $100 a bottle. Most of the wine is Japanese, and the remainder is Chinese. The largest wine-tasting exercise of 1979, with an international panel of sixty-two, came to a verdict on the world's worst wine producing countries. The joint winners of this dreaded award: China and Japan.*

The temptation to 'twit' and relabel is strong. A shipper's profit margin on honest, down-market wine is around fifteen per cent. Wine, duty, tax, bottle and label account for forty-four per cent of the wholesale price. Cork and packaging take sixteen per cent, transport seven per cent and the shipper's overhead eighteen per cent.

A fancy embossed label may add four per cent to costs, but it can inflate the profit to 200 per cent. The temptation is increased because it is difficult to prove that a wine is not what it is said to be.

Wine can be 'got at' in legitimate ways, used by growers throughout Europe and the US.

Tartrates, for example, are thin flakes or small crystals which fall to the bottom of the bottle. Wine which has been stored in too cold a cellar commonly suffers from

---

year of origin and could be sold for 25p a dozen to a man who bottled them with false labels.

A favourite Victorian trick was to sell aerated gooseberry wine as champagne. A fake Port was widely advertised in London in 1886 as 'pure as the tears which bereaved affection drops upon a new-made grave'.

* After an unsteady start, Japanese whisky has improved steadily in quality. Not so with wine. Despite heavy investment and applied technology, the 1980 Japanese vintage has been described thus: 'A veritable disaster. Worse that 1979. Can one say more?'

this, for the tartrates are precipitated. The crystals are harmless, but people in restaurants – who seldom recognize real sharp practice, but who are big on appearance – will often refuse to pay for such wine and send it back.

The wine is easily repaired by being disgorged and refrigerated for a week at –8 degrees C. It is then diluted with cologel or metatartaric acid. This does little for the taste, but it works wonders for the appearance.

Protein haze harms the appearance of wine by making it cloudy. This is a particular hazard in sherry. It is 'got at' with bentonite and singlass. Tartaric acid is added to wines that are 'flabby', lacking in taste on the palate. Citric acid cures the haze and sharp taste of wine suffering from excess iron. Ascorbic acid and sulphur dioxide are added to improve the taste of oxidized wine.

Other methods are banned but still practised. Sodium nitrate prevents a second fermentation of delicate white wines on a lengthy journey in uncertain temperatures. This is particularly important in tourist areas which import their wine over great distances, notably Hong Kong, Singapore and other Far East areas, Kenya and West African tourist countries like Gambia, and the Caribbean resorts.

Sodium nitrate is, however, banned as a stabilizer. This is because it can affect the stomach, nerves and blood circulation in amounts of 2mg per litre. The less effective sulphur dioxide or sorbic acid should be used instead. It has, however, been found in Frascati, Bordeaux and Alsace wines. The Italians are the most liable to use it and 45,000 gallons of dangerous wine were confiscated by police in the Alban hills, home of Frascati. The prevention of fermentation is a problem, and carrots have been used to get round the regulations. The faster the fermentation of an immature wine can be stopped, the faster it can be got on to the market.

The French are fond of filtration, another process that accelerates the journey from vat to bottle. The alternative is the careful and lengthy process of 'racking', in which wine is allowed to settle and is carefully decanted several times before bottling. This is expensive in time and storage space.

The problem with filtration is that asbestos fibres from the filters can contaminate the wine. A report issued by the French Federal Union of Consumers showed that fifteen out of twenty-nine wines examined for asbestos were contaminated. The list included names like St Emilion and Côtes-du-Rhône.

A significant amount of port, and some brandy, is fortified with coal and petroleum by-products rather than grapes. Bromine is added to some Spanish wine.

More common is wine that has had liquid sugar added to it to convert it to a higher category and price. In one case in 1980, seven businessmen were fined for selling 74 tonnes of inverted sugar to wine growers. A local joke has been doing the rounds in the Rhineland. 'How much will you get for your 1982 Spätlese, Johann?' 'Three to six months, if I get caught.'

The trade also 'hypes' wines to catch wine and travel snobs, talking up both the reputation and price.

Beaujolais Primeur, or Nouveau, is the classic example. This light and refreshing young wine was a popular drink in Lyons, a city said to be watered by three rivers, the Rhône, the Saône and the Beaujolais. With an alcohol level of only 9.5 to 11 per cent, it was rather weak. The grapes were not particularly distinguished, but it was good to drink it from the barrel during a game of boules.

Indeed, it was important to drink it from the barrel. The wine is drunk very young, going on sale on 15 November not long after the harvest. With a barrel, a loose bung meant that the young wine could continue to give off carbon dioxide without blowing the thing up.

But the wine became fashionable beyond the workers of Lyons. A Great Beaujolais Race to Britain was dreamed up, with much publicity going to the entrant who brought the first bottle of the year from Beaujolais to London by fast car, aircraft or helicopter, or combination of all three. Sales increased five and a half times in ten years.

To take advantage of the new market, it had to be sold bottled rather than barrelled. The build up of carbon dioxide would explode a corked bottle. So the newly popular wine had to be 'stabilized'.

Sulphur dioxide was used to kill bacteria and yeasts. This could cause headaches and leave an unpleasant taste if added when fermentation had started. Never mind. 'Twits' were queueing up to buy the stuff.

The 15 November deadline for sale left no time for the usual method of clearing wine with fining or filtration. So the Beaujolais Primeur was savaged with centrifugation or freezing or both.

As if that was not enough, the wine was bombarded with ultraviolet rays and cooked to 85 degrees Centigrade to make sure it behaved in the bottle. The trade term for this is 'actinization', but pasteurisation is a better description.

It was not the bottling process alone that was making Beaujolais Primeur unrecognizable from the pleasant wine the Lyonnais had been knocking back happily for years. It did not come from the same vines. The last two decades have seen a sixty per cent increase in the amount of land under vines in Beaujolais. Most of the increase has come in land previously considered too poor, too high or too exposed to produce good wine.

This land was also being squeezed to produce to the last grape. The finest vineyards should yield only thirty-five hectolitres to the hectare.* A Beaujolais classified as a 'Cru' is restricted to forty hectolitres and a Beaujolais Villages to forty-five. The theoretical top limit of fifty hectolitres for ordinary Beaujolais can be and frequently is raised to eighty-five hectolitres.

* That is around 311 gallons to the acre, or some 1,900 bottles. At 85 hectolitres, the yield goes up to 4,600 bottles.

The French have an apt phrase for pushing up the yield: 'on fait pisser la vigne'.

Whisky is counterfeited on a lesser scale than wine. Nevertheless, the turnover of faked and misrepresented whisky is thought to exceed £350 million a year.

Scotch whisky is the main target. It was once largely restricted to crofters who knocked it back with milk for breakfast. Gentlemen drank brandy. But phylloxera devastated French vineyards and the brandy trade in the 1870s, and Scotch became fashionable. It has been faked ever since.

Some 'whisky' is totally false, the alcohol being distilled from wine and molasses. 'Million Pipers', a noisy enough thought in itself, is a wine-based whisky sold in Central America, where other fakes include 'Glasgow Rain', 'Scottish Delight' and 'Scotch Skirt', a reference to the kilt. The most aptly named is 'Highland Reel'.

Others are made from grain that has never seen Scotland. Thus ' "Black Label" as supplied to the House of Commons' has been found in West Germany. Inquiries revealed that the 'London and Glasgow company' named on the label did not exist, and that the whisky had been distilled in the Soviet Union.

The Scottish Whisky Association reports that Johnnie Walker, misspelled in various ways, is a favourite trademark. Counterfeits include 'Loch Ness' in Italy, 'Edinburgh' in Japan and 'Scotland Kilt' in Germany. The Association, with its inquiries run by lawyer Quintin Stewart, has taken legal action against fakes in Holland, Italy, Belgium, France, Germany, Portugal, Spain, Greece, Australia, Israel, Angola, Pakistan, the Philippines, Brazil, Surinam and Japan. The label of a brand named 'Tartan', sold in Japan, claimed that the product was 'made 100 per cent from genuine imported Scottish grapes'.

With Suntory Old now the world's best selling brand, Japanese whisky producers have to look to imitations themselves today. Their whisky is faked in Thailand and the Philippines.

The fakers' task is made easier by the public obsession with colour. The colour of whisky is simply a matter of fashion and has nothing to do with the spirit itself. Pure whisky straight from the still is 119 degrees proof and colourless. Whisky stored in sherry casks takes on a slight yellow colour. The spurious idea arose that the more colour a whisky had, the longer it had been aged in cask and the better quality it was.

In fact, artificial caramel colouring is added to whisky using spectrometers, colorimeters and tintometers. A skilled tintometer operator puts a light colour into an eight-year old Scotch, a fullsome yellowness into a twelve-year old and a darkness into a twenty-year old.

The fakers do the same, knowing that a drinker is likely to be more impressed by the colour of 'real' Scotch than by its taste, particularly after a night club has drowned it in ice and water.

Water also plays a part in beer. 'Beer is over ninety per cent water anyway,' says the British-based Campaign for Real Ale. 'If the percentage is played about with a bit, the majority of drinkers probably would not notice.'

Landlords do not water their beer as frequently as they did, though fourteen publicans in the English Midlands were fined for this in 1979. A more common trick is to pour back the dregs and slops from under the taps.

But much modern beer and lager comes legally from breweries at a lesser strength than a traditional ale that a landlord has watered. In Europe, visitors to Britain will note this problem particularly since Continental beers are generally stronger.

Keg beer is largely responsible. This insipid liquid owes its existence to the East Sheen Tennis Club in Surrey. Little beer was sold during the week and it was in poor condition by the weekend. So Watneys came up with a pasteurized beer in a sealed container that was impregnated with carbon dioxide gas. It was known as Red Barrel and what it lacked in taste it made up for in long shelf life.

Heavy advertising pushed this 'keg' beer up from one per cent of beer sales in 1951 to surpass two thirds by 1976. Duty is levied on beer according to its strength. Keg beers became weaker and weaker to save duty. The Sunday Mirror wrote of Watney's Special Mild in 1971: 'This brew is so weak that if it dropped in strength by about one per cent alcohol it would be classed as "near beer" and could be sold to children.'

Lager in Britain has little to do with Continental lagers except for a light colour and a bought-in name. *What's Brewing?* tested the original gravity of Dutch Heineken and found it to be 1048.6. Whitbread's 'Heineken' had an original gravity of 1033.

In Germany brewers keep a Reinheitsgebot, a Pledge of Purity, introduced by Duke Wilhelm IV of Bavaria in 1516. Beer may only be brewed from malted barley, hops, water and yeast.

British and American brewers are concerned with technical advances since Duke Wilhelm. Potato starches, pasta-flour, wheat, malt extract, flaked maize and rice grits are used as substitutes for malted barley. The good Duke would not have approved of other additions, such as the p-heptyl-p-hydroxy benzoate used as a preservative in the beer.

It has been suggested that, in the US and Britain, brewery shares should be listed under the Chemical Industry.

Water itself is faked in France, Spain and Italy. The 'mineral' water sold in restaurants for 75p a throw is tap water served up in the correct bottle.

This is because travel snobbery now extends to mineral water as well as wine and food. Perrier water has become so fashionable in New York that hostesses make ice cubes from the stuff. Yet the differences between brands are almost undetectable, particularly when chilled. The wine and food writer of the *New York Times*, Craig Clayborn, arranged a tasting of expensive mineral waters, including Perrier, Vichy, Apollinaris, Rambosa and Badoit water. He included plain commercial soda water with the fancy imports.

The blindfolded tasters agreed that the most satisfying was Canada Dry Club Soda, a humble soda water.

Pouring out and raking in – mark-ups and other devices

It is difficult to know with much precision what is being poured out of a bottle. The restaurateur will know if his mineral water comes out of the tap, or at least his manager will. But with wine, he can be fooled by his wine merchant who in turn can be fooled by his shipper and by the grower.

But the structure of a wine list does give the customer a group of clues as to the restaurant's profit margins.

Some only mark up wines by a third. The hundred per cent mark-up is more common, and restaurateurs generally reckon on charging for their most expensive wine at one hundred per cent more than the price of an average meal for one. Thus a restaurant charged £33 for its top wine, a Château Margaux 1967. Food for one averaged £16. The wholesale price of the wine was £17. At the other end of the scale, a bistro in a resort, where a meal worked out around £4, was selling its top wine, a Côtes-du-Rhône worth £3.80 wholesale, for £8. Both used the hundred per cent basis and were thus known as 'doublers' in the trade. Those who mark up three times are 'treblers' and four times 'quads'. Quads are by no means unknown, particularly in Spain and Italy where the basic cost of wine is low.

There is generally a higher mark-up on cheaper wines than on expensive ones. The management make more on wines than spirits, and most on the cheap wine, so the wine waiters are under orders to 'push' wine and particularly cheap wine on the customers. 'From the point of view of mark-ups, the customer is best off drinking a 1947 Montrachet,' says a restaurant owner. 'The mark-ups are biggest with Spanish plonk.'

The worst rip-offs occur in restaurants catering for tourists and travellers where no repeat trade is likely. Even the house wine, normally a safe bet, may be poor. 'Shrinkage', or stealing by staff, is a problem in places like these and some solve it by serving packaged miniatures instead of house wine. The customer pays more and the staff steal less, because the loss of a miniature is less easy to explain than the 'evaporation' of house wine bought in bulk.

Where wine is sold by the carafe, the measure must be stated. If it is not on the wine list, the customer must be told the measure if he asks. There is no similar rule for glass sizes. Wine bars notoriously take advantage of this. But there is no legal comeback if a 'glass' of wine is served in a thimble.

Beware of the second and third cheapest wines on the list. These are the wines the inexperienced go for, being too mean to buy the expensive wines and too snobbish to buy the cheapest. They are thus fast-moving. Wine the restaurant wants to get rid of, or on which it is making a particularly high profit, occupies this slot on the list.

This trick has become common because the ignorance and snobbery of clients has driven good restaurants to despair. One West Country restaurant famous for its excellent but expensive cooking compensated by offering fine old vintages at retail prices. The customers avoided them like the plague. In despair, the owner doubled the prices of these excellent burgundies and clarets, which promptly began to sell well.

The costs of keeping a cellar are now astronomical. Old-established restaurants, with lots of storage space and long-standing arrangements with wholesalers, can be more competitive than new ones.

The difficulties that new restaurants have with storage and cellarage often make it a nonsense to buy a very expensive wine, particularly a red. There is no point in buying a wine which has been rushed about from pillar to post, upended and turned frequently, for immediate drinking. The taste is badly affected.

The basket cradles found in many snob restaurants are also pointless. They should be used to remove the cork from a bottle of wine without upending it and disturbing the sediment. Many wine waiters take the bottle out of the cradle to uncork it, thus destroying the whole object of using a cradle in the first place. Once the cork is removed, the wine should be poured from the bottle in its cradle into a decanter in one movement.

Leaving the wine on the table in its cradle and serving it into the glasses is absurd and the sign of a poor restaurant, though doubtless an expensive one. Each time the cradle is jerked up and down to fill the glass the sediment is disturbed and goes straight back into the wine. If sediment is a worry, the wine should be decanted.

The presentation of the wine list gives further clues to the restaurant. The fully printed list is out of place today. One smart London restaurant and a few in Paris still have them. They are not generally in the customer's interests since they are drawn up to take future inflation and price rises into account.

The loose-leaf catalogue favoured by the French, where the local wine gives precedence only to champagne and the rest of the world follows by order of cost under 'vins divers', is much more practical and a good sign.

Wine lists are notorious for hyperbole: 'vineyards basking in the Mediterranean air' are likely to be found in North Africa and if there are any references to 'growing under the Southern sun', the wine has probably come from South Africa or Chile. The list should tell the customer where the wine comes from, and who made it, where and when. More than this is likely to be a smokescreen to get rid of rubbish. Less shows an awareness that the least said the better.

It is surprising how seldom customers check that the bottle brought to the table tallies exactly with the one on the list. 'Little mistakes' about vintages happen frequently. They are invariably to the customer's disadvantage.

The profits on wine can far outstrip those on food. The owner of a bistro in the South of France buys cheap Algerian wine at three francs a litre. She adds black ink to turn it from harsh red to ruby and calls it 'réserve maison'. She gets six pichets, small carafes, out of it at seven francs the pichet. That is a mark-up of fifteen times. She sells three francs of raw materials for forty-five francs. It is the Midas touch.

A bistro owner typically pays £1.10 for a litre of bad bulk red. He adds 1p of ink and gets six small carafes from it at £1.30 each. That is £7.80 on £1.11, a profit of over 600 per cent. On an average turnover of eighty carafes a day, he is getting a profit on carafe wine of £89.20 a day.

Even better margins are available with wines by the glass. A busy wine bar can make substantial profits on the house wine in this way.

Fiddling the optics, the expectancy effect and the liquor butt hustle

Bars are as adept at short-changing as restaurants, and this is not restricted to obvious clip-joints.

The mighty film and leisure group MGM owes drinks to three million people. It admitted serving doctored drinks at its Grand Hotel and Casino in Reno, Nevada.* Federal alcohol agents discovered alcohol-free cocktails, recycled drinks poured back into bottles and 16,000 bottles of expensive spirits refilled with cheap brands.

The management blamed barmen and other staff for a conspiracy. MGM was ordered in 1981 to pay back two free drinks worth $5 to customers who could prove they were at the hotel and casino between August 1978 and July 1979. The estimated three million customers, to be

* *Daily Telegraph*, 23 December 1981.

contacted through advertisements in sixty-eight news-papers, are also to be allowed into a musical show at half price. MGM also has to pay a civil penalty of $125,000 and the alcohol agents' bill of $475,000. Judge Grant Bowen gave an example of recycled drinks: 'taking the wine left by a couple at dinner and pouring it back into another bottle'.

Nicholas Marshall of *Catering Times* went to the St George's Bar at Brown's, one of London's oldest and best hotels. He and his companion had two gimlets each, followed by two small martinis each. He was charged £8.60. He asked for a receipt and one arrived for £11. It had no details as to how it was made up.

Marshall asked for a written, detailed receipt. He got one for £11 for four gimlets and four large martinis. He demanded to know what he had paid £8.60 for. A third receipt arrived. It showed four gimlets at £1.10 each, making £4.40, and two large dry martinis at £1.70 each, making £3.40. The bar staff refunded him 80p at this stage. The excuse was that somebody else's drinks had been included by mistake.

He then told the hotel's deputy manager that they were definitely small martinis. The manager refunded £1.70. What had begun as a bill for £8.60 ended as one for £6.10 with receipts for £11 and £7.80 along the way.

Short changing is easiest with foreigners and natives who have had too much to drink. 'Expansive, that's what I'm looking for,' says a barman. 'Customers who are in an expansive mood. Then I expand my wages.'

Short measures and substituted bottles are another source of income for some barmen. A coin placed in the optics of a spirits bottle gives the barman a free bottle for every seven he serves. He can put ordinary whisky into a bottle of Black Label, keeping the difference in price for himself. Or he may serve no spirits at all.

An experiment by Dr Alan Lang, a psychiatrist at the University of Florida, has established that fake drinks can have the same effect on behaviour as real ones. What a person thinks he's drinking is more important than what he actually drinks. Lang experimented with twelve students. One test group was told that it was being given vodka and tonic. All accepted this as true. They began to behave in a drunken way. Inhibitions were released, dirty stories were told, driving standards deteriorated. In fact, they had been given straight tonic.

Another group was given vodka and tonic, but was told it was tonic only. Nine out of ten accepted this, and behaved in a thoroughly sober fashion. Unlike the other group, erotic photographs failed to rouse them. There was no laughter. Tested safely on a private road, there was little effect on their driving. The only exception was a light drinker who noticed the alcohol and its effects.

The hardened drinkers were easily taken in by the tonic. Dr Lang commented on the 'expectancy effect'. 'The pharmacological action of the alcohol is not all that important,' he said. 'What is important is what people believe.' Those who are used to drinking expect it to have an effect, and they imagine it readily even if not served with alcohol.

Barmen have known this for generations. Gin and vodka are the easiest drinks because of their lack of colour. The barman pours in tonic and serves it straight if the customer looks expansive. For others, he wets the rim of the glass with the liquor, running his finger round it. The rim trick is also used for whisky, to give bite and smell to a well-watered Scotch. It is most common with Bloody Marys, where tomato juice, pepper, salt and Worcester sauce easily disguise the lack of vodka. It has been estimated that ten per cent of all the Bloody Marys served in New York contain no alcohol.

The more exotic the drink the easier it is for essential ingredients to be left out. Daiquiris and Pina Coladas, being both exotic and fashionable, are made up without a rum base. Mulled brandy punch in the US is often an obnoxious combination of rough red wine and herbs, without brandy.

In the 'liquor butt hustle', staff collect the leftovers from bottles left on tables and in rooms. These are then sold to night clubs. The average bottle of whisky reconstituted in this way could contain five or more different types of Scotch, but this is difficult to tell whilst the senses are being assaulted in a disco.

Night club staff are also adept at imitating the sharp plop of a champagne cork being released. This is done within earshot but out of sight of the table. The customers are then served, with much aplomb, a sparkling white wine.

In their defence, barmen say with some justice that they have been corrupted by the public, rather than the other way round. Dishonest tourists will shrug off an unsuccessful attempt to pay short by claiming they do not understand the local currency. They will deliberately order a round in the most complex way possible in the hope of confusing the barman. They may also work in pairs. Pretending to be strangers, one will back the other up in any arguments over change.

Sharp practice in the travel game is by no means only on one side.

Hotels

Planning for profit

A hotel is a money machine.

'You have to design it to get the maximum cash out of it,' says designer Philip Brown. 'You get in as many bedrooms as you can. That means they are small, so you furnish them to look large. Light-coloured walls, carpets and bedcovers and curtains. Plenty of mirrors. Gilt light fittings. Simple table, chair and bed with a headboard. Headboards are important: they make a room look substantial without taking up space.

'And a simple watercolour or abstract painting. Reproduction of course, but simple. If you have any complicated designs in a bedroom, it shrinks.'

Rooms like this are said in the trade to be 'wide look'. The principles are the same as the conversions done on narrow jets like the Boeing 707 to make them have the same 'wide body' look as the 747 and DC10. Lighting, mirrors and fabrics are all chosen to increase the illusion of size.

The same thing is done on the ground floor. The public rooms, the lounges, drawing rooms, reception halls are smaller in modern hotels than in older ones. The designer works hard to make them look bigger than they are. Thus a hotel like the London International has disguised its small public rooms with a circular reception surfaced in polished beige marble with well-lit panels decorated with 70,000 dyed magnolia leaves imported from France. The Elizabetta is themed in Rococo and velvet brocade, which even covers the air conditioning, the electric candelabra and the Muzak outlets.

Though this fails to subdue the Muzak, it does give the

impression of generous size. 'You really want your ground floor to make you money,' says Brown. 'And you don't make money from people sitting round a drawing room reading the newspapers.

'The most basic point is that you don't want people to spend money anywhere else than in the hotel. So you cram in the concessions on the ground floor. A news kiosk, a chemist, a flower shop, a boutique, a jeweller, a tailor, a car hire and ticket agency, a hairdresser and beauty salon, a sauna centre and gym – very fashionable and profitable, that. And of course, you have to get in a couple of bars and a coffee shop and a restaurant.

'The average tourist spends a quarter of the total cost of his trip on shopping. With some people, that is a lot of money. So you want the shops inside the hotel. That is why modern hotels have such lousy public rooms. A lot are down to just a lobby with a couple of chairs. Its because they have brought the shopping street into the hotel.'

Corridors, kitchens, offices are all kept as small as possible since they do not generate money. Brown talks of the 3,000 room, 6,000 guest Hotel Russia in Moscow with dismay. 'The Russians built the world's largest hotel but they put in four huge and almost identical entrance lobbies and there are several miles of chocolate and beige corridors. All that wasted space cuts into their profits.* A Western designer could have got another 750 rooms in with no problems.'

The designer must also try to trap the guests in the hotel gardens or beach. 'You don't want people wandering off to have lunch on somebody else's beach or a drink at

* A lot of the profits go to Stockmann's department store in Helsinki. Travellers in the know in Russia order all their essentials from Stockmann's, which are sent up from Helsinki's central station on the seventeen-hour Moscow 'Express'. It carries cornflakes, milk, records and tapes, lavatory paper, roach killer, cocktail sandwiches and canapes, avocados and a pair of dentists to fix foreigners' teeth.

somebody else's open air bar,' says Brown. 'You can use the approach roads to the hotel to keep guests in. They don't like crossing roads, so you bring the hotel drive in a wide sweep that keeps them in your garden or beach. You make sure that the pool is the prestige point of the hotel, not tucked away but easy to get to.'

Hotels call their pool areas 'tanning yards'. They are good sources of profit, particularly in Florida where they are exploited more cleverly than in Europe. The pools are in shapes that are attractive to look at but not good to swim in. The width, for example, keeps altering as the pool curves and there will only be one or two points where a decent swim is possible.

The diving boards, though clearly expensive and quality made, are rather high for the average swimmer. The pool is thus something that is nicer to look at than to venture into. This means guests stay in their 'tanning stations', relaxing on comfortable sunchairs and eating the salted nuts and crackers thoughtfully provided free on the tables next to them.

The combination of salty snacks and the sun rapidly leads to a raging thirst which the pool stewards can profitably quench. 'People who swim don't drink nearly as much as people who only sunbathe,' says Brown. 'You want them looking at the water, not in it.* Most pools play Muzak. It keeps the tanning yard awake and drinking and prevents it slipping off into profitless slumber.'

Canned music is an important aspect of the money machine. It is used to lure guests into spending their money in the way that best suits the management.

Muzak is orchestral, with no vocals. Each tape is made with a particular spending pattern in mind. Fast, snappy music encourages the speed and quick turnover that a fast

---

* That is seldom a problem in British resorts. Only 3.8 per cent of visitors to Great Yarmouth and four per cent at Blackpool ever swim. The North and Irish Seas keep them on dry land spending money.

food joint or hotel coffee shop need. Slower, more classical music is best for an expensive hotel restaurant, because it encourages people to linger, and whilst they linger, they spend.

Music may be the wrong word. Muzak, for example, deliberately takes out all the entertaining parts of a tune and reduces its pitch and scale. Otherwise, staff and guests would be tapping out the beat with their forks or cash registers instead of getting down to the serious business of spending.

Thus the tapes for a hotel restaurant will be watered down classical, a soft sound of violins that helps the customers to relax. Strauss, castrated of all rhythm and panache, is reckoned the best composer to induce an intimate and expansive feeling. The guest feels no urgency, continuing to spend as he whiles away the meal, and is not alarmed at the thought of a big bill at the end of it. Turn off the tape, and restaurant takings will be down.

The coffee shop, particularly at breakfast and lunch, wants the reverse. The music must set the customers nerves on edge, remind them they are in a hurry, persuade them to eat up and pay up and leave.* The tapes play rock and disco numbers. Turnover increases. But in mid-morning and mid-afternoon, the coffee shop wants people to stay. It has fewer customers and could look empty and unattractive. It wants to tempt the customers it has to stay longer, so that they will tempt other people in. The music changes, to quieter and more sophisticated rock music like the Eagles and Neil Diamond.

Some hotels have their canned music programmed in twenty-four-hour cycles. As many as ten different tapes are used for different locations, with each tape itself changing the character of the music as the hotel's own inner

---

* 'When people have finished eating at my restaurant, I want them to get up and go,' the owner of the fast food Chicago Pizza Pie Factory told the *Daily Mail*'s Simon Kinnersley. He plays loud, frenetic music. 'It motivates people to get out.'

tempo progresses through the day. The lifts and reception will be bland, probably with a national theme, Gilbert and Sullivan for London, subdued flamenco for Spain. The restaurants and cocktail bars have slow and classical tapes, the shopping arcades medium tempo Lawrence Whelk, the 'tanning yard' what is called 'multi-generation pop', which may not thrill but will not offend customers of any age group. The main bar will have a multi-generation rock tape, faster than the tanning yard, old Beatles or Monkees numbers.

Other systems depend on a barman or *maitre d'* selecting the right tape for the right moment. The canned music company will provide tapes numbered in terms of customers present – the more, the stronger the beat and louder the soundtrack – and time of day.

The music helps to establish the right mood. So does the light. 'You want as little pure daylight as possible,' says Brown. 'If a modern hotel has a window on the ground floor, it makes sure it is smoked glass. That is to keep them cool and dreamy, in a permanent twilight. People don't spend so much so easily in harsh daylight.'

The designer is thus less an architect than a 'hotel themer'. He can invent new styles of building, like Miami Beach French. This was started by Ben Novack, the modest owner and conceiver of the Fontainebleau, who said: 'I overcame more difficulties than the pioneers who built the West.' Its massive tanning yards take 1,000 chaises longues on the 'pool deck' and another 500 on the beach. It is part of the 'Strip', eight miles of lumbering, gaudy money machines that rub shoulder to shoulder along the Atlantic coast of Florida in pastel concrete and neon.

Novack's French theme means there are fleur-de-lys on the linen, the lavatories are for Dames and Messieurs, the coffee shop is called Chez Bon Bon and the gardens are patterned on the real Fontainebleau. 'The French theme is like Muzak,' says a hotel consultant. 'It embraces the guests, relaxes them and gets them used to the idea that they are going to have to pay French prices.'

Wages are by far the biggest item in hotel costs.* An engineer is second only to the designer in improving profits. A good hotel engineer will provide systems that keep the wages bill down. The Holiday Inn in Strasbourg was the first in Europe to cut right back on ground floor staff.

There is no doorman, for the doors are automatic. The guest fills in his own card at reception, which will also double as the signature for the bill. He takes his own luggage upstairs on a trolley. There are ice-makers and vending machines in the corridors. The rooms have impregnated shoe cloths, mini-fridges with a bar, and direct outside dialling telephones. There is no room service. When the guest leaves, he calls his own taxi on a Taxiphone in the lobby. Should he want breakfast before he goes, he cannot have it in his room. He goes to the coffee shop, and serves himself.

A good engineer can cut back in other ways if he works for a 'sleep factory', as the trade calls second class hotels that do not boast of their service standards. Baby listening devices run through to the receptionist, who can warn the parents if a child begins to cry. Morning calls are telephoned automatically with co-ax ring circuits. The minibar in the room has every bottle in an individual cradle and directly it is removed its price is registered automatically at reception.

Electronic guides keep an eye on room vacancies and the status of residents. At a hotel like the Royal Garden, blue lights show unoccupied rooms, red those being redecorated, green those who are part of a group, pink those

---

* Payroll and staff expenses account for 32 per cent of the average international hotel's turnover. Food costs 9.1, drinks 2.8, departmental expenses like running a sales office 12.4, general administration 6.1, marketing 2.6, heating and energy 3, building maintenance 3.3, rent 6.9, property taxes and insurance 2.9, interest charges 2.7, depreciation and amortization 4.4, with an income before taxes of 10.9.

who have not booked and in whom the credit manager is interested.

There is a key card system with plastic cards electronically coded for each guest, which eliminates the old problem of previous room occupants hanging on to the key and returning to ransack the room. Automatic alarms sound in reception for forced entry into any room. An override enables the manager to flash emergency warnings on room TVs even if the set is switched off.

A 'service centre' will provide fourteen kinds of food and drink, from Coca Cola to Continental breakfast, in the room. It has its own cooker and refrigerator. All purchases automatically register at the cashier's desk and go straight on the bill. Mini-bars in rooms have boosted hotel liquor sales by an average of 400 per cent.

A hotel computer cuts back further on the need for staff. The French PLM hotel group owned by Baron Elie de Rothschild has one it calls 'Arthur'. It stocktakes every day, to see if it is short on eggs or Mouton Rothschild. It keeps an eye on the temperatures in each room, checking the 1,000 fire zones in the hotel every seven seconds.

Arthur costs dishes, and works out how much each sort of guest spends – Americans are now spending less than either Germans or Arabs. The Japanese and Belgians are big spenders, the British parsimonious. Arthur also churns out bills like confetti.

Guests are issued with a computer card. At the various restaurants, they hand it over to the waiter at the end of the meal. Arthur debits their account and automatically adds service.*

Closed circuit television is used to watch progress in restaurants and banqueting rooms. The manager can check

---

* This avoids the nasty question of service charges and tips. The actor Terry-Thomas was pestered by a waiter in a Swiss restaurant after he had paid the bill. 'But the bill included the service charge,' said Terry-Thomas. 'Service, yes,' said the waiter with menace. 'Tip, no.'

on reception without leaving his office. Machinery keeps down the wage bill in the kitchens. Automatic chipmakers produce 1,400 three-ounce portions an hour, with a special potato mix going in one end, and either long and thin or short and fat chips coming out the other.

There have been experiments with a liquid nitrogen freezer system which means that meals can be prepared months in advance, sealed and placed in special food cassettes. These can be selected electronically by guests, put on a belt which passes through a microwave heating tunnel and appear at table on robot cars.

Big is beautiful as far as profits go.* The average profit margin for a hotel with up to fifty 'sleeper places', or beds, is 7.1 per cent. Up to 120 beds, it is ten per cent, and over 120 it rises to 12.8 per cent. Hence the tendency for hotels and hotel groups to get bigger. The single, small unit cannot cope with the likes of Sheraton – which started in 1937 as a single 200-room hotel in bank receivership and four decades later had twelve million guests a year in 418

---

* Holiday Inns are easily the largest group with 303,578 rooms in 1,755 hotels. They could put up everyone in a city the size of Nottingham. The next largest is Sheraton, with 107,996 rooms in 418 hotels. The rest of the top ten are Ramada, Trust House Forte, Hilton, Howard Johnson, Balkan Tourist, Days Inn of America, Grand Metropolitan and Inter-Continental, and Quality Inns. All these have more than 40,000 room apiece.

More to the point, for the traveller, is the number of rooms to each hotel. The US-based international chains go in for the biggest hotels. Inter-Continental averages 385 rooms in each hotel, followed by Hilton with 350, and Sheraton with 258. Below these giant installations, Holiday Inn averages 173, and Ramada, Days Inn, Quality Inns and Howard Johnson all average over 100 rooms. Reflecting its many older hotels, Trust House Forte averages 90. For real intimacy, Balkan Tourist runs the smallest hotels with an average of 75 rooms.

hotels in thirty-five countries, and hotels planned in a further fifteen countries – or Holiday Inn and Hilton.

The Hotel Russia has been outstripped in Moscow by a 10,000 bed monster in the suburb of Izmailovo. Many countries have hotels which average more than 100 bedrooms each.*

The big groups make money through plugging each hotel into a world-wide reservation system. These can be very sophisticated. Sheraton's reservation computer in Boston can be tapped from round the world. It gives instant details on Sheratons all over, from Paris to the wonderfully named town of French Lick, Indiana. It spells out room availability, rates, hotel facilities, the distance from the neighbouring airports and motorways. It gives that moment's rate of exchange, in Netherlands Antilles guilders, Dominican Republic pesos, Guatemalan quetzals, UAE dirhams and Venezuelan bolivars. It gives the 'wash down' at each hotel, the difference between gross bookings and net, or the no show rate. It will search for partial spellings, looking for similar names when there has been an error over a guest's name. At any time, it will reveal who is staying at a Sheraton.

Thus, one night there were thirty-seven Johnsons and sixty-one Smiths, from Dow Chemicals' Mr Johnson of Missouri at the Sheraton Baton Rouge to the less prestigious Mr Smith of Newcastle, where the computer had warned the Frankfurt Sheraton that his travel agent's voucher should only be accepted 'at hotel's discretion'.

The computer will even say who is not staying at Sheratons. Thus Mr Johnson of Brentford had cancelled from the Atlantic Zurich, and was thus missing the Doltschis-

---

* Bulgaria, Hungary, Monaco, Portugal, Rumania, Turkey, Puerto Rico, the Philippines and Thailand. A report says there is a move in the US to small hotels 'of l'Ermitage type'. This Los Angeles hotel sports a jacuzzi whirlpool filled with mineral water and transports guests free in Rolls Royces. Alas, not a common type.

tube Swiss Restaurant, the Barber'n'Beauty shop, the heated indoor pool, the curling and skating, the night club and the view of the Old Town. He might, of course, have been on to something much nicer.

Variable rates

The expensive computer hardware is necessary. The Sheraton money machine is complex. Though the Sheraton Munich has only one rate throughout the year, the more tourist-conscious Sheraton Waikiki has twelve different seasonal rates. Neither is a bed a bed. There are nine different types of bed, each with its own computer code: singles, doubles, Queens, Kings, studios for one, studios for two, rollaways for children, rollaways for adults and cribs.

Not that a rate is a rate in many hotels, particularly out of season or during a recession. Receptionists are frequently authorized to give discounts to guests that can go as high as two-thirds off printed rates.

'Of course, we're trained to say that *we* don't give discounts in *our* type of hotel,' says a receptionist. 'We say that our prices are the ones printed in the tariff. A lot of people will go along with that, even in London in the disastrous season of 1981 or Spain in 1980.

'Most people don't think you can haggle over hotel prices. They think they are fixed. We like to give that impression. But they aren't. Nothing in travel is. I was giving discounts of up to sixty per cent to people who asked.'

What is a rule when a hotel is nearly empty can also apply when it is nearly full. Hotels with occupancy rates as high as ninety per cent will still agree to discounts to get nearer the manager's grail, one hundred per cent on his occupancy schedules. This will normally be restricted to a 'walk in', someone who simply arrives at reception and asks for a room. Those who have booked through an airline or travel agent have already cost the hotel ten per cent in commission.

The hotel may also insist on a discounted room being paid for in cash or by cheque, since a credit card could mean the loss of a further five to seven per cent to the card company.

A local hotel member of an international chain, like Hilton or Holiday Inn may give discounts up to twenty per cent, provided that the reservation is made to them directly rather than through the chain's international offices, which will also cost in commission.

If a receptionist will not give a discount, it is worth persevering and trying with the duty manager. A 'walk in' should realize that most of his fellow guests already have discounts, even if the benefit is going to a travel agent or credit card company rather than to themselves.

'Of course we like people who come off the street,' says Claudio Buttafava of the Savoy in London. 'If someone books a room with us through the US and pays by credit card, we lose right down the line. There's eight per cent for the travel agent, a $5 booking fee to the handling agent and three per cent minimum for the credit card company, plus fifteen per cent VAT and fifteen per cent service charge for the staff.'

Overcharging varies from hotel to hotel. Bill padding is not as common as in restaurants. It is a rarity in chain hotels, since the accountant and management would have to be in complicity. It is difficult to siphon off money from a single account paid by cheque or credit card at the end of a stay. Inclusive package tours are also relatively immune.

But some mark-ups are absurd. A room rate may seem reasonable, but the hotel claws back a good profit by charging highly for meals, particularly à la carte breakfasts and for small items like soft drinks and laundry that the guest may not notice when ordering.

Telephone charges in European hotels are so high that the Bell Telephone System launched an advertising campaign urging Americans to make a brief call home to get their family or office to ring them back in Europe. Savings can be considerable.

A businessman from Dubai who called his office for ten minutes a day for two weeks from an expensive London hotel would pay £225 above the normal rate, thanks to the mark-up.* If he had made collect calls, on which the hotel cannot make such a profit, he would have paid only £7 above the standard rate.

The German hotels in one international chain charge DM 26 for calls that cost DM 10 at standard rate, a 160 per cent mark-up. London averages the same surcharge, where Geneva is one hundred per cent and Paris is only twenty-five per cent with no handling fee for collect calls. Surcharges are illegal in the US.

A Teleplan has been introduced by American Telephone and Telegraph to reduce European surcharges. Free publicity is given to hotels which reduce their rates. Not that Teleplan is over-generous to the guest: Hilton Internationals joined with an undertaking not to surcharge more than one hundred per cent.

Overbooking is another common flaw. Most hotels do it, for the same reasons as most airlines. A certain percentage of people who book do not show up. It should be safe to overbook by this amount. Peter Clark, the Sheraton UK sales manager, says that the Brussels Sheraton has an average 'no show' rate of thirty per cent of those who book by phone or telex.

The problem arises when everyone does turn up. The circumstances can be embarrassing. The Inter-Continental in Wellington sold off the rooms booked for the Queen's entourage on her State visit to New Zealand.

Most hotels fall into three categories. There are grand hotels of great luxury and often fading style; chain hotels that may glow with rich fittings but can never totally be

* *8 Days* 23 June 1979.

free of the sleep factory image; and package hotels thrown up for the great tourist swarms.

Savoy: Grand Hotel

It is easy to tell a Grand Hotel. Each tells the same story about itself. An Indian potentate is staying with them. He orders a bullet-proof vest, and the hotel is happy to get one made for him. When it is delivered in his suite, he rings for a porter.

'Put it on,' he orders. 'Now, step out on the balcony.' He produces a pistol. 'I want to make sure it works.'

Even here, the Grand Hotel says, service does not go that far.

It has all the elements that a Grand Hotel should have: a trace of the exotic, a little mystery, power, and the willingness to do anything for a client except die for him. The Savoy claims that it happened there, in the 1920s.

The Savoy, overlooking the Thames from the Strand, has the right statistics. Luxury comes by the ton. In a year, the Savoy goes through fourteen tons of smoked salmon at £160,000 wholesale, two tons of Strasbourg foie gras, thirty-nine tons of Normandy butter, and half a ton of Beluga caviar. Its customers consume 3,500 dozen quarts of champagne a year, and it keeps 100,000 bottles of claret on hand in the hotel at all times. The hotel serves fifteen dozen gull's eggs a day in April, half a million oysters between September and April and thirty brace of grouse a day, including a few brace flown down from Scotland on 12 August. Grouse fresh from the guns are not particularly pleasant, but with an upstart like the Hilton importing grouse by helicopter and Rolls Royce, the Savoy has no choice but to keep up.

It is a small city in its own right. It has a two megawatt power station, which produces 200 million pounds of steam a year. Its refrigeration plant supplies six tons of ice a day, and its own well 500,000 gallons of water. It employs painters, decorators, plumbers, carpet-layers, carpenters and bricklayers. It makes mattresses and bakes bread, 3,000 loaves and 45,000 rolls a week. Its printing presses produce three million items a year, and its laundry cleans eight million pieces of linen a year.

Its switchboard handles 6,300 telephone calls a day. It has forty-six lifts and its own theatre. It employs people of twenty-eight different nationalities who speak sixteen languages, including the now important Japanese and Arabic.

People have been born there. 'I think the women do it to say their children were born in the Savoy,' says a receptionist. Many people have been married there. Some have died there.

It has played host to enough royalty to have worn out several red carpets. It had a murderer who killed a masseuse in a room in 1980. 'I admitted him,' says a receptionist. 'I made him pay £200 deposit. I thought if he had that amount of money, he would be alright. He wasn't.' In between, 'we've had singers from Callas to Jagger, and a similar spread in everything else.'

Like other Grand Hotels, it has been hurt by mass tourism and the arrival of the chain hotels. Some of the apartments have been sold off for offices, and it now has 346 beds.

A Grand Hotel has a hierarchy all its own. The General Manager is at the top, in this case Claudio Buttafava. A big hotel can turn over $22 million a year, and a General Manager at a top hotel in London or Paris can earn $80,000 a year. With school fees, accommodation, clothes and meals provided, that is often money straight in the pocket.

Resident managers, responsible for the day to day running of a hotel, can make $50,000. 'They earn it,' says an executive. 'They have to run the rooms, the food and beverage, hire and fire staff. It's fourteen hours a day, seven days a week, particularly in the Middle East and Far East.' The sales manager may earn $35,000 a year.

'Everyone thinks it's so easy, just kissing people's hands, and bowing and scraping,' says Buttafava. 'There's more to it than that. You've got to be a bookkeeper, a diplomat, a dishwasher. You have to know how a kitchen is run, and how to greet the Queen. You have to watch the costs and percentages, and still find time to change your tie four times a day.'

Buttafava himself has peeled potatoes, made soup and tended bar at the Grand in Paris, washed up and run the switchboard at the Principe Savoia in Milan, and was porter and linen keeper in Frankfurt.

'I do not consider myself to be a servant,' he says. 'I sell human services, and that is very different. The less I am regarded as a servant, the more people will get from me. That is why the English rarely make good waiters. They confuse service and servility.'

The duty managers come below him. 'We are here to prevent problems getting as far as the general manager,' says Andrew Hirst, a duty manager. 'And we get them. We have the lowest of the low dealing with the highest of the high – at least, that's the way some of the highest think. You get difficulties with nationalities and language.

'A Grand Hotel has to absorb everything. Not just murder. In a week, we had David Bowie, Mick Jagger, Elizabeth Taylor and half the aristocracy here. Also, a drunken boxer who spent half the night destroying his room. We charged him £2,000 to repair it and he paid up like a lamb. But it does require a certain diplomacy.'

The duty manager is the last line of defence. 'We prefer to keep ourselves in reserve,' says Hirst. 'The *chef de brigade* and the other receptionists deal direct with the customers. We take the decisions.'

Receptionists bear two rules of Grand Hotels in mind: people must appear to be married, in double rooms, and solvent. Hotels care rather less about the first than the second. As long as adultery is not blatant, and the couple are paying for a double room, most hotels are not sensitive. They have not been for some years: casualties at the Savoy during the Blitz included a prominent Belgian diplomat and his secretary, bombed in bed.

This does not mean that a man can entertain a lady in a room for which only he is booked. The Westbury in London quaintly insists that gentlemen leave their doors ajar if they take a lady upstairs. Others will not let them get as far as the lift – unless they have a suite. 'It's one law for the rich, and another for the very rich.'

The receptionist will know if a guest has stayed before. Claridges keeps cards on all who have been there, including Mussolini whose card notes his fondness for large pillows and his demise in 1944, 'hanged upside down'. The Savoy keeps details of the last six years of customers in a 'live' file with 60,000 names.

The cards note preferences and eccentricities: 'Chivers marmalade *not* Tiptree', 'foam pillows', for this obsession is a common one. The cards also note anything removed by the client during his last stay, a flannel, a coat hanger. 'A lot of hotels now use coat hangers with special hooks that will not work at home,' says Hirst. 'It's rather sad. The Lancaster in Paris buys its ashtrays by the crate specially so people can take them.'

With new arrivals, the receptionist checks addresses against the world telephone directories held by the switchboard. He also looks at business guides: 'the client may not be in them, but his company will'. Credit cards are checked. Bad debts plague Grand Hotels. One couple at the Savoy paid with a cheque on a non-existent account, and left with all the covers and curtains from their suite.

Potential big spenders are given preference if rooms are tight. Those staying only one night are not popular, because the hotel will only take bed and breakfast from them. The average guest staying for a few nights will spend half as much again as the room on food and drink. 'People with a religious thing against going out' are welcomed. This is hotel shorthand for Arab families where the women stay in the hotel, spending up to £500 a day on fruit and flowers.

133

Established clients and VIPs get gifts from the 'goodies box': chocolates from Charbonnel et Walker, flowers or champagne.

The head porter rules over the linkmen, luggage porters, liftmen, messengers, pageboys and chauffeurs. His key item is his contacts book, which will enable him to get a seat for Wimbledon or to hire a yacht for Cowes Week at short notice.

It is an international business, and he is a member of the *Clefs d'Or*, the society of concierges or porters. It has a headquarters in Paris, and 4,000 members in nineteen countries. Each entrant is grilled by a Selection Committee on subjects like Customs duties, postage rates, airline routes, dates of public holidays and visa requirements.

A good concierge should be able to fix most things. Alberto Pinto, the chef-concierge at the Excelsior in Rome, was said to be the second most important man in Rome, after the Pope. The porter at the Grosvenor in London was able to get an Oscar ticket for Bianca Jagger in California in a few hours, through his contact with his opposite number at the Beverly Hilton in Los Angeles.

The Savoy has 180 staff on the twenty-four-hour-a-day room service which Buttafava says is 'the hallmark of the Grand Hotel'. These include housekeepers, chambermaids, housemaids and valets. The night service staff number sixty-four. A full à la carte menu is available throughout the night.

The complex hierarchy comes out strongly in the restaurants. The restaurant manager, Mr Antonio, is God. Beneath him come first, second and third head waiters, reception and station head waiters, wine butlers, *chefs de rang* and the lowly *commis de rang*.

The manager greets the guest, and the first or second head waiter shows him to his table. The wine butler takes the order for aperitifs. The station head waiter presents the menu.

The station is the sideboard. There are normally eighteen guests to each station at lunch, and twenty-five at dinner when people are in less of a hurry. The station head waiter takes the order, in triplicate, and hands it to the *commis*. One copy stays on the sideboard and the other two go to the kitchen.

Orders in Grand Hotels are always taken in French, even if the staff is Italian. Tradition, and clarity in the kitchen, demands that a note is taken even if a customer leaves out a course. RA, *rien avant*, means no starter and RES, *rien en suite*, means no main course.

The *commis* takes the food from the kitchen to the sideboard. He does not get to serve it, however. That is done by the *chef de rang*, either on his own or assisting the station head waiter.

A first buffet chef is in charge of the meat trolley and carving. The demi buffet chef is responsible for the sweet and cheese trolleys.

The *chef de rang* clears the table to the sideboard. The *commis* takes it out to the kitchen to be washed up. 'He is the mule,' says Mr Antonio. 'He doesn't get near the guest but he carries a lot.'

A guest can rate his own importance in the restaurant. If high, he will be served by the station head waiter or head waiter. If low, he will get the *chef de rang*. A station head waiter has tails, a *chef de rang* a dinner jacket with waistcoat and white apron, a *commis* a high-buttoned white jacket.

The Savoy has its own uniform, red jackets for senior staff, green for station heads, but the system is the same elsewhere. 'In general, if you are served by someone in tails, that is high prestige,' says Mr Antonio. 'A dinner jacket is not.'

A *commis* notes sourly: 'Guests don't usually thank people in white jackets. They just complain, particularly if the place is half-empty. They've got nothing better to do than look at the staff. In a crowded restaurant they are grateful to get served at all.'

The hierarchy is reflected in the division of the tips. All the money is put into a box called the *tronc*. Each morning, it is shared out on a points system where the first head waiter rates twenty-four points down to a commis at eight.

The kitchen also has its rankings. There are sauce, roast and fish chefs, *hors d'oeuvriers*, soup and omelette specialists, larder chefs, *legumiers* to prepare vegetables. There are buyers, important men where a typical Savoy banquet for 300 requires 80 dozen oysters, 10 pounds of caviar, 140 pounds of salmon, 65 pints of turtle soup, 30 saddles of lamb and 300 quail. Above it all is the mighty *chef des cuisines*, a dictator in a tiny office, microphone in hand.

It is the detail and the hierarchy that clearly distinguish the grand from the chain hotel. The big chain hotel will often have a better site and more lavish bedrooms but it does not compete in service.

Holiday Inns – chain hotels

Holiday Inns is the largest hotel group in the world. It has more than 1,750 hotels and a quarter of a million rooms. Investment has run at $650 million in one year. It is also rather curious. It was founded by a popcorn vendor, Kemmons Wilson. He looks for evidence of a belief in God, regular Church attendance and disfavour to divorce before hiring a new man. His partner is a former carpenter and home builder, Wallace Johnson. He will not hire anyone with flat feet. 'It spells slow thinking,' he says.

The first motels were designed and furnished by Wilson's mother, Doll, a former stenographer.

Its expansion has been remarkable. Wilson opened the first motel with borrowed money in Memphis in 1952, after a family holiday had convinced him that there was a market for reasonably-priced motels that would cater for families. He called it the Holiday Inn after a Hollywood film. By the 1970s, a new Inn was sprouting on earth every two-and-a-half days.

Wilson achieved this by being precisely the opposite of the Savoy. He did not believe in experience. He had none himself and few of the first executives he hired had worked in hotels before. He did not believe in individual excellence. He believed that whatever the limitations of the individual, by working for Holiday Inns a kind of fusion would take place with others, making the group invincible. 'Two and two equals five or more' is how he put it.

Above all, he did not believe in the unique qualities of a great hotel like the Savoy. Wilson believed in a system of identikit hotels, where the light switches would be in the same position (to the right of the door) from Swiss Cottage to Bermuda, the towels would have the same number of threads to the inch from Marbella to West Bend, Wisconsin, and the staff would have learned their craft from the same instruction manual.

The founders attribute much of their success to God. Wallace Johnson confers with Him about company affairs before leaving for the office every morning. He says he puts his questions to the Lord 'loud and clear'.

'Well, Lord, where are we going to find those $84 million we need to finance those new hotel projects in Western Europe?' The Lord's replies, Mr Johnson has stated, enter through the back of his head and rise up through his subconscious.

At Holiday City, the company's sprawling, seventy-seven-acre headquarters, the executives gathered every Wednesday morning to be led in prayer by its chaplain, the Rev. 'Dub' Nance. Every year, an inspirational address is given in Memphis by a prominent evangelist such as Billy Graham.

Rivals think that godliness has helped. The moral fervour helped keep up the enthusiasm that Wilson rates much higher than ability amongst employees. It encouraged thinking in simple slogans – 'When you're feeling low, try to force a smile from the inside', 'Your attitude is showing.' A rapidly developing group in the mass travel and catering field invariably depends on young and relatively ill-educated and poorly paid staff. A new Holiday Inn in Abu Dhabi cannot recruit or train on the same level as the Savoy. Rapid indoctrination is essential, and the fast food operators have borrowed widely from Holiday Inns.

The company also went out of its way to emphasize that, unlike the normal sleazy image of motels, it was a fount of morality. It started an 'Open Bible Policy'. Every bedroom must have an open Bible on the dresser, and its pages must be changed each day by the chambermaid. It is laid down that it should be open at the Book of Psalms one day, the Old Testament the next, the New Testament the next. Any Innkeeper, as the hotel manager is called, who fails to enforce this will quickly receive a chiding letter from the Rev. Dub. The chaplain claims that the policy has resulted in several conversions, plus the fact that many errant husbands have been saved from adultery at the last moment by the sight of the opened scriptures in their motel room.

It has also been good for business. Although the group has no 'morals policy' as such, wives worried less if travelling husbands stayed at an Inn. Wallace Johnson told a reporter: 'I find that a man who has been to a tomcatting party knows he's wrong. When the sun is down, and he has sobered up, he'll say: "I wish I had the principles of Holiday Inns." '

The group is now active in casino hotels, and the religious fervour is wearing a little thin. But rivals have always considered that much of the success was due to another bible, a thick book called the *Holiday Inn Standards Manual*. Each hotel has one, individually numbered and highly confidential.

Like most of the major hotel and fast food groups, Hilton, Sheraton, McDonalds, Holiday Inns is largely a franchise operation. Wilson sold franchises to dentists, real estate men, lawyers, petrol station owners, bankers and others with no hotel experience. The Manual told them everything they wanted to know, from how to control the algae in the swimming pool to how to run a credit check on a guest.

The franchise costs about six per cent of the gross rooms

revenue. It is made up of an initial franchise fee of $15,000 plus $100 for each room over one hundred rooms, a fee of $2,500 for the Holiday Inn sign, $3 per month per room for the use of the reservations system, one cent per room per night for training, three per cent of ground rooms revenue as a franchise revenue, one per cent for advertising and one per cent for sales office.

The franchisee finances the building of the hotel, reckoned at from $2 million for a hundred-room suburban hotel to a minimum $21 million for a six hundred-room high rise with conference facilities in a city centre. A new Holiday Inn in Aberdeen cost £35,000 per bedroom.

The Manual lays down exact building and furnishing standards. Japanese Holiday Inns got a waiver to allow them to build their rooms smaller, because of the high cost of land and the small height of the Japanese. The Chelsea Holiday Inn also had smaller rooms than are allowed elsewhere, and has no car park, because no other site was available.

Otherwise, the rules are rigidly uniform. Every room must have a writing desk, double bed, two easy chairs, a standing light, two bedside lights of one hundred watts, a television and, of course, a Bible. During building, drawings must be submitted to the Inspections Standards Department in Memphis. There are standards for everything, from the weight of bars of soap to the availability of book matches.

Many franchisees buy a furnishings and equipment package, so that Memphis supplies them down to ashtrays and face flannels. For $229, the eager franchisee can buy a Holiday Inn worship kit, which includes a lectern, altar cloth, gold cross, electric candlesticks and attendance certificate blanks. It should also keep him in with the Rev. Dub.

Once the instant hotel is up and passed by the men from Memphis, the franchisee can acquire an instant-trained staff. If he himself is going to manage the hotel, he can take the Holiday Inn University course for Innkeepers.

The University has a staff of sixty and takes 150 students. The principles of Innkeeping are poured into them rather as a foreign language is taught in a language laboratory. There are self-paced instruction manuals on subjects like food and beverage control. Sound booths and tapes work up skills on reception. Videos explain the art of the coffee shop supervisor.

They are taught how to use the group's Holidex reservation system, said to be the largest privately-owned communications system in the world. It can make and confirm a reservation to any Inn in thirty seconds. The computer terminal in Memphis is surrounded by three-inch thick concrete, so that Holidex will survive a nuclear holocaust.

The rest of the staff can also be trained *en masse* by the University. Thus, someone setting up a Holiday Inn in Swaziland – and there is one there, of course – can conjure up a washing machine or a waiter through Memphis.

He keeps the name only if his hotel passes quarterly visits by a team of inspectors who have a check list of over 500 items to be passed. Any failure involves penalty points. Poor hygiene rates highest. Lavatory rims are checked with a dentist's angled mirror or tissue. This can count forty points per rim. A peeling ceiling in a laundry costs sixty points. There are penalties for rattling doors, holes in carpets, wrong wattage light bulbs and stains or hairs on upholstery.

Towels must come in the right number, size, colour and fabric. Fabric damage is heavily penalized. Mattresses must have been turned regularly. They have months printed on the corners so that this can be checked. Food service must be working a minimum of sixteen hours a day and the air conditioning in all public areas must be fully functional. The algae count in the compulsory pool must be low.

Three months is allowed for faults to be put right. The penalty points are doubled if they are still uncorrected on a second inspection. A short extension is granted after this. If there are still faults, the hotel is reported to the International Association of Holiday Inns, the corporate body of the franchisees. It will then issue an edict to withdraw the Holiday Inn sign and services.

About thirty hotels are banned or drop out each year. Some cases are treated leniently where the guest can identify the reason for the drop in standards. Thus the Holiday Inn in Beirut survived the inspectors until the gunmen finally put paid to it. Guest questionnaires in every room are sent to the head of sales and marketing. Trends are evaluated, not by an individual, but by a computer which will warn the inspectors if there is a persistent run of complaints.

The result is a slick system that should work anywhere, even if it is short on any individual skill. A chef, for example, is trained and checked with Army thoroughness.

He will have passed basic kitchen tasks. He will know how to prepare basic sauces. He will be able to boil, fry, sauté, roast and bake potatoes. He can boil, scramble, poach, omelette, coddle or fry eggs. He can prepare that handsome source of hotel profit, the club sandwich. He can make fruit salad, crème caramel, trifle, compôte fruits and custard. He will have been checked in grilling, roasting, frying, stewing, boiling and braising meat.

A waiter is trained and checked on his 'special skills' as well as his serving abilities. He is taught to recognize hosts, light cigarettes, converse, and deal with customers who are either intoxicated or unable to pay, or both. He is also taught to give guidance to customers on the menu or wine list, an important point when hotels are pushing a special food promotion or a cocktail of the month.

Security men must see that all television sets are bolted down, that the French windows on ground floor rooms do not open wide enough for furniture to be pilfered, that a customer who has walked in without paying does not 'do a skip', as the midnight flit is known in the trade.

It may not be Grand Hotel. But with only 0.7 staff to each guest, where the Dorchester has 2.5 to one, and with a staff turnover of more than seventy five per cent a year, the system is efficient. The Holiday Inn University is a joke

141

to graduates of Lausanne, but it sets instant standards most package hotels cannot match.

Package hotels

The customers in package tour hotels are known as 'geese'. This is a misnomer. Geese tend to hiss if they are too rigorously disciplined and kept in line. 'Sheep' would be more accurate, for the ambition of every package hotel is to have uncomplaining guests who fall in with its plans.

A 150-room hotel in Corfu begins its planning for the summer season the previous November. The owner, a Greek who lives in London, starts negotiating with tour operators then. 'I look to make £800 profit a room over the year. We run at a loss out of season, so we need £1,000 profit from each room from April to October,' he says.

Ideally, he wants to do business with a single operator. 'There's less room for chaos that way. You get a nice, integrated package. One lot of guests arrive by the same aircraft as another group leave on. All the geese are the same nationality so you don't get any friction between them, and you know the cash take outside the room.'

The take in the bars and discos is important and varies with nationality. Spanish hotelier Paul Benvenuto says: 'The Germans and the Dutch are the biggest spenders at the bar, followed by the Scandinavians. The Germans are very rowdy when they've been drinking. They sing a lot, and that can annoy other people. The Scandinavians can get very destructive and smash the place up. The British aren't too bad at all, not the hooligans they are made out to be.*

* Not true of some British football fans. In one case, sixty-three Glasgow Rangers fans had to be repatriated from Barcelona after devastating the Costa Brava in a manner that reminded Spanish editorial writers of Drake's attack on Cadiz. 'Oh my God,' said a repatriate on arrival at Glasgow airport. 'I just remembered. I went out in my car.'

There are other factors. 'The Dutch are terribly mean when it comes to food,' says Benvenuto. 'They'll bring two suitcases, one for their clothes, the other full of cold meats, pastes, bread. The French don't make good package tourists. They are far too fussy, they demand too much. It's essential for a profitable package hotel to operate on a slim staff, so it's difficult to slot in a big French group.

'The Belgians are far less bother. They are important. More hoteliers go to the annual trade fair in Brussels than anywhere else. The Japanese are the easiest, but they are difficult to come by outside London, Paris and Rome.'

Tour operators are well aware of the attractions of a single block booking, and drive hard bargains. Most hotels have to accept bookings from several operators in different countries.

'That means you've got to be firm with guests,' says the Greek. 'I've got one load of Germans arriving half an hour after some Belgians leave. Actually, there's no need for the Belgians to go for another two hours, as far as the airport and check-in are concerned. But I have to get them off the premises, so they go.'

There is no pretence that guests are individuals. 'You think of them in terms of their package. You think, that's a Blue Sky, that's a Neckarmann. If you ever thought of them as people, the whole system would break down.'

That has happened, most notoriously in Spain during the mid-1970s when a combination of overbooking and air traffic controllers' strikes led to people sleeping in schools, halls and on the beach.

Turnover is the name of the package game. At its best, a package tour is as remarkable value as a modern pocket calculator. Two weeks in Majorca with full board can be had for less than the cost of the scheduled return airfare – yet the flight is also included, sometimes there and back on a scheduled flight. Hotels shave profits to a minimum. Volume, and a full hotel, are vital.

'You think of the hotel as a factory, a tanning factory.

A gaggle of people, all pale and wan, arrive one week and leave bronzed the next. Everything is programmed to a plan. It has to be. The rooms and the beds and décor is all identical, so you don't get complaints about other people having better ones.

'At the same time, if you've got a sea view on one side of the hotel, you charge for it. Any extra you can get is worth having, because it all adds up during the season.

'We clean the rooms for eight minutes every day, and we change the sheets every four days. We allow for thirty rooms to be done after midday for people who stay in bed late. It's all laid down in the work schedule for the chamber maids, it's all automatic.

'So is the food. The menu was worked out back in December and we stick to it. It's standard for everyone in the hotel. We tried doing different menus for different nationalities but it didn't work. The Germans complained that the British were getting sausages for breakfast and the British were mad when the Germans got Wienerschnitzel.

'For the set menu, we feed them 60p worth of food for breakfast, £1.10 for lunch and £1.65 for dinner. They get a good hot dinner and then we serve it again cold for the buffet lunch. Suitably disguised, of course. Most tour operators insist we have something à la carte as well. It looks smarter. We have steak, scampi and trout, easy to store and easy to serve. We also work out an allowance with the tour operator for birthday and anniversary cakes to give the spontaneous gift touch.

'We used to have room service for drinks and breakfast, but we packed it in. A solo, a guest who's not on a package, will always tip even though he's paying way over the odds. But a goose won't tip for breakfast in bed, even though we're making a crummy £15 profit off him in a week. A package is a package, and he thinks it includes everything.

'We throw in one evening of Greek music. We get a band and a singer in – they do two hotels a night right through the season. Some of the waiters dance. The geese have a go. We don't regulate that, or tanning or drinking. If a goose wants to burn himself, he can. If he wants to get drunk, he can. We prefer him to do it in our bar, that's all.

'It may seem cynical, but it's not. People like to be regimented. Why else would holiday camps be such a success?'

Greek hotelier Spiro Flamburiari says that nationality is important. 'The biggest complainers are the Italians and the French, but they come out with it at the time. The British store it up and then go behind your back. They'll thank you for a marvellous holiday and a few hours later, when they are home, they'll be writing to the tour company demanding a pound back here because a meal was late and a pound back there because a sheet wasn't changed.

'They are very petty. However, they also organize themselves well so on balance they are popular in the package trade.'

A one hundred-bedroom hotel on the outskirts of Torremolinos gets by with a staff of sixteen. It has two receptionists, a head waiter and four waiters, a chef, under chef and two skivvies, a housekeeper and four chambermaids. The waiters double as barmen.

Former Costa del Sol hotel owner Phillip Knightley says: 'Running a package hotel is a very fine balanced thing. There is a lot of pressure to open up as soon as possible. Our manager changed out of dungarees half an hour before the first guests arrived, and some of the paint was still wet.'

The building was not completed when the tour brochures were printed, and the tour operator used an artist's impression. 'He had a lot of imagination,' says Knightley. 'He showed a girl sunbathing on the beach outside the entrance to the hotel. Actually, the hotel is three-quarters of a mile from the beach, and there is a railway line outside the entrance. To get to the beach, you had to cross the line, walk through some sugar cane fields and by-pass a TB clinic.'

The change-over of guests is a delicate operation. 'We changed every second Monday. The buses with people leaving used to pass the new arrivals on the road to the airport. We had forty-five minutes to clean all the rooms. It wasn't enough time, so we used to give the newcomers a glass of wine to delay them going to their rooms.

'Everybody overbooked. You had to because of cancellations. Hotels help each other out, and you just had to pray that somebody else had some room. The main psychological point was the last day and evening. You give the guests a farewell party, and send them off in a haze of champagne. Spanish champagne, of course, but it's last impressions that tourists remember.'

The receptionist is a key figure. He has to deal with complaints and the nightmares of overbooking, groups stranded by airline strikes, departure dates confirmed in error and the other natural hazards of the business.

'It's a bit like being an air traffic controller,' says a receptionist in a large Majorca hotel. 'You've got all these groups circling round, and you've got to find somewhere to put them. You can keep them in the stack for so long, sitting in a bus or in the foyer, but eventually they have to land in a room. And that can be painful.'

Complaints run highest in new resorts, because the staff is ill-trained. 'So are some of the guests,' says Spanish hotelier José Fernandez. 'They have never been in a hotel before. When you've got a factory worker from Bruges or Birmingham being served by a peasant's son from Galicia, it's a recipe for trouble. They don't understand each other's background, let alone language.

'So you keep things simple. A simple menu, simple drinks, so everything can be done by just pointing at a list.'

A difficulty is that staff tend to leave package hotels as soon as they are experienced enough to move on. 'The prestige is higher, and so are the perks', says Fernandez. 'Package hotels work on such a straightforward basis that there is little room for tips, bill padding and all the rest.

Most things are paid for in advance, so there isn't much scope for staff initiative. They move to a better class of hotel.'

The building itself can be a problem. Many package hotels were put up fast during a boom: the Costa Brava in the late 1960s, the Costa del Sol in the early 1970s, North Africa and Greece more recently. A fishing village with no building above two storeys becomes a resort with twenty multi-storey hotels, largely built with fishermen's labour. Hotels are often poorly built.* Examples include a Majorca hotel where the balconies had a tendency to part company with the facade, a Greek establishment where a hairbrush could be put into the gap between window frame and wall, and a hotel in Cyprus where the lights went out whenever the lift was used.

Fire regulations are often skimped. Following a series of disasters, a leading independent consultant on hotel fire prevention visited Spain.† Bill Bunday reported that he would have closed every hotel he visited. He found 'eggbox type doors instead of fire resistant ones', 'dead-end corridors where guests would find no escape from a blaze' and 'stairways that would funnel inflammable gases and dense smoke from blazing furniture and decoration in ground floor public areas to the floors above'.

Bunday found that fire extinguishers, marked in Spanish only, were out of sight on service staircase landings. There were no visible fire alarms in the hotel corridors and no notices in rooms of what to do in an emergency.

The Hotel Volga at Calella de la Costa on the Costa Brava had over 100 rooms, but no fire alarms or visible fire instructions, and just one extinguisher per floor. The

* Outright collapse is rare. However, part of the Hyatt Regency Hotel in Kansas City collapsed in July 1981, killing 111.
† Daily Mail, 23 July 1979. Spain's record is poor. Even the US has problems. A fire at the MGM Grand Hotel in Las Vegas in November 1980 killed 84.

management said: 'Guests would be contacted by telephone in the event of fire and told to leave the hotel.'

A hundred phone calls would take time, even if the switchboard was not affected by smoke and fumes. Perhaps the Volga would follow the example of the Rosamar in Lloret del Mar, also on the Costa Brava. When a fire broke out in its night club, sleeping guests were roused by banging on bedroom doors. Fortunately the fire spread slowly.

Also at Lloret, the Hotel Flamingo and the Imperial Park have much in common: no fire doors, no fire escape instructions, few extinguishers. The Imperial Park marks its service stairs Private. The 287-room Flamingo does not mark this potential escape route at all.

One 17-storey, 400-room hotel in Benidorm had several hazards. Bunday found that the guests in twelve rooms on each floor, between a cul-de-sac and the main staircase, would be completely trapped if smoke cut off the stairway. A stairway at the other end of the corridor was partially blocked by foam rubber mattresses. It was not marked as an emergency exit. On the ground floor, there were foam plastic chairs and settees in the lounge at the base of the stairs, all highly toxic.

The apt name of this package hotel: the Titanic.

Eccentric hotels

There are also, of course, eccentric hotels although by definition these do not fall into any category.

There is indeed a hotel that is fit only for dogs, the Kennelworth Luxury Hotel on East 72nd Street in New York. It is quite an establishment. The 'spacious private rooms' look like gaily painted chateaux ranged around an indoor village green. Costs range from $11 a night for a twenty-eight-square foot single to $15 for a fifty five square foot suite.

There are lobby shops. A boutique 'features a unique selection of pet apparel and accessories from around the world'. The Grooming Salon does 'both classic and contemporary cuts for all breeds to perfection'. A hotel photographer provides framed colour pictures of guests. They can be dressed for the occasion by the boutique, which sells everything from satin baseball caps for chihuahuas to straw hats with sunglasses for spaniels and 'foreign intrigue trenchcoats' to add to a Dobermann's air of menace.

The à la carte menu covers most tastes from dogmeat to peanut butter, but special requests have included chicken legs with no skin, roast beef sandwich on rye bread, sirloin steak for a Yorkshire terrier, and applesauce and boiled eggs.

The Kennelworth, which would cost a million dollars to replace, was started by the actor Les Weiner. He was never satisfied with ordinary kennels for his own dogs when he went on holiday. He was to have called it the Waldog Astoria, but he was afraid the hotel might sue.

The cheapest rooms are in the new Japanese 'capsule hotels'. The guests sleep in reinforced fibre capsules, about the size of a railway sleeping berth or a large coffin, which are stacked in rooms. The capsules are big enough for one person to lie down in. They are lockable from inside and have colour TV, radio, alarm clocks and fire sprinklers built in. The better capsule hotels also throw in a telephone, and communal swimming pools and saunas.

They can be rented by the hour, convenient for railway stations and airports. They cost a fraction of a hotel room to build, at around £1,400 a capsule where a room in a Mediterranean resort hotel averages £26,000 and in a European city centre hotel more than £60,000.

At the other end of the scale, the world's most expensive hotel was opened in Paris in December, 1981. The Nova Park hotel, in the old *Paris Match* building close to the Champs Elysées, has a royal suite that costs 37,500 francs a night. That is more than £3,000 and it does not include breakfast. However, the suite does come with five bedrooms, seven bathrooms, an office, a sitting room and a kitchen.

Its glass is armoured, it has special security staff, its own direct telex on a red line confidential system, a telephone bugging detector, a direct lift to the car park so that a guest can drive his motorcade into the hotel and enter the suite without being seen. Anyone taking the suite could lay himself open to attack by kidnappers or political terrorists, so such precautions are necessary, although it seems pushing matters a little that the security room should overlook the master bedroom.

The suite comes with a complimentary Rolls Royce and driver. It has a free TV video service, with a hundred films available round the clock.

The Madonna Inn at San Luis Obispo, between Los Angeles and San Francisco is a motel with 110 different rooms of common eccentricity. The Cave Man Room has rock ceiling, walls and floor and a rock waterfall. It has stained glass portraits of cave men, a selection of clubs and the bathroom is hidden between two rocks. The Austria suite has a seventy-foot long room with an antique Belgian wedding veil in the shower door.

The Swiss Bell room has cattle and edelweiss painted on the windows and the lavatory has a waterfall and giant clam-shell basins. Safari Land has leopard wallpaper and tiger, zebra and elephant trophies. The Irish Hills suite is entirely emerald green, including the ceiling. The king-size green bed has a king-size shamrock shaped headboard. This makes a pleasant change from the rest of the motel, where the basic colour is pink. Even the bread for the sandwiches is pink. The Cloud Nine room is almost entirely pink, with cupid lamps and angels on the plastic shower doors.

The designer and owner, Alex Madonna, is proud that it is usually full. He thinks it is a very practical concept. 'In our coffee shop,' he says breathlessly, 'the waitress only has to move her arm an average of 5½ inches per cup of coffee. In a normally designed restaurant, she must move between 36 and 44 inches. That means that here she has five times less travel and can therefore pick up approximately $1 to $1.50 per seat per day and with fifty three seats, she can make at least $50 a day on top of her wages.'

Mr Madonna also has a good gimmick to encourage couples to turn up by the trio. The Inn has 'Ron', 'De' and 'Vous' suites.

The Astroworld Hotel in Houston has a Crusader suite based on a medieval castle. The eight-foot-square bed has a King Arthur striped awning which hides two TV sets in the raftered ceiling. The walls are stone. The Gladiator bathroom has three separate baths next to an eighteen-foot heated swimming pool with a 2,000-year-old bust of a gladiator inside the shower.

The hotel may be a bit haywire with its historical dates, but it tries hard. The two-storey Tarzan room has a twenty-foot tree, a bamboo staircase, zebra-skin wallpaper, stuffed heads and furniture covered with real tiger skins.

The Barnum and Bailey bedroom has a seven by eight foot bed, which is a replica of the bandwagons used by circuses to trundle on musicians, midgets and freaks. It was designed by a well-known film set designer, Harper Goff.

The Shangri La in Singapore has put its money into uniforms. The swimming pool staff wear matelot suits, the bell boys have red Chinese jackets, the waiters have yellow Chinese pyjamas, the page boys wear Persian waistcoats, the room maids purple cheongsams, the receptionists Malay sarongs, the security men Los Angeles Police Department outfits, the doormen Genghis Khan jackets and the waitresses Charles I lace.

'I wanted to discuss something with the manager,' says a guest. 'But I couldn't take the strain any more. He'd probably have been dressed up like Louis XIV.'

In Acapulco, the Las Brisas has 200 swimming pools and a fleet of 150 jeeps for guests. The jeeps are pink and white. So is everything else. 'Everyone likes pink, don't they,' says owner Col. Brandstetter. From the brochures to the bed sheets and the blossoms floating on the pools, the place is pink. Acapulco is famous for the American developer who said of his project: 'Here we are creating a typical traditional Mexican village. There won't be anything else like it in the whole of Mexico.'

Reasonable and unreasonable expectations

Most countries have official grading systems, which should make it easy to class a hotel. They can, however, be confusing. Spain gives one to five stars for hotels, one to four stars for apartment hotels and one to three stars for pensions. De luxe can thus be applied to a four-star apartment hotel as well as a five-star hotel.

There is a major difference between a one-star pension and a one-star hotel. The pension needs only one telephone for general use, one common bathroom and one lavatory for each twelve rooms. A one-star hotel needs a reception area, a hall porter, laundry facilities, a bathroom for every seven rooms. A two-star hotel must have telephones in every room, almost half of which must also have their own showers. A three-star hotel must have bathroom *en suite* in half its rooms, and such refinements as separate passenger and luggage lifts.

Four- and five-star hotels need much grander public rooms, bathrooms and numbers of staff. Standards for apartment hotels are considerably lower.

Things should be easier in Italy, Greece and Yugoslavia which have five categories. They start with de luxe: the Italians then number them to 4, the others letter them to D.

For tax reasons, however, many foreign hotel owners try to keep a lower official rating than the actual standard their hotel deserves. So British tour operators dream up their own ratings, a mish-mash of red and blue stars, As, Ts and Xs.

Curiously for a major tourist country, Britain has no official compulsory classification system. True, the English

Tourist Board has six classifications. But since they do not inspect the hotels, relying on the owners to fill in the details themselves, nobody takes much notice of it.

The AA star system is the most useful. It is drawn up on strict lines. A one-star hotel gets by on hot drinks in the evening, a cooked breakfast, two main dishes at lunch and dinner, a wine list with two reds and two whites, a lavatory for every six bedrooms, and rooms large enough to 'allow freedom of movement of guests occupying the room'. The AA is keen on the hierarchy of shoes. A one-star hotel must provide shoe cleaning materials.

The five-star place needs a uniformed porter, a writing table, TV, radio and bathroom for every room, a cocktail bar, drinks at all hours, à la carte breakfast, at least seven hot dishes at lunch and dinner, full floor service of meals and drinks in rooms for twenty four hours a day, dinner to 9.30 p.m., a wine list including Chateaux bottled wines, luxurious rooms, early morning tea service and a twenty-four-hour laundry service. Shoe-wise, a cleaning service must be provided: 'Boots' lives.

The real break is between two and three stars. Three and four have much the same as five, though less of it — less service, less choice of wine and food, less room. A three star can, for example, close its dining room at 8.30 p.m. and it does not have to polish shoes. A two star is better than a one only in having to produce a choice of vegetables at lunch, a luggage stand in every room and a lavatory to every five instead of six bedrooms.

The most important aspect in any hotel or its restaurant is how well the guest is treated. This is largely the responsibility of the guest himself. Hotel staff have some very nasty ways of getting their own back on guests they do not like. They are often given sophisticated training, based on mass psychology, to help them get their own way with complaining guests. Equally, there are things a guest can do to make sure he is welcomed and lands up with the best service and the best table in a hotel.

Staff do not like people who complain, particularly if they do so at the top of their voice and with threats to take the matter to the manager or the directors.

'The simplest way of getting your own back is to put the guest in a "noise chamber",' says a receptionist at a big London hotel. 'Every hotel has them, near the lift machinery, over a kitchen, above or below the night club, by the air conditioning plant. The night club is best because the guest won't know its there until 10 or 11 at night and then he probably won't feel like changing his room and just has to grin and bear it.

'If he complains that it's the wrong room, you just say you are redecorating the right one. Redecorating is the hotel equivalent of airlines "technical reasons". Whenever there's a mix-up with rooms, it's redecorating that gets you out of the hole. People believe it, even if its the height of the season and the last thing any sane hotelier would do is to take rooms out of commission.'

There are more subtle means than noise chambers.

'The early alarm call is a classic,' says the receptionist. 'The guest can raise hell if an alarm call is late, but there's not much he can do if it's three-quarters of an hour early. It means he's stuck in his room waiting for his breakfast with nothing to do, which is very irritating.'

There are many small things that annoy guests and that appear to be deliberate. Over-boiled eggs, cold coffee, the wrong morning newspaper are the ones hoteliers are most conscious of. 'Particularly eggs,' says the receptionist. 'You get apparently well-adjusted men and women reduced to incoherent fury by a badly boiled egg. But these things are never deliberate. The guest is obviously in the right, the hotel is in the wrong, so the staff don't try anything on, though slow service, being indefinable, can be deliberate.

'You can affect a rude guest by making him pay full rate if he checks out late, even if he's only a minute or two after checkout time. No matter what they may say, all hotels will allow favoured guests to check out late without any fee, provided a new guest is not within ninety minutes of arriving for that room. That gives plenty of time to get the room ready.

'Noon is a typical check-out time, although it would make no difference at all in most hotels if it was extended to 1 p.m. Most new guests arrive after 5 p.m. So there is plenty of room for latitude. But a guest who's made a nuisance of himself won't get five minutes grace.'

Another squeeze is ringing up each day to ask the guest to confirm that he is not leaving. Hotels make their living through understanding the basis of human nature. They are well aware that it is unsettling to come back to a room in the evening, after a hard day on the beach or in the office, to find the red message light on and a query from reception asking whether Sir wants to stay.

If the hotel is full, or if the guest has been vague about his date of departure, most hoteliers will check even though they know that in an ideal world they shouldn't. But if the hotel is not full, it is a sure sign that the staff are having a niggle at the guest.

'People don't believe that hotels can be so petty. Well, they should see how petty people can be to hotels. I have had a woman demand that we sack a chambermaid because she had rearranged her pills and potions when she was dusting the bathroom. She had the chambermaid's name, everything, and she was determined she should go. We transferred the maid to another floor.

'A man tried to have a doorman thrown out because he failed to recognize him – even though it was a new doorman who'd never seen him before.'

If a hotel does not wish to see a customer again, it is in a sensitive position. It cannot refuse him entry unless it has a positive and legally sound reason, like a bad debt in the past. It can, and will, claim to be full when he tries to make a booking but this may not convince him at off-peak times of the year.

The best method is to ensure that he does not wish to stay there again. This is not as easy as it sounds. 'We had a guest who was loud-mouthed, bossy and domineering,' says the owner of a luxury hotel in Scotland. 'We could take it but the other guests couldn't. They would retreat to far off tables in the dining room and empty the bar when he was around.

'We gave him the worst room in the hotel. No effect. He rebooked. We tried giving him poor service but he enjoyed complaining. He hadn't propositioned the chambermaids or got drunk so we couldn't ask him to leave. We finally did it by querying his credit. People get very upset if you suggest their credit isn't good, particularly bossy people. You can query their morals, their marital status, their manners and they don't mind.

'Their money is something else. We asked him if he would settle his bill every three days. He got mad and left. Bringing in the credit manager can do wonders to shift unwelcome guests.'

Your rights

Travellers do have rights, however unlikely that may seem in the light of experience. Few people in the industry advise them of this. Many actively conceal it. Travellers also have obligations, as the industry is swift to point out.

A hotelkeeper is required by law to give food, drink and a room to anyone who arrives in a fit state and with enough money. The penalty for refusal without reason is imprisonment or a fine.

Alas, there are exceptions to this wonderful rule. It does not apply to residential hotels, boarding houses or pubs. The hotelkeeper is off the hook if the hotel is full, or if the traveller is drunk, disorderly or has a contagious disease, or wants the room for illegal purposes. This includes adultery.

A hotel can demand payment in advance, and a guest can be evicted if he refuses to pay the bill whenever he is asked to do so. The guest can also get his marching orders if he indulges in immorality or conduct offensive to other guests. Necessary force can be used to remove a guest who is behaving badly and who refuses to leave when asked.

The law considers it reasonable for a hotel to turn away a traveller who has no luggage or proper identification – even though both these may just have been lost by an airline. Absence of luggage alone is not enough justification to refuse a room.

Hotels are allowed to have any rules about animals they wish. Although they must take in and guard a customer's luggage, they need not accept 'something exceptional which is not luggage – such as a tiger or a package of dynamite'.*

If a traveller does not pay his bill, the hotelkeeper can seize his luggage, but not his car. 'Flitting' without paying can lead to up to two years in prison. It is larceny to leave intentionally with hotel linen, towels, glasses and so forth.

Most hotels have notices claiming that they are not responsible for any loss or theft unless articles are deposited for safekeeping. This is nonsense. At common law, the innkeeper is an insurer for the loss of the goods of a guest in his inn, unless the loss arises through the negligence of the guest, an act of God or the public enemy. Not locking a room door is negligence.

A hotel can limit its liability to £100 with a maximum of £50 for any one article, if it displays prominent notices both in the rooms and at the check-in desk. But it will still be fully liable if anything is stolen, lost or damaged through staff negligence or theft, or deposited for safe custody.

The position improves when it comes to restaurants and night clubs.

First the guest has to behave. Reasonable force can be used to throw out a customer for intoxication or disorderly conduct, even after the meal has been ordered.

Otherwise he is in a strong position. The restaurant must use due care to furnish wholesome food: if failure to

* *Robins and Co* vs *Gray*, 2 QB.501 (1895). History does not relate why Mr Gray found it necessary to travel with a tiger and dynamite.

do so results in an injury to the customer, the restaurant is legally liable. In short, if the food makes you throw up you can sue under the Sale of Goods Act, 1893.

Everything must be of the nature, substance and quality demanded by the customer. All prices must include VAT. If there is a minimum price, a course charge or a service charge, they must be listed on the menu at least as prominently as the price of the food. A magistrate can impose a maximum fine of £400 for failure to do this. A jury can fine what it likes.

Read that again. The next time a restaurant tries the minimum price or cover charge ploy, and this is either not on the menu or in a smaller typeface than the rest of the menu, refuse to pay. If pressed, threaten to take the restaurant in front of a jury.

No minimum quantities for food are laid down by law. But if the menu says a steak is six ounces, it must be that. If the restaurant claim that it started off at six ounces but shrank and lost weight during cooking, laugh and refuse to pay. Carafe wine must be 25 cl, 50 cl, 75 cl or one litre. The customer must be told which, and the amount must be marked on the wine list or on the carafe. Many restaurants get away with this. Equally regrettably they are allowed to sell wine by the glass in unspecified amounts.

If the food is inedible or the wine rotten, complain. If there is no satisfaction, you are entitled to reject the meal and to refuse to pay for it.

You must, however, pay for what you have eaten. If you eat half a course before sending it back, you have to pay half. If you refuse to pay anything, the restaurant can demand your name and address with a view to civil action. Only if you refuse to give your name and address can the restaurant detain you and call the police.

Remember that provided you give your name and address, a restaurant has no right to hold you. If the police are called, they will take no action beyond perhaps prosecuting the restaurant for wasting police time. If a waiter or manager uses physical force or verbally threatens you, this is actionable.* Insulting language that only humiliates and embarrasses is not.

A firm booking is a contract. If a customer turns up and there is no table, he can claim breach of contract. Note that if the customer doesn't turn up he can be sued himself.

The words 'Not Responsible for Hats and Coats' do not relieve the restaurant of its responsibilities. If a waiter or cloakroom attendant takes a coat the restaurant is liable for its damage or theft – though not for anything left in its pockets. If the customer hangs up his own coat, he is responsible for it. Similarly at a parking lot, if the attendant takes the car and keys, the parking company is responsible no matter what may be printed on the ticket.

There are plenty of safeguards for dealing with travel agents. The main one is that travellers can sue for loss of enjoyment as well as getting their money back.

If an agent does not provide the holiday described in a brochure he has broken a contract and is liable to pay compensation for disappointment.

A holiday or travel booking is a contract but it depends only partly on the terms and conditions printed in the contract. If anyone is killed or injured through negligence, the conditions do not take away the right to compensation. If a travel agent's negligence causes loss or damage – through a false brochure and so forth – the conditions will only protect him, no matter what they say, if they are fair and reasonable.

Thus a tour operator was fined £1000 for recklessly making false statements by claiming a hotel had a private swimming pool, a children's paddling pool and a night club. The swimming pool was not private and there was neither paddling pool nor night club.

Brochures should have easily readable conditions, and should show very clearly how travellers may have to pay surcharges. If a holiday has to be cancelled, the agent

* The restaurant is also responsible if a waiter spills food and drink over a customer.

should offer alternative holidays or a prompt refund of the money. If the circumstances are beyond his control, such as the invasion of Cyprus or revolution in Portugal, he may keep the amount of his reasonable expenses.

Since surcharges are allowed only if prominently stated in brochures, keep the brochure. If a hotel turns out to be a nightmare, photograph it. Evidence is important in all claims.

Airlines need only compensate for what will obviously arise from a delay, such as a night in a hotel. They are not responsible for 'unforeseen damage' like missing a vital business meeting, overstaying in a country and being hit for tax, or simply a messed-up holiday.

And they are not liable at all if they can show that a delay was not their fault or that all steps had been taken to avoid it.

If an aircraft breaks down, the lack of proper mainte-nance leaves the airline open to blame. Although most airlines will pay for hotels anyway, if the delay results from striking air traffic controllers, bad weather and so on, they are not obliged to do so.

Overbooking is now common. A passenger who is 'bumped' from a flight is entitled to reasonable expenses for hotel, eating and phone calls whilst he is waiting. Some airlines will refund half a fare for the leg of the flight that was overbooked, for a minimum of £10 and a maximum of £100. They are advised to do so, otherwise a magistrate could impose much stiffer penalties.

Generally speaking, if the airline manages to get a pas-senger to his destination within two hours on domestic routes and four hours on international flights of his orig-inal overbooked flight arrival time there is not much point in sueing.

Compensation for lost luggage is fixed at £11.70 a kilo. This is regardless of what the luggage contains. Seasoned travellers fill their bags with bricks to get them to the maximum weight and thus to the maximum compensation level.

If your suitcase goes missing, the airline should provide spare pyjamas, toothbrush and razor. It should also pay for the extra journey to collect it if it turns up.

If luggage turns up on the carousel damaged, complain at once. Otherwise it can be considered to have been delivered in acceptable condition. If damaged inside, such as smashed bottles of Scotch ruining clothes, you are not expected to notice this on collection. But claim compensation within seven days or the airline will no longer be liable.

3 RESORTS

The life and death of a resort

A resort can change its character with great speed.

Torremolinos was a poverty stricken village in 1955, with a population of a few thousand getting a hard living from the sea and the land. It had a couple of pensions and a handful of villas, and in the summer a few families motored down from Madrid to spend the school holidays on the Mediterranean.

They were not rich. They stacked their luggage on the roofs of old cars and they had no chauffeurs. If they ran to a maid, so did the rest of middle class Spain. The rich went to the Atlantic resorts, like San Sebastian, and the very rich stayed on their country estates or went to France.

That year, the first foreigners began to arrive in Torremolinos. They drove up from Gibraltar, coming on Torremolinos before they got to their real destinations, inland towns like Granada. In those days only fifteen per cent of visitors to Spain stayed on the coast. The rest explored the countryside, the cities and the museums. Or they had travelled down from Barcelona and on past Malaga.

They were mainly British and American. They wanted to spend their summers as Gerald and Sara Murphy had done in 1923, when the Murphys had persuaded the owner of the Hotel du Cap at Cap d'Antibes to stay open in the summer for the first time, and had themselves cleared the La Garoupe beach of seaweed. The Murphys and friends like the Fitzgeralds and Hemingways had dressed like French fishermen, spent their time swimming and getting brown, and had invented the billion dollar phenomenon, the beach holiday.*

* From the beginning of recorded history to 1923, society was heliotropic. People kept out of the sun, and the suntan was

The people coming into Torremolinos did not want to walk in the Swiss Alps or look at châteaux on the Loire or view Dutch tulip fields, which is what most tourists did in 1955. They found the French Riviera crowded. Some of them decided to found their own little Cap d'Antibes in Torremolinos.

They were rich and the first hotels reflected the luxurious peasant style: 'It looks back to Nature,' says architect Pedro Imbert. 'But it's really back to the cheque book.' It was expensive by Spanish standards, but Spain was cheap. By 1957, luxury villas were being built. The Madrid families who owned beachfront property had seen values climb twenty fold in two years.

By the early 1960s, Torremolinos was highly fashionable. Playboy described it as: 'Home to movie stars and smugglers, heiresses and the disinherited, the eccentrics and the ephemera of five continents.' James Michener wrote of it in the bestseller, *The Drifters*. One of the original villas, worth £1,000 in 1955, was sold as a site for a hotel for £146,000 in 1963.

But Torremolinos no longer resembled an upper-class fishing village. By the mid-Sixties there was no pretending

---

the stigma of labourers. Those with pretensions were pale. Victorians unfortunate enough to have been exposed were advised to use Dr Locock's Cosmetic, a 'delightfully fragrant preparation for removing all freckles, Sunburn and Tan'. The reversal is remarkable. The lotion industry that now promotes suntans turns over an estimate $2 billion a year. The artificial tan business is flourishing, from bottles and ultraviolet machines.

This is odd for, besides turning old social taboos upside down, sunbathing is bad for the skin. Clinically, tanning is the production of melanin by the pigment cells in the skin following over-exposure to the sun's ultraviolet rays. Ultraviolet leads to ageing, peeling and occasionally to an easily treated form of skin cancer. Peeling is a first degree burn and the mechanism is no different to a thermal burn from a match or hotplate.

that it was not simply a resort. A nice resort, classier than the Costa Brava, but awash with people from the more expensive package tours who rode the shuttle buses in from Malaga airport.

The rich, and the artistic types and layabouts who lived off them, shuddered and moved on. Some went as far as Morocco and Bali. Others moved to the nearby enclaves of Marbella, or to a brand-new purpose-built fishing village, with marina and choice of golf courses, at Andalucia del Neuva.

Torremolinos continued to go down-market. The beach-front sprouted fish and chip shops, Dutch, British and German bars, pinball joints and fast-food takeaways. The nightclub where the rich had drifted on the favourite drink of champagne and cognac, echoes now to bingo callers, disco music and a ten minute Authentic Flamenco spot.

'We started off with expensive hotels,' says Torremolinos hotelier Paul Benvenuto. 'Four and five star, because they had the best return and Torremolinos attracted people with money. Then the place started going honky-tonk, so we built one- and two-star hotels, and they went like a bomb. But now it's reversed. We've overbuilt, and the five-star hotel is selling at two-star prices. That keeps it full, but a two-star man would have to give his rooms away to compete.'

Benvenuto says the resort has changed almost beyond recognition. 'It used to be very smart, very chic. Now its just sangria, flamenco, birds, sun, the Costa Cheapo.'

Torremolinos has been described as being more of an enterprise than a town. It turns over a million and a half tourists a year. Their main intention is to get brown.

'I get down to the beach at 7.15 a.m.,' says an English girl. 'I lie on my back until it gets nice and warm at eight. Then I do an hour on my front and an hour on my back until one. I have half an hour off for lunch. Then its really hot, so I change from front to back every half hour until four. After four I change every hour and I pack it in at six.

'No, I can't swim. Anyway, the water is very smelly. I don't read. I mean, sunbathing is what its all about, isn't it? There isn't time to do anything else. Of course, its agony for the first few days, but anything worth doing needs effort. I really work at it and the lotions stop me burning too much.'

The assistant manager of the Penina Golf Hotel in the Portuguese Algarve says: 'In general the standard of people is dropping. It's a pattern. First come the people with money. Then the masses follow.'

The once smart Algarve is now full of hitch-hikers. The Secretary of State for Tourism, Luis Nandim de Carvalho, attacks them: 'They are the tourist trash of Europe, an uncontrolled invasion of parasites. They camp on the beaches and spend nothing.' That is the final horror of a declining resort: an invasion of visitors without money. The Portuguese are considering the introduction of a law that would ban any tourist who cannot produce 500 escudos (around £4) a day for each day he intends to stay. Nudists, banned by traditionally strict Portuguese morals, are to be encouraged to perk up the flow of escudos once assured by well-heeled British, American and German golfers.

The decline in the status of Ibiza has been matched by a rise in prostitution, theft, pornography sales, price-rigging and villa rackets. English stallholder Clem Hill says: 'the local Mafia here have twice threatened to chuck me in the harbour with weights on my legs if I don't match the prices in the stalls they control.'

Argentine-Italians control prostitutes in the old hotels near the port of Palma. Atracos, robberies with violence, and robos, without, have increased more than 150 per cent since the death of Franco. Bag snatches in Torremolinos average forty a day, and a thousand robberies were recorded in Marbella in the first six months of 1980. Every June, the Ibicenos burn pagan effigies of the 'tourist evil' they feel is entering the community.

Greece is going through a similar process. The early

beneficiaries in a resort boom are local land owners and property dealers. As the boom picks up, construction bosses and builders' merchants stand to make their fortunes. Hoteliers do well whilst the resort retains its original, expensive image and attracts the rich.

But the success itself changes the nature of the resort and of the people who visit it. It becomes overcrowded. Pricey restaurants that flourished with the 'pioneer' tourists move down the coast or over to another island where the boom is still beginning. Hoteliers see their profits shaved as competition increases and the cost-conscious package tourists arrive.

In the final, popular stage, the original groups do not fare well. Land prices are inflated to the point where sales slow down. There is over-capacity in both the building and hotel side. The haste and inexperience of the early days come home to roost, with a polluted beach and sea, sweaty traffic jams, inadequate or non-existent health clinics, garbage disposal, and housing, soaring prices, rapidly decaying buildings.

The supermarket and disco owners, part of the secondary boom, are now hit along with the car hire agents and water ski men and pedalo operators. The new tourists do not spend. 'Most of our customers come in, buy some bread and butter and a Coca-Cola and go out,' says a supermarket owner in Quarteira, Portugal. 'If this goes on, we'll have to sell out or go bankrupt.'

The only ones still to make money are the chemists, selling potions to the tourists. 'I should have been a chemist,' says Portuguese hotelier Joao Figureido. 'Two things happen to every tourist. They burn themselves and they get the runs. The mark-up on some sun lotions is better than on a bottle of champagne, and we don't sell much champagne here now.'

Columnist Nigel Dempster keeps track of resorts that are still chic, at least for part of the year. During January, Barbados is in, though Dempster's guest list includes some very unhousehold names. (Chubby Benson? Bill Tyrwhitt-Drake?) By February, the clientele has become more recognizable and has gone skiing.

Those who intend to climb the slopes go to Verbier, former racing drivers like James Hunt and Jody Sheckter, and the younger financiers like John Bentley. Those more concerned to be seen make for Gstaad. They include Gunther Sachs, Roman Polanski, Adnan Khashoggi and a leavening of Americans, Edward Kennedy, J. K. Galbraith. These resorts are not cheap: a gin and tonic in Gstaad can cost £9.50. But St Moritz still attracts the big industrial and shipping money, Gianni Agnelli, Christina Onassis, Stavros Niarchos, and deposed royals like Constantine of Greece.

By March, the fashionable have followed Princess Margaret to the Caribbean island of Mustique. The chic summer resorts in July and August include Marbella in Spain, St Tropez, Ibiza and Southampton, Long Island. Marbella is strong on actors, Stewart Granger, Sean Connery, writers like Harold Robbins, and bent financiers. St Tropez attracts rock musicians, Mick Jagger, Bryan Southcombe, and would-be degenerates, and has Brigitte Bardot as a long-term resident. Ibiza sees King Juan Carlos of Spain being protected from one of the higher crime rates in Europe, and Southampton, Long Island sees a bit of everything, from Charlotte Ford, she of the Motor Company, to the Bee Gees.

Kenya comes into its own in October, a blend of aristocrats, Arab financiers and TV stars. And anyone with pretensions to maintain ends off the year that month in Paris for the Arc de Triomphe weekend.

In truth, even some of these ultra-chic resorts have tottered far enough for them to be, for the outsider at least, indistinguishable from upmarket package resorts. Indeed Marbella, a development of rancho villas between an ersatz, custom-built Andalucian fishing village and a crowded town with a candy floss centre, no longer looks particularly upmarket. It had *élan* when Prince Alfonso

Hohenlohe formed a club there, and the first big villas went up on an empty beach that had cost him a few pence a square metre. But the intervening twenty years, the land profits that reach fifty-fold, the coast highway, the building and the constant halving and quartering of land plots, have left the place shell-shocked.

Already, some of the new resorts of the 1960s have faded out. Dempster mentions Sardinia in August, though he lists just two fashionable people who go there: the Aga Khan, who has little choice since he has developed it, and the ubiquitous Chubby Benson. The much-vaunted Costa Smeralda, designed a few years back as the last ditch of the very rich, the place where they would hold out against the package hordes, is now best known for its kidnappings. Corfu, one of the smartest destinations on the Mediterranean ten years back, now outpulls Benidorm for package tourists.

The resorts of the future may not grow and decay in the same haphazard manner. St Tropez was a small fishing village in the 1950s when Roger Vadim shot a film there because the beach and the village were isolated and empty. It grew, and grew, and is now choking itself. The modern resort is planned and built at one time and to one purpose.

Custom-built resorts

The Club Méditerranée shows the extraordinary growth in the custom-built resort business. It was started by a Belgian water polo player, Gerard Blitz, in 1950. He bought surplus US Army tents and cooking equipment, rented a train carriage and a field near Palma that had no facilities beyond water, and recruited his clients from his swimming friends and through a small ad in a French sports paper.

There was no question of elaborate service or food in the tented village. The guests fended much for themselves. They were young, and relatively poor, and the place had the air of a slightly upmarket youth hostel. The locals objected to the girls wearing two piece swimming costumes, which they reckoned indecent. It was several years before the Club was allowed back to Spain.

It was not a financial success. Within four years, the Club had a new managing director, Gilbert Triganon, who had supplied it with tents and camping gear when the war surplus ran out.

But the Club had tapped a vast new market. It had broken the monopoly of the rich on holidays in the sun, and the new clients loved the Mediterranean well enough for many to be recorded in Club annals as bursting into tears when they boarded their Third Class carriage to go home.

By 1981, the Club had 16,000 employees servicing 772,100 guests in twenty-four countries on five continents. It turned over £250 million in 1980 and the former tent-maker, Gilbert Trigano, reported profits of £11 million. Club resorts were important enough to local economies for the British government to underwrite the building of a jet runway in the Turks and Caicos to bring Club tourists into that area of the Caribbean. Few people cried as they left. Sunshine holidays were part of the Western way of life, and there would always be a next year.

The Club bases its success on its belief that there exists a 'multinational lifestyle', in which holidays play an important part. Trigano dreams that there will soon be a translation computer, a sort of Esperanto by machine, that will erase the only real national difference between his clients, language. He seeks to make his resorts as classless and similar as possible.

From the start, the Club has not had servants but a staff of equals known as GOs, or *gentils organisateurs*. These 'kind organizers' are, like superior Butlins Redcoats, reckoned to be of similar standing to the clients, who are known as GMs, or *gentils membres*.

This is a neat device. It gives the 750,000 members a sense of belonging, increasing repeat business and bringing in a useful £2.25 million a year in membership fees. 'Membership,' the Club says, 'symbolizes the togetherness people have with each other, the ethos of the Club.' It also helps to put GMs and GOs on the same level, 'not as clients and servants, but as friends'. Many of the staff began as guests.

This cohesion is helped by pushing the staff round the network of eighty-three 'villages'. There is a compulsory change in posting, often to another continent, every May and November. That leaves little time for local peculiarities to get established. To encourage cohesion amongst guests, money is banned in the resorts and is replaced by plastic beads.

'Social standing cannot be based on money, because there isn't any,' says the Club's Patricia Mortaigne. 'There are different standards to judge people. Someone is the best at waterskiing, the best looking, the best tennis player. People relax more with beads instead of money.'

All this togetherness leads to the 'multinational lifestyle' much envied by other resorts. 'Basically, everyone is the same,' says Patricia Mortaigne. 'It doesn't matter if its a Japanese executive, a Belgian civil servant, an American teacher, the lifestyle is similar. They play tennis, golf, bridge. The differences are superficial, languages or clothes.'

The resorts are called villages because: 'The village is the human scale *par excellence*. Those responsible for it can get to know everybody in a week. It may actually be a hotel block, but there is always a village atmosphere. Man wants to live together.'

Apparently, he does. Having progressed from tents to straw huts, the Club opened its first permanent hotel-village in Agadir in 1965. Edmond de Rothschild became a major shareholder after most bankers had turned down Trigano's requests for development finance. They have doubtless regretted it since, for the Club has expanded from its largely French base to include the American, Japanese and Australian markets.

It takes two years to build each village, but the spread is wide. In 1980, new villages were opened in Egypt, Brazil,

New Caledonia, France, Malaysia and Haiti. The following year, there were new developments in Colorado, Santo Domingo, Mexico, Sicily and Egypt. The Club has its own architects and construction company. In many cases, governments submit proposals to the Club inviting it to build villages in their countries.

Sport is an important promotion point for the Club: it has 1,228 sailing boats and 500 instructors, 130 tennis instructors who gave 1,700,000 hours of lessons in 1980, 90 diving instructors, 110 water skiing instructors, 650 skiing instructors, and 400 horses. The Club thrives as a resort chain because it is homogenous. It may be upmarket and multinational, and have more sport and less passive entertainment, but it is based firmly on Butlin and the original holiday camps.

Where the first villages cost $50,000, new ones are between $9 and $12 million. But this scale of investment is modest compared with the $750 million Walt Disney has spent to create its fantasy world in Florida. Walt Disney World near Orlando has 27,400 acres, employs 15,000, can park 12,000 cars and had 22 million visitors in its first two years of opening.

Theme parks and fantasy worlds, complete resorts built to cater for or pander to the imagination, have become people-pullers on a massive scale. Since it started in 1971, more than 125 million have visited Disney World. That includes at least one member of forty-four per cent of all American householders with earnings of $20,000 a year, the kind of statistic that makes marketing men drool.

Disney is now building an Epcot Centre on the site. This stands for Experimental Prototype Community of Tomorrow. It will cost $800 million. Some of this is going on a 5.5 million gallon saltwater tank, the largest built, for a Living Seas exhibit. 'Imagineers', artists, architects, engineers, planners and designers, are making 'audio-animatronics' figures, walking, talking replicas of characters such as Benjamin Franklin and Mark Twain. The waters in a new lake are monitored for level, flow rate and chemistry by a satellite 23,000 miles above the equator.

With Disney World attracting fourteen million visitors in 1980, making it 'the number one resort vacation destination on the globe', and the company turning over $433 million, fantasy resorts will expand. This is despite the fact that the huge investment required makes them a gamble.

Gambling resorts

A different gamble, and a very different resort, exists in the casino cities. Gambling is an integral part of the tourist industry. Two resorts, Las Vegas and Monte Carlo, owe their existence to the gambler-tourist. A third, Atlantic City, saved itself from extinction by legalizing gambling. Until they were swamped by their own greed, London casino operators were making more than £200 million a year from tourists.

The 300 gambling houses in Las Vegas win $2 billion a year. The city now has more slot machines – 30,000 – than residents. Founded in 1885, the US Government's intention being to 'build a fort there to protect immigrants and teach them how to raise corn, wheat and potatoes', it was not an agricultural success, and has never been much good at protecting visitors, but has boomed since gambling was legalized by the State of Nevada in 1931.

The gang leader Bugsy Siegel opened the Flamingo Club on the three-mile strip between Vegas and its airport in 1946. He filled the sand with flamingoes, lawns, cork trees and artificial ponds.

Siegel was murdered a year later, and his successor Gus Greenbaum soon followed, but development accelerated. There were twelve luxury hotels along the strip by 1956, including the Desert Inn, the Sahara and the Sands. They offered free flights, free transport by Rolls Royce, cheap food and showbusiness stars to attract gamblers.

The strip itself is now a six-lane highway lined by hotels, casinos, restaurants, nightclubs and bars. All is designed to encourage and excite gamblers, with poolside craps tables and terrace roulette so that the sunbathers can lose money.

Play stops for thirty seconds a year, on the first stroke

of midnight on New Year's Eve. It resumes promptly at a half minute past midnight. Vegas lures its patrons with motor racing, world championship boxing, and stars like Sinatra and Tom Jones.

A casino boss says: 'We have some of the finest entertainment in the world here. Our tourists like to lose their money in style.' And lose they certainly do. Honours in the hotly contested convention business between Las Vegas and Miami were even in 1978, with some 345,000 conventioneers each. The Las Vegas visitors spent $92 million. Only $46 million was paid out in Miami Beach. The difference is accounted for by gambling losses.

Monte Carlo was created by François Blanc, a French speculator who specialized in starting casinos in near-bankrupt principalities. His first, in Homburg, was closed in a fit of Teutonic morality in 1872. Dostoyevsky was on hand to record the croupier's final, sad call as midnight struck on 31 December: 'Messieurs, á la dernière.'

Blanc had already picked up the apparently useless concession for the Principality of Monaco. The Grimaldis, forbears of Prince Rainier, had recently lost most of their territory in a Franco-Austrian peace treaty. They retained a rock, an oblong peninsula, a lesser promontory forming the second side of a natural harbour, a narrow strip of land connecting the two, and a great many debts which they had little prospect of paying.

A casino already existed, but Monaco was a squalid place that attracted few visitors. So Blanc built a new casino, with the Hotel de Paris next to it, and put roads, gardens, a harbour and a new town round them. The town was christened Monte Carlo in 1866. The casino did so well that the Grimaldis were able to abolish direct taxation within three years. Blanc left eighty-eight million francs, over $100 million in modern terms, when he died in 1877. This should have served as a warning to generations of future tourists, but his family emphasized that François was a philanthropist at heart. He was the first casino boss to pay *viatique*, or journey money, to any gambler who had lost his rail fare home. He also installed a psychiatric clinic in the casino for those whose nerve had broken with their fortunes.

Monte Carlo barely survived the war. It was described in 1949, at the time Las Vegas was getting going: 'On the point of death. It is a slowly expiring country given over to retired generals, drab gamblers and stray cats.'

It was saved by Aristotle Onassis. He won control of the casino company, and the high rollers returned. After friction developed between Onassis and Prince Rainier, the Greek was bought out for 39,912,000 francs. Though Onassis said, with his customary magnanimity, 'I was gypped', this represented a profit of 35 million on his original investment.

The moral was ignored by gamblers. So is that of Atlantic City. It had been a booming resort town in the 1920s, but then the tourists moved down to Florida, Mexico and the Caribbean. The wind moaned along the rotting broadwalk, the sea ran into empty sand, and it had the air of Skegness in winter.

In 1978, gambling was permitted and the first casino opened. By 1981, houses worth $15,000 'B.C.' (before casinos) were selling for $150,000. A garbage dump valued at $36,000 in 1977 sold for $20 million in 1980. The beaches were still empty, since the new tourists were not interested in swimming. But the town had become, in the proud words of a leading citizen, a 'people factory'.

At the Resorts Casino, three thousand tourists at a time can play craps, blackjack and fruit machines, watched over by the 'spy in the sky', a surveillance room with 108 TV monitor screens. The company is planning a 1,000-room hotel to house its gamblers. A new airport and twenty-six new 500 bed-hotels will be built by 1990. The three original casinos were winning $500 million a year by 1980.

London was no slouch when it came to profits, either. A million pounds was spent restoring the Ritz ballroom for the new Ritz casino in 1978, with stucco, goldleaf and plasterwork in Edwardian baroque. The management emphasized its expectations at the gala opening, providing 300 lobsters, 200 crabs and 25 pounds of Beluga caviar. Baron Henri de Montesquieu, a director of the House of Moet, removed the corks from champagne bottles with a sabre and poured the fizz over a pyramid of 500 glasses.

The 'drop'

The temptations were too much for some. As the volume of the 'drop', the money converted into chips, approached £1 billion a year, several London casinos lost their licences. The Coral casinos made a profit of £11.5 million in 1979. Both they, and another large operator, Ladbroke, were breaking regulations in an attempt to extract yet more cash from visitors.

No more than fifty really high rollers turn up in a gambling centre in a year. They are chiefly Arab, Indian and Japanese and can lose £100,000 and more on a 'trip' of three hours play. Three Saudis lost £350,000 in an hour's play: 'Sheikh the dice', said the wags.

To get them, London casinos started paying commission to those who introduced them, based on the amount of their losses. The registration numbers of cars parked outside rival casinos were noted, and their owners traced through the illegal use of a police computer. The gamblers were then tempted to transfer loyalty with lavish gifts and free dinners.

Playboy acquired licences as Ladbroke and Coral lost them. Its London boss, Victor Lownes, reported that there was no shortage of high rollers to underpin the 'grind action' of small stakers. 'There are two new pigeons coming up the stairs for every one fluttering down,' he reported. But in 1981 Playboy itself lost the licence for the Playboy Club, which had made profits of £11 million a year, for infringing the gaming regulations.

It is difficult to understand why casinos should have risked their licences so regularly, since the profits from them have been as high as in that original 'licence to print money', commercial television.

A casino is only vulnerable to fraud and cheating by its own employees. Players represent no long-term danger, unless they are in league with employees. Honest staff are crucial, and the Monte Carlo casino school spends eight months training them. They need, says casino expert Henri Galliano, to 'concentrate on developing computer brain speed, psychology, elegance in card handling and a poker face'.

They are taught to be nice about taking the punter's money. Instructions to dealers and croupiers in a London casino run: 'Deliberately adopt a friendly attitude. Convey a spirit of good will and *mean it*. Don't forget, a sincere smile is a valuable asset. Maintain the same courtesy and friendliness in winning and losing. You are expected to exercise all your courtesy and tact in putting patrons at ease.'

They normally work in relays, an hour on, twenty minutes off, to keep them sharp. They are well paid. Shift managers make around £16,000 a year. The men in charge of each game, the 'pit bosses', earn £12,000, the shift captains £10,000 and the top card dealers £9,000.

Monte Carlo expects its croupiers to be 'thoroughly trustworthy, well behaved, obliging and courteous, tidy, clean in their habits, and simply but well dressed'.

In case they are not, casinos either sew up their pockets or give them clothes without any. Monte Carlo croupiers cannot accept social invitations or gifts from, and must have no contact with, patrons outside the casino. They must not talk to strangers in the street. Each table has a *chef de partie* who checks both patrons and croupiers.

Mongrels of delinquency

In Monte Carlo the Casino's police force is independent from that of the Principality. Every day, the names of all visitors and job applicants to the Casino are checked against a list of wanted and convicted men. Expert physiognomists are employed to watch croupiers and players.

They are trained to spot anyone on the Casino's lengthy blacklist of welshers, suspected cheats and sharps.

The chief physiognomist at Monte Carlo was a Monsieur le Broq, who claimed to know at least 60,000 people by their characteristics. He could give names to half of them. The normal police method is to study the eyes and nose and, with women, the hair. Le Broq disagreed. He said that the most recognizable and identifiable trait of all was gait, the way a person held himself and moved.

The finance officers on the first floor are at the end of a corridor so narrow that only one person at a time can approach. Players must leave hats and briefcases in the cloakroom. There is an independent stand-by electricity system, so that there is no chance of a black-out if the lights go out in the rest of the Principality. Croupiers need only press a button for the contents of their cash boxes to drop through pneumatic tubes into a basement vault.

Nevada has a larger police force than any other State of comparable size, largely to check on what happens in the two square miles of Las Vegas. A special inspectorate visits every casino and gambling club at irregular intervals to look for cheating.

Inspectors on raised chairs watch the croupiers, and managers watch the inspectors.

Such precautions do not always succeed.

The Ruhl Casino in Nice lost £800,000 in the first six months of 1978. There was collusion between twenty croupiers and eight 'barons', gamblers secretly in league with the croupiers. The croupiers, besides hiding tokens in their socks to be cashed in later, would simply push a 'baron's' chip on to a winning square at roulette. Winnings were shared out after closing time at an all-night café.

Croupiers also allow late calls from barons, enabling them to back a number after it has landed. One London club had £12,000 and £30,000 taken from it in two successive nights like this.

Ruhl croupiers also used sticky pads on their sleeves to

take chips from the Casino's winnings, later transferring them to accomplices who brushed past them at the table. The Court President who sentenced them, described them with magnificence: 'Mongrels of delinquency, destroyers of the beautiful orchestration between gambling and chance.'

Lavatories figure in frauds at American roulette. Each player has differently coloured chips. A player with green chips excuses himself from the table, and meets a player with yellow chips in the men's room. They exchange a number of chips.

As a winning number comes up, the first player puts a stack of green chips on it, covering a single yellow chip. The croupier tells him the bet is too late. So he takes away his green chips leaving the yellow. The second player is too far away to have placed it himself, so the croupier has to pay out on the yellow chip.

Croupiers will also use stacked cards for the benefit of a baron amongst the players. The cards are arranged to give the baron winning hands. The British Gaming Board confirms that 'a full shoe of stacked cards has been switched into a game of blackjack'. Most casinos use Spanish-made patterned Fournier packs, known as super 818s, not available on the open market. They are locked up before use, and shredded after. But super 818 reject packs were sold by Harrods, with painful results for Casinos.

Pretty bra-less girls, arguments, any diversion allows crooked croupiers to hand out extra cash for a baron's winning chip, or to allow it to be 'top hatted', an extra chip placed on top to increase the winnings. A £100 chip 'top-hatted' like this wins £3,500 extra.

Detectives using marked £20 notes played roulette at the Victoria Sporting Club in London. The Club was raided, and police found two of the notes in the wallet of a senior employer. The total cash in his wallet was £4,000, part of a skimming fraud estimated by police at £1,800,000 a year. On a secondary 'skimming level', overtime bonuses of £50,000 a year were said to have been paid illegally to cashiers.

How to cheat

The sad fact is that cheats have always preyed on tourists. A pair of loaded dice were found under the lava of the Roman resort of Pompeii. A typical medieval diceman, Elmer de Multon, was sentenced in twelfth-century London for 'enticing strangers to a tavern in chepeside and there deceiving them by using false dice'. Elmer's descendants, of whom there are many, are more likely to entice tourists to a casino in Mayfair than a pub in Cheapside but otherwise the modus operandi has changed little. The American river boat gamblers have moved on to the ski and sun resorts and casino cities.

The tourist is vulnerable when he gambles. Away from home, disorientated, relaxed or over-tense, he is a soft target for the sharps, dicemen, street-men, top-stockers, French shufflers and hold-out artists who populate the resorts.

The best defence is to examine their methods.

Dicemen are the most common of the breed. They operate wherever tourists congregate, from the Costa Brava, which suffered an epidemic of them in 1979, to Florida and the sacred halls of Monte Carlo. The casino has special green dice made in Reno which should be impossible to counterfeit.

An American named Jason Lee had a long run of luck at craps. He staked only modest amounts, but two other Americans backing him picked up more than three million francs in two hours. A suspicious casino Inspector checked the dice. Lee, and his associates Philip Aggie and the aptly named Arif Shaker, were arrested as they were boarding a plane for Morocco at Nice airport.

In the oldest trick in the game, the dice were loaded. They were set to make a three and four on every throw, and 200 pairs of other loaded dice were found in their luggage.

A small hole is drilled and filled with mercury, so that the weighted side falls to the bottom when the dice is thrown. This can be detected. The dice is held at diagonally opposite corners. If it then rotates on its axis, it is loaded.

'Unloaded' dice have a drilled out cavity to lessen the weight on one side. They drop on the opposite side to the cavity. Others have rounded edges on some sides, coming to rest on the flat sides. Dice that are not exactly square land on the longer sides. A pig's bristle stuck into a corner performs the same service.

Production runs of loaded dice are long enough for them to cost little more than the honest item from the same manufacturer. They are, of course, sold as 'practical jokes'. The largest recorded loss due to loaded dice in 1980 was £35,000 in Las Vegas. A fine joke.

Dicemen also use 'dispatchers'. These are dice that do not have the correct number of pips. Since it is impossible to see more than three sides of a cube at a time, only three numbers need be used. Thus the side opposite a six, which should have a one, can be another six. A diceman convicted after cheating a Plymouth casino in 1979 had dice with two 6s, two 5s and two 4s, so that he could not throw less than eight.

Dispatchers have to be introduced into the game, a process known as 'ringing in'. It is done at the moment the cheat picks up the dice after the dupe has thrown. The false dice are concealed in the thumb joint. The fair dice are picked up in the fingers, but the false ones are dropped into the box. The fingers holding the fair dice are then turned inwards and the dice taken into the thumb joint where the false dice were.

The process is reversed at the end of the play, so that the dupe gets the fair dice.

There are special ways of throwing dice. In the 'Greek-shot', one die is thrown to land on top of another which has not been spun and remains as it came out of the palm. The 'slide throw' involves a die being held by the little finger so that it slides rather than rolls.

'Slurring' involves using a cup with a false interior which holds the dice so that they come out as they were put in. When squeezed, a V-shape extends from the side and holds the dice securely. The rattle comes from another cup held in the left hand or, in the case of a Lebanese who had extracted large sums from tourists in Marbella, from a tape recorder in his jacket. American-made slurring cups cost $50.

Backgammon is the major growth industry for dicemen. The number playing in the US has increased from under a million to thirty million over the past decade. A professional backgammon circus tours from Las Vegas to Palm Springs, the Costa Smeralda in Sardinia, Marbella and Gstaad.

There is plenty of money to be made. The professional Philip Martyn won £2,000 on the short jet flight from Acapulco to Mexico City from a man who chanced to be sitting next to him. At major tournaments, where players meet by appointment, wins exceed £100,000. The international backgammon championships at Paradise Island in the Bahamas are worth $250,000. Whilst the top professionals like Martyn are totally honest, there are plenty who reckon to pay for their holidays by cheating at dice.

Cardmen, or 'sharps', make their money at poker, trente-et-quarante, baccarat, chemin-de-fer, and bridge and whist if the stakes are high enough. They are found particularly in Italy, Florida and Spain, and are present in force in more exotic destinations, including. Hong Kong, Macao, the Philippines and Brazil.

'Streetmen' are the lowest form of sharp. The most common ploy is the three card trick. Three cards are laid on the pavement. One is a Queen. A crowd gathers. A man starts betting and wins steadily. Others in the crowd join in. They lose steadily.

The first to bet is an accomplice, a 'starter' or 'bear leader' whose job is to incite the crowd to bet. The crowd does not win because the streetman palms the Queen. Aimed at strangers and tourists, it is most often seen in places like London's Oxford Street, Benidorm's Calle Mayor and near airports and railway stations.

'I use a City gent as my starter,' says an Oxford Streetman. 'Foreigners go for that. He has an umbrella, stiff collar, watch chain, the lot.

'I let him win £20 or £25. Then I say to the crowd — "Come on, let's see if you're as good." My starter says: "It's easy, friends, try it." Then he clears off to keep an eye open for the law.

'The Iranians used to be a great touch, but not any more. The Arabs are good, and so are the Swedes. The Yanks are hopeless, far too street-wise. I reckon to make around £70 a day at the top of the season in July and August. My starter gets £20 of that. My best week was over £500, in 1978 when the tourists weren't so suspicious.'

Sharps in card games often work in teams, although feigning not to know each other. Those who specialize in signalling an opponent's hand to their colleagues are known as 'itemers'. They were notorious in riverboat days, when the itemer James Ashby signalled his accomplices by playing tunes on a violin, and they still exist. The modern itemer relies on the flutter of an eyelid, a yawn, a scratch or finger drumming. The best defence is to conceal one's hand.

Marked cards are produced commercially in some countries, notably the US and Taiwan. Tartan backs are often used, since the lines of tartan show the value of the card. The suit is shown by the band of lines ending in the top left hand corner, a wide space between the first two lines meaning diamond, between the second two lines hearts, and so forth.

Genuine cards can be altered with 'shading'. A 'shading box', a tiny dye pad looking like a dinner jacket button, is used to mark the cards during play. The box is lightly fingered and the dye transferred to the card.

Ultraviolet dye was used to defraud the Charlie Chester casino in London of £11,000. A man in violet-tinted glasses sitting next to the croupier could tell whether the next card at blackjack was high or low. He 'itemised' his colleague by moving his chips. Cards marked with ultra-violet that shows up with special contact lenses have been recorded in Britain, Yugoslavia, Italy, West Germany and the US.

A simpler way to find out an opponent's hand is to look at it. Sharps use reflectors, known in the trade as 'shiners'. Originally, a dealer would drop a little wine in front of him and read the cards in the reflection as he dealt.

Baize table tops put paid to that. In came snuff boxes with convex reflectors in the top and pipes with 'shiners' in the bowl. Neither snuff nor pipes are much in vogue in Vegas or Monte Carlo now. Sharps use special shiners that are designed to be dropped inconspicuously in a pile of chips.

Other equipment is used for 'holdouts', where the sharp conceals one or more cards for use later. A 'ring holdout' is a watch spring with a clip that fits onto a ring. It holds a card in the palm of the hand. The 'deck topper' is a pair of jaws inside a shirt sleeve that holds cards. When the release is pressed, it drops the cards onto the top of the deck.*

It is said that the best sharps use itemers, the second best marked cards, and the third best machines and shiners. The worst are the 'dealers'. They work with the pack to win and stand the highest risk of being caught.

---

* The more informal clothes used for modern gambling killed off the elegant old 'Coat and Vest Machines'. Worn with evening dress, they had a breastplate that concealed a card down the shirt front and that released it upwards into the hand when a cord fastened to a loop on the back of the sharp's shoe was pulled.

In the not unlikely event of detection, the 'breastplate' had the advantage of being if not bullet proof, at least bullet resistant. Swindling equipment is still known in the US, the principal place of manufacture, by the charming name 'Advantage Goods'.

A 'bottom dealer' puts a good hand on the bottom of the pack. He deals with his fingers below the pack and thumb on top. He deals top cards to his opponents with his thumb, and bottom cards to himself with his fingers. This can be detected because there is a slight click as a card is drawn from the bottom of the pack.

A 'second dealer' draws the second card from the top if it suits him. He observes the top and second cards by drawing them slightly over to the right, whilst leaning to his right, generally to an ash tray. Beware of right-handed smokers who keep an ashtray on their left.

Impudence is used to avoid the cut with cards that have been 'stacked' in an order favourable to the dealer. He picks up the bottom half of the pack with his right hand and puts it in his left hand. He then picks up the top half and places it on top. This usually works. If it is detected, the sharp apologises and 'low profiles' for a few hands.

The cut is also avoided by crossing hands, picking up the right half of the pack with the left hand, and the left half with the right hand. The two are put back in order, but crossing the hands confuses the other players.

This is low-class sharping, if effective.

'The victim is called the mug, the mark or the pigeon,' says a British sharp. 'You look for a precise type. A fat man or fat lady. Fat means rich. Slightly drunk. Preferably someone who thinks they are good at the game. It's difficult getting money off a complete novice. They look around too much and ask too many questions.

'You want somebody who is acting a bit out of character, living out a holiday fantasy. Then, when they start losing heavily, it won't be *them* who is in trouble. It's the fantasy figure. They get a glazed look and you know you've got them, as sure as if you had knocked them out in the ring.

'Of course, you don't cheat all the time. You get by on skill whenever you can, knowing that you have all your knowledge waiting in the wings if things do go wrong. Oddly enough, I've only been accused of cheating when I was playing dead honest. I'll clean a guy out shirt and all if I'm beating him on skill, and he'll get very upset. But I never go too far if I'm cheating. It would be too risky to clean them out.'

It is possible to doctor roulette wheels. One organization successfully altered wheels from Holland to the Middle East, winning several million pounds. It is thought to have cleared £3.5 million in Cannes alone.

The basic idea was simple; loosening the dividers between certain numbers so that the ball would settle in more easily.

A gang was sent over to fix the wheel at the Palm Beach Casino in London. It was an odd bunch: a Las Vegas gambler, a Sunbury on Thames old age pensioner, a Streatham croupier, a Viennese nightclub owner and an Austrian mechanic based in Germany.

Detectives, tipped off to the gang, watched the mechanic through a hole in the gaming room ceiling as he worked. He took the wheel off its base. He carefully took out six dividers between numbers, and the twelve screws fixing them. He refitted them with twelve screws he had specially made in his workshop in Germany. This widened the dividers. He glued them in so that a casual test would not show any give or flexibility. He filed the dividers at the top. He polished the bottom of the wheel with a paper tissue and left after an hour's work.

He should, by slightly widening the dividers, have made it likely that one number would come up repeatedly. A 'bagman' flew into Heathrow from Dusseldorf with the 'investment', 70,000 DM and $7,000. This would be used as stake money. The gang had calculated that they would win £600,000 in an afternoon.

In fact, the mechanic got his work wrong on this wheel. He had not widened the dividers enough. The gang lost all their stake money in two hours and then, still looking puzzled, were arrested. 'But we lost!' said one. 'You can't arrest losers!'

This scheme was a variation on the more normal

'Wedge'. Extra padding is put in the bottom of some slots so that the ball keeps bouncing and leaps on into other selected numbers where the sides of the slots have been slightly widened. A croupier at Le Cercle Club in Park Lane, London operated the 'Wedge' telling clients to back the middle numbers of the Number Two table in return for a forty-five per cent share of the proceeds.

Sometimes, it is the house that does the cheating. Roulette balls have been coated with metallic paint and electro-magnets under the table control where the ball will fall. Police in Britain uncovered a £1,800,000 a year fraud of skimming off profits.

There are commonly used methods of short changing winners and ensuring that big winners do not go home with their money.

For the first, a casino will speed up the spin of the wheel. A winner is passed fewer chips than he is entitled to. Instantly, the wheel is spun again and, in his haste to get another bet on, he does not count his winnings. A big winner is plied with drinks and the casino suggests he plays card games, with the intention of getting their money back.

The odds
The fundamental point in gambling is that the casino always wins. Should they start losing, they alter the rules or ban the player.

Thus, roulette wheels can suffer from the Jagger syndrome. This is named after an English engineer who discovered that poorly maintained wheels develop a bias towards certain numbers, which can be detected after two months of continuous observation. The odds then slide from the casino to the gambler.

Dr Richard Jarecki, a Heidelberg professor, assembled a team of table watchers on Jagger lines in the 1970s. The results were run through a computer at the London School of Economics. Dr Jarecki cleared £80,000 on three consecutive days at San Remo.

He was promptly banned from playing both there, and at other casinos in London and Las Vegas where he had registered heavy wins. This was despite the fact that Dr Jarecki had played in an entirely legal manner.

A casino can be vulnerable to 'counters', gamblers who keep track of cards in blackjack as they are played. Counting is based on how many high and low cards have been dealt. The more high cards left in the deck, the better the chance of a winning total or a blackjack. The gambler raises his bet. When there are many low cards left, he reduces it.

This can give a one to one and a half per cent advantage against the house. Thus, throughout the world, blackjack dealers shuffle the pack when they see a gambler keeping a count.

However, in New Jersey, the State laws prohibit shuffling. Blackjack schools started, which teach card counting, basic blackjack strategy and money management. Students have come from as far afield as Czechoslovakia and the Philippines. One counter, a former insurance salesman, won $80,000 from the Brighton casino in Atlantic City over five months.

'Blackjack has become a game of skill here, not a game of chance,' said the Vice-President of Resorts International casino. It was a revealing statement. What he meant, of course, was that blackjack had become a game in which the player as well as the casino had a chance. 'We believe that if we are going to build a big, expensive casino, we should have the mathematical advantage in every game.'

The month he said that, August 1980, the Atlantic City casinos had made $76,900,000 gross winnings. Nevertheless, the insurance salesman was banned from blackjack, along with 440 other counters in the city. They can play craps or slot machines only. Beards, glasses, weird haircuts and hats have failed to outwit the casinos' security men and TV cameras. The counters are currently supported by the American Civil Liberties Union in trying to get the bans declared unconstitutional.

That cuts little ice with casinos. They rig the odds in their favour, and Bernouilli's Law of Large Numbers does the rest. This states that the average will always be maintained in an infinite sequence of roulette spins, card deals and so forth. By giving itself above average odds on bets that are ruled by averages, the house will always win in the end. A gambler's Lady Luck is a short fling, not a live-in mistress.

If no chances are equal, however, some are less unequal than others. By choosing the right bet on the right game, the tourist can make his money last longer.

Casinos normally return 97.5 per cent of stake money as winnings. It seems modest, but they rely on continuous play to swell their profits. Over an evening's play, they expect to make nineteen per cent of the 'drop', the amount spent on chips.

Blackjack is the safest bet. A report of the Royal Commission on Gambling used statisticians, accountants, engineers and computer specialists to deduce the true odds in gambling. Professor E. Downton of Birmingham University produced a system that reduces the house edge in blackjack to 0.6 per cent.

This requires skill and a good memory, and blackjack pays badly. Roulette offers a simpler chance of bigger winnings. Sean Connery won $30,000 at St Vincent, Italy on three consecutive spins of the wheel by betting on seventeen. The odds against this are 46,656 to one, but the scale of the pay-off explains the popularity of roulette.

A single number is the best bet at roulette, reducing the casino's advantage to 1.35 per cent. The worst is covering the maximum of twenty-four numbers, where the edge is 2.7 per cent. Thus the apparently greater risk of going for one number is less than spreading it over several numbers.

The simplest roulette system yet devised was seen at Monte Carlo. A gambler put a spider in a match box, painted half red and half black. Before each spin, he removed the lid and bet on the colour the spider was sitting on.

Breaking the bank

There are many systems, but they all have in common the fact that they do not work. The casino industry always claims that a few lucky players could bring it to ruin. It lives off the idea that the bank can be broken. It may be beautiful, but it is a myth.

The Spaniard Tomas Garcia got closest to it. He arrived in Homburg in August 1860, with his brother and his German mistress. He won £56,000 on 24 August, £338,000 on 25 August and £220,000 on 26 August. On 27 August, he lost the lot.

On 28 August, he won £520,000 in less than an hour, losing £88,000 later in the day. He won again on 29 August, bringing his profit to £800,000.

He briefly left the casino, returning on 9 September to win £488,000. He went into a decline on 10 September, losing £914,000 in six hours. He had won it all back by 12 September. He left Homburg on 14 September with £2,010,000. He had not broken the bank, but he had wiped out its profit for the season.

Garcia could not leave well alone. He returned to Homburg in October 1861 and lost that part of his fortune that had not been spent in a year's high living. He was later caught playing with marked cards at baccarat, was imprisoned and died in poverty.

Woolf Joel won 250,000 gold francs in fourteen minutes when red came up twelve times running at trente-et-quarante at Monte Carlo. The South African millionaire gave an all-red dinner at the Savoy in London. It was held in a red room, with waiters in red serving red wine and red food, beetroot salad, rare beef and tomatoes and strawberry mousse. A few months later, Joel was shot dead by an angry employee.

The most famous winner was Charles Deville Wells, the Englishman immortalized in the song:

As I walk along in the Bois de Boulogne with an independent air,

You can hear the girls declare, he must be a millionaire,
Oh, and then they sigh and wish to die,
And they wink and turn the other eye,
It's the man who broke the bank at Monte Carlo.

Middle-aged, bald and bearded, he entered the Monte Carlo casino on 19 July 1891. By 21 July, he had won over 500,000 gold francs. He played the 'coup de trois' system, allowing the stakes to accumulate for three successive wins, and then starting again. At the start of the winter season, he broke a trente-et-quarante table at 11.30 a.m., half an hour after it had opened. He broke several roulette tables.

Alas, he never broke the bank itself. The casino, encouraging the legend that it could be broken, made a considerable fuss. Tables were closed with much ceremony and publicity but the casino itself never ran out of funds.

Wells returned in 1892 in a magnificent steam yacht, the *Palais Royal*. He broke tables six times shortly after arriving. Then he started losing as steadily as rain falls in the West of Ireland.

At the end of the year, he was arrested aboard the *Palais Royal* in Le Havre, so poor that he was trying to sell the coal in the yacht's bunkers to a local merchant. He was later sentenced to eight years at Bow Street court for obtaining money under false pretences.

Inexorably, the roulette wheel spins in favour of the bank. Deviations are the gambler's only hope. But a worthwhile deviation, where 6,000 more reds than blacks occur in a sequence of a million spins, will only happen once in 500 million spins. In the meantime, the zero grinds away in favour of the casino 27,000 times every million spins.*

* Nevertheless, it is a myth that gamblers frequently kill themselves after losses, and that special patrols clear the corpses daily from the Monte Carlo casino. The suicide rate for gamblers at Monte Carlo is 0.049 per 1,000, several times better than the average for New York or London. A gambler may lose his shirt but seldom his life.

At craps, the bank has an advantage of from 1.414 to 16.7 per cent, depending on the betting strategy of the player. His chances are considerably improved if he remembers the probabilities. The odds against throwing a 2 or 12 are 36 to 1; a 3 or 11 are 18 to 1; a 4 and 10 are 12 to 1; a 5 and 9 are 9 to 1; a 6 or 8 are 7 to 1. A 7 is 6 to 1 against.

Easier money?

Fruit machines are very big business indeed. They keep Las Vegas alive, since the 'slots' account for more than seventy-five per cent of casino profits, with 400 and more machines running twenty-four hours a day in the big casinos. Without them, much of the Vegas travel industry, the hotels, airlines, restaurants, clubs, would come to a halt. British fruit machines ring up gross annual revenues of £350 million a year, more than casinos, bingo or football pools.

Nobody has much to say for them.

The Hudson Institute in New York terms them a 'low-skill gambling device', a category they share with mouse-racing, lotteries and pinball machines. The Gaming Board describes them as a 'form of unequal chance gaming in which turnover is rapid'.

Most machines have twenty symbols in each of three reels, giving 8,000 possible combinations. The odds are never good. The recommended payback in Britain is eighty per cent of the stake, a recommendation that is seldom heeded. The payback in Las Vegas is nearer to sixty per cent.

There are occasionally big payouts. Jerry Somer and his son Paul pooled $30 and were betting the maximum $3 a time on a Las Vegas machine in 1980. On the fifth pull, they hit the jackpot on all three lines, including the five sevens in the bottom line necessary for the jackpot. The machine itself will pay out only $250 in cash. But as long as bells ring and lights flash, it keeps on registering money. It stopped at $300,000.

In July 1981, Jeff Randall, a salesman, invested $23 in a machine in Lake Tahoe and won $1 million.

The odds seem generous. The Somers were paid 100,000 to one. But the British Gaming Board estimates that the odds of winning a substantial jackpot are eight million to one against, so this is scarcely charity. And it seldom happens.

In general, a gambler can expect to do five times better at roulette than at the 'slots'. The odds are worse if the fruit machine operator or his staff are dishonest. A Royal Commission in Britain discovered three fiddles that it described as 'widely practised'. The mechanism can be altered to give a lower pay-out than the manufacturer built into it. Staff can open the machine, move the reels to the jackpot, put in a coin and collect. A percentage of coins can simply be removed. Auditors do not find any evidence of this since few machines have foolproof counters. It is thought that £250,000 was 'skimmed' from machines in Northern British clubs in 1978: the Royal Commission criticized club officials for refusing to give it information.

Players try to get their own back by cheating the machines. 'Reel timing' was a favourite device. The player memorized the sequence of symbols on each of the reels. He found the exact time each reel would spin for after the handle was pulled. By setting the reels spinning at a precise time after the coin had started the clock mechanism, he could guarantee a winning line.

This is not possible on electric machines, though these are themselves vulnerable. A man was spotted tampering with a machine at the Holiday Inn in Slough at Christmas in 1979. He ran off, leaving behind a collection of wires in a Golden Virginia tobacco tin that would, or so it was said, have guaranteed a jackpot every spin.

'We are at this man's mercy,' said a spokesman for the amusement trade. That is doubtful. It is men who are usually at the mercy of the trade, those who take that sad phenomenon, the fruit machine holiday. It is estimated that twenty million people go on holiday each year with nothing more in mind than playing fruit machines in end-less repetition until their money runs out. The majority are Japanese and American.

Europeans fall for bingo in a similar way. In Britain, £340 million was staked on bingo in 1979. At an average of £1 a card, that represents much devotion from a large audience. The game, originally encouraged in the military because it taught innumerate conscripts how to recognize the numbers on gun sights, was exported by British tourists to Spain.

The Spanish took to it with greater passion, gambling £1 billion on it in 1980 with stakes of up to £100 a card. Fraud in Britain has seen bingo callers ensuring that accomplices in the audience win, or skimming the stakes. Nothing has compared with Spain.*

Bingo was legalized in 1977. By 1978, the Government had been forced to close forty-nine of Madrid's fifty-eight gambling parlours for rigging games, fiddling the take, skimming and tax avoidance. El bingo is not the quiet, harmless flutter it seems.

Neither are lotteries. It is common for the street sales-men in Italian and Spanish resorts to sell tourists tickets for non-existent or past lotteries. The prizes may appear good, paying up to a million to one, but the odds against winning have reached 48 million to one in Spain.†

Bingo and lotteries are also popular in the other big category of resort, the floating one, the cruise liner. Morals at sea differ little from those ashore.

---

* Spanish civil servants, military personnel and all those handling State funds are barred from bingo. So are minors, drunks and lunatics. It might be felt anyone playing bingo in Spain falls into the last category.

† State lotteries are no better a bet. Louis XII of France, for example, sold 500,000 tickets on a lottery on the date of the completion of Milan Cathedral. Started in 1386, there was no longer a French monarchy by the time it was completed in 1805. A promoter's dream.

Cruises

Cruises were worth $20 billion world-wide in 1979. In that year it was the biggest winter leisure industry in North America, filling more berths than there were hotel beds in the West Indies. More than twenty-five cruise liners operate from Miami alone. On some Saturdays, the normal change-over day, ten cruise liners leave Miami with 500 to 750 passengers aboard each hour.

The other popular cruising areas are also booming: the Mediterranean, the South Pacific and Australasia, South America between Rio and Buenos Aires, the West Coast of the US and Round the World. Mini-cruises, first brought in by car ferry lines anxious to fill their ships out of season, vary from short luxury trips to all-night disco dancing sessions in the Channel. Education Cruises improve the minds, or at least the suntans, of schoolchildren and pensioners.

This is not just good news for the shipowners. It is very good news indeed for some of their employees, who have used their ingenuity to extract more from the business than their owners do. It can be bad news for the passengers, from whom this cash is subtly extracted.

Caution should start at the point of sale, the travel agent. Two factors agitate against travel agents recommending the best lines. The three best lines out of Miami, for example, are generally reckoned to be Royal Caribbean, Norwegian Caribbean and Cunard from San Juan, although the last has had its knuckles rapped on health regulations.

These are often sold out well in advance and, because they are popular, the cruise lines have no need to pay a high commission to travel agents. So they are not well liked by many agents, who get more commission and kickbacks, such as free cabins for themselves and staff, from the questionable lines. If a client enquires about a good cruise, he may well be told that it is sold out and find himself on the line that pays that agent most.

Good lines pay from seven per cent to ten per cent of the cost of the cruise to the agent. Cunard and Chandris, for example, pay ten per cent. Some lines pay a higher commission on winter cruises from 1 October to 31 March. The big P & O line gives seven per cent in summer, eight per cent on fly cruises where the passenger flies out to join the ship, and 8½ per cent in winter.

Agents thus push winter cruises. Even more, they recommend third rate trips on Eastern Mediterranean and Communist bloc ships where their commission will start at twelve per cent at peak periods and hit fifteen or sixteen per cent in the off season.

A former cruise director puts it bluntly: 'Ask a travel agent for advice, and the odds are that you will wind up on a bum boat or in a bum berth.' A passenger, he says, should always ask round for recommendations from people who have been cruising before. He should insist on seeing a full diagram of the ship with the location of engines, elevators, lavatories, bars, night clubs and other things that are noisy. Some ships stack the night club, disco, cinema and dining room over each other, so there is little trouble.

Others spread them through the ship and the noise affects many cabins into the small hours. Engine noise is not so bad as the vibration and rattling. It can be difficult to sleep in the worst cabins, on a low deck, in the centre of the ship slightly towards the stern. If the passenger cannot afford a higher deck, from the main deck and up, he should try to get an outside cabin slightly forward. But there is a great deal of motion on a high deck towards stern or bow, so a high cabin is not necessarily the ultimate.

'Outer' cabins with a porthole are invariably much more expensive than 'inner' cabins without. This was important before air conditioning when it was an advantage worth paying for to be able to let air in. Nowadays, portholes are firmly shut and are not used for air. However, shipping lines report an increasing demand for them. It is all part of the oneupmanship and snobbery that are noticeable in cruising.

'The same codswallop applies to decks,' says a travel agent who specializes in cruises. 'You get Bridge, Boat, Saloon, Promenade, Stadium, Sun Decks, even Captain's Decks. None of it is any more than a name. It only makes sense if a passenger looks at deck plans properly, but they often don't.

'Say somebody decides on the Stadium deck. It sounds nice and it's the right price. It could be the bottom one, for all he knows, with some grotty keep-fit gym that the line calls a Stadium. The passenger doesn't check it out with the ship as a whole to see where it is.

'He doesn't go through the symbols either. He sees a couple of beds and he thinks, good. He sees an area with what looks like a bath, and he thinks, marvellous. A twin-bedded room with a bath, just like a hotel. But it isn't. Those can be symbols for bunks, upper and lower, so that's four in the cabin, not two. The bath isn't a bath, its the symbol for a shower. And it's the deck nearest the bilges.

'So he complains to the cruise line. They say, why shouldn't we call it the Stadium deck? It's got the gym. And the symbols are what they say, symbols – they aren't beds, they are the artist's impression of a bunk seen from above. And it isn't a bath, it's a shower base. So there.'

Class at sea is just as complicated as class on land. The cruise business sports First, Tourist, Economy, Fourth, Luxury, Cruise and Basic Classes, and not necessarily in that order. What is First on some lines would rate steerage on others: the Transatlantic class on Cunard's QE2 is reckoned superior to First on many lines. The South Atlantic routes have their own Cabin Class, which rates somewhere between First and Tourist elsewhere.

The most honest description is Deck Class in the Far East. It means just what it says: enough space for a bedroll six feet by three on deck and, sailing from Hong Kong at least, a lavatory for every forty passengers.

That's entertainment

Everyone wants a 'fun ship', and entertainment is one of the great divides between ships. The best lines will have ten people working full-time on entertainment – two sports directors, a cruise director and two assistants, a hostess, a dance team of two, and two entertainers. Poor lines only have three or four and tend to monotony.

Menus reveal much about standards, which is why experienced cruise passengers ask to see a typical lunch menu in advance. Many travel agents fob people off with a very untypical Gala Dinner menu, a once-in-a-cruise affair dolled up with gold tassels. 'The crappier the lunch menu, the sloppier the line will be,' says the former cruise director. 'If it's mimeographed, little choice, cold buffet round the swimming pool, there will be problems. If it's properly printed and there is hot food, that augurs well.'

The professional entertainment is another indication. Royal Caribbean will fly in a package of four entertainers and change them every four days, a standard only matched by Cunard and its world cruises.

Others only sign up acts where a couple of entertainers do the whole show night in, night out. 'Say it's a magician and a comic,' says the former cruise director. 'For his first act, the magician does paper magic, tearing telephone directories apart. Mental telepathy is good for about twelve minutes. Then he does a dove act. Finally he has the audience participation bit, losing a $1 bill and finding it down someone's blouse.

'The comic will do three or four spots. There will always be one on the cruise itself and it will always have the standard cruise jokes. I tell you, you hear the same jokes so often on the bad lines you want to jump over the side.'

Don't be a schmuck

Having checked out the line for general reputation, menus, entertainment and a good quiet cabin, canny passengers sound out the dining room. On a Transatlantic trip or a smart cruise, they send the *maître d'* a note before they sail, containing money and details of the table they want to sit at. If there are two sittings, they go for the second – only 'schmucks and shoe factory owners', as the cruise industry calls dullards, attend the first. Priming the *maître d'* is the accepted way of getting on to an interesting table. Much cachet still attaches to the Captain's Table on a cruise ship and a £10 tip will often get a passenger on it.

The 'split tip', half in advance and half at the end, gets the best service. The food on good ships is excellent. To get the best, an advance of £15 to the *maître d'*, with a word about wanting some suggestions off the menu, is an investment that pays off in terms of cuisine.

Waiters have their own well-tested ways of maximizing their tips. A classic is to offer a 'favoured' passenger boeuf Wellington. This is the biggest and hence the most glamorous dish that, in league with the chefs, they can provide. They will offer it to the most likely looking passengers – the man with a gold coin ring or a digital watch on a gold strap, the woman with the most jewellery, or by nationality in descending order of the big cruise tippers, first Germans, then Venezuelans, Americans, South Africans, Italians, British, Canadians and Scandinavians. Belgians and French are considered mean. The Swiss rarely tip at all.*

The chef is on a 50:50 split. The waiters make sure that other promising looking passengers see the boeuf Wellington as it is brought in. Anything that can be flambéed is

---

* A seventeenth-century Swiss traveller wrote of his visit to a Bedfordshire inn: 'As I was going away, the waiter who had served me with so very ill a grace, placed himself on the stairs and said "Pray remember the waiter." I gave him three halfpence, on which he saluted me with a hearty oath. At the door stood the cross maid, who also accosted me with "Pray remember the chambermaid." "Yes, yes," said I. "I shall long remember your most ill-mannered behaviour and shameful incivility." She gave a contemptuous loud horse-laugh.' That was in 1684. The Swiss have little changed. Nor, the Swiss might argue, have manners in English hotels.

popular for the same reason. Not only does the waiter or *maître d'* have to perform at the table – thus ensuring a good tip – but he can make sure that the flames shoot high enough for the surrounding tables to see it and scent it.

'Crêpes Suzette is the ultimate because the ladies go for it too, where they might find our boeuf Wellington as tough as the noble Lord's boot. If Table A gets Crêpes Suzette, then everyone else is going to feel a schmuck until they get it too,' says a *maître d'* with a British line.

Food standards on the best lines are as good as anything ashore. On the bad lines, the food can be a hazard to health. The worst are the Russian and Yugoslav lines, followed by the Greek ships and Italian. The British have their problems as well. Passengers normally only realize this when they get ill: they do not check out a glamorous cruise ship in advance, as they might a restaurant on dry land. On some cruises, in the late 1970s, more than two thirds of passengers came down with chronic diarrhoea and mild typhoid.

There was a severe outbreak of gastro-enteritis and typhoid aboard the Russian cruise ship *Litva* in 1978. On an Atlantic cruise from London, many passengers flew home rather than complete the trip. 'Bread from breakfast was still on the table, stony hard, in the evening. Bacon and sausages were served raw. Everyone was disgusted at the food,' said a passenger. The Master was fined for breaking health regulations.

Food poisoning affected more than 100 passengers and crew on the Chandris Line's *Ellinis*. The P & O's *Oriana* has failed to pass US health regulations. The cruise liner *Jupiter*, owned by Epirotiki Line, was on a British-based cruise in 1977 when 300 out of her 350 passengers got diarrhoea, two had typhoid and three paratyphoid.

A report in 1976 by the Sea and Air Inspectors Group of the Environmental Officers' Association said that many cruise ships were 'filthy'. Several ships were infested with cockroaches and mice. Others had filthy galleys and state-rooms, with piles of refuse left lying in kitchens. Dr J. W.

Carter, a ship's doctor, has said that cruises are 'comparable to army assault courses rather than restful holidays at sea'. Any ship with more than twelve passengers aboard must carry a ship's doctor, which is why most cargo-liners take less than that.

The age and background of a ship give some clues to hygiene. Although some old ships are adequately rebuilt, like the Costa Line's fifty-eight-year old *Franca C*, many 'modernizations' consist of a new funnel and a coat of paint. The cruise ship *Galaxy Queen* started life as *HMS Fencer*, a 15,000 ton aircraft carrier. Generally speaking, the more modern a boat, the more likely it is to be clean (and the bigger a boat, the more comfortable since it is likely to be turbine rather than diesel-powered, with less vibration). But no ship is cleaner than the cleanest cook. It is the line that matters.

Skimming the bingo

Separating cruise passengers from their money is a developed art. An observant passenger would notice that one person is usually last back on board before the ship sails from the ports on its route. It is the cruise director. He will often be wearing a hat, because he is not too keen on being recognized. And, almost invariably, he will be carrying paper bags. These will be full of cash and curios. They represent the commission he has just been paid on the goods the passengers have bought ashore. He is late back because he wants to be sure he gets his take on all the passengers' purchases, including last minute ones.

Some sort of rake-off is perhaps inevitable for pursers and cruise directors. How else do you get a bright executive to work at sea nine months a year on low pay? A cruise director sums up his craft: 'You have to be knowledgeable. Sincere. Likeable, or able to hide your distaste. You need organizational ability and the gift of the gab. No self-doubt about the rubbish you are saying. The success of a cruise is largely in your hands. These are qualities that deserve reward.'

The rewards used to be blatantly obvious a few years back. Cruise directors would stand outside the liquor shops on the duty free Caribbean island of St Thomas, counting off their passengers with those click-click machines they use for head counts on aircraft. They were paid by the head.

Things are a little more subtle now, but just as profitable. Pursers and cruise directors average $300 to $500 a week in salary from the lines. Few make less that $1,000 a week cash on top and some make more than $2,000 a week 'reward money'. To get it, they do everything from skimming the bingo to selling off their own curios at 'passenger' auctions. It is common for the shipowners to know that the director is skimming twenty-five per cent off the bingo and horse racing, and splitting it 50:50 with the purser, although on some Greek ships the pursers freeze out the cruise directors.

'If you see the purser or his assistant in their white jackets handling the bingo and horses, when there is plenty else for them to do, then you can be sure that they are just taking care of their action,' says a director. 'And you can be pretty sure that the Captain will be taking his cut from the purser.'

Horse races are the easiest to skim. These are normally six-horse races, either on film or with mechanical models. The cruise director's greatest assest is that he can fix the odds. Say 390 passengers each put £1 on a race. The cruise director can simply pay out £340 by manipulating the odds. Unless a passenger is taking notes and adds up the numbers of people placing bets and the amount staked, nobody will be any the wiser. Since the cruise director will whip up a hurly burly to give excitement to the betting, it is effectively impossible for the passengers to know what has been staked.

A take of £50 out of £390 is, in practice, modest. Twenty-five per cent, £95 or so, is a more normal skim. And, unless a passenger actually manages to add up the number of bets placed on each race, and ignore the embarrassment of calling the crew's honesty into question, the skimming is all but foolproof.

Not only the cruise director makes on the horse racing. So do more humble members of the crew, as long as they have a passenger they can persuade to act for them. With filmed races, the crew get to recognize each race. They know which horse is going to win. Tip off a passenger, and there are guaranteed winnings to be shared.

Most tickets are in colour sequences, a particular colour for a particular horse. By keeping discarded tickets until that sequence comes round again a cruise or so later, a crew member can slip the ticket to a passenger and again split the winnings.

Bingo is not so easy to cream. 'With horse racing, nobody knows how much has been wagered. But if there's an audience of 100 for Bingo with a £1 stake, and you say the pot is worth £70, someone is going to ask what's going on,' says a former cruise director. 'You have to hold fire for the Snowball Bingo.'

A percentage of earlier pots is kept back for the big 'Snowball' Bingo. Interest gets higher and when Snowball time comes, with its big pot, people will buy three or four cards. 'The amount of money no longer corresponds to the number in the audience, and bingo, you're in business. You may not have seen the cruise director around for the first games. But you can be damn sure he'll be there at Snowball time.'

A powerful cruise director will dictate when the bingo takes place, normally before a big show to maximize the number of players. There is a favourite time for 'Snowballing', as skimming the big bingo games is called. It is after the Captain's farewell cocktail party at around 7 p.m. and before the traditional farewell show at 8.30 p.m. The director pushes the Snowball over the ship's PA system. 'You tell them how big the pot is standing, £300, £400. People think you're doing them a favour by blasting on about it. Actually, you're helping yourself,' says the director. Over the length of a cruise, the director makes £500 to £600 from bingo.

The 'Elephant Sale' is another source of income. Towards the end of a cruise, passengers realize they have acquired a lot of junk they do not need: swimsuits, straw hats, curios like carved elephants (hence the name). So the cruise director announces an 'Elephant Sale' to auction it off.

'It can be one of the funniest things on a cruise,' says a director. 'You wait until everybody is in a good mood and feeling generous, and then you palm off your own junk. You stock up with bracelets, candlestoppers, carvings, your own junk that you have picked up cheap or as commission from shops ashore. You need to control things, though. If the audience spend too much on things that actually belong to other passengers, they have less spending capacity for yours. So you feed your junk in carefully.'

One director who specialized in carvings had a set ploy to reduce interest in carvings belonging to passengers, thus increasing the value of his own. He would hold up a passenger's carving and say: 'This is fine, as long as you don't have anything wood in your house.' He would then play a tape recording of crunching sounds – 'death watch beetle, I'm afraid.'

Directors collect free perfume and eau de cologne samples in the French ports in the West Indies, Guadeloupe and Martinique. They tape them together into sets of three – 'the nicer the boxes and the smaller the bottles the better'. Then they announce during the Elephant Sale: 'To help the boys get a little bit of coffee money, we're selling these perfumes off at a real modest price, just £5 a set.' These are always best sellers.

A good Elephant Sale will net a director £100 with another £75 to be distributed among his staff.

Commission from ashore

'One or two lines don't allow any crap with Elephant Sales, mileage, bingo. No messing around on board,' says a director. 'But there's always plenty to be had on shore.'

Indeed there is. Most passengers spend upwards of £100 ashore on duty free liquor and perfume, jewellery and souvenirs, hire cars and sightseeing tours. A hard-working director will take a cut on all of this.

Take liquor in the Caribbean island of St Thomas. There used to be just one liquor store, Christie's, that controlled the trade. Now there are five competing for custom. The liquor merchants pay a director 75p for each box of four bottles bought by a passenger off his ship, plus a £75 incentive for each hundred boxes.

It is relatively simple for a cruise director to get his passengers to buy at the store that is giving him the best rate. Before the ship arrives, he gives them a sales talk. 'You want them all to hear. You could lose a lot on a sunny day, so you make sure you blast the talk through the loudspeakers to the pool. You always blend your sales pitch with information the passengers have got to have, like Customs regulations. That way, they have to listen to you,' says a director.

'Then you give them a good blend of shopping tips and history: who discovered the country and all that junk, and where to shop. How do you get them into one store, when all they want is liquor, and the liquor is exactly the same? You put in a gimmick. You say that Store A will give the passenger a free replacement bottle if it breaks any time on the cruise, even going back through Customs at the end. You say that Store A has given you fifty bottles for this very purpose.

'Only Store A does this. You tell them that Store B is just as fast and cheap, though they might not find it quite so elegant, they may not be looked after quite so well, and of course they get no replacement bottles. There isn't much doubt which one they will go to.'

The director also introduces curios during his lectures.

One always toys with a £1.50 musical key ring during his talk, playing it through the microphone and tossing it into the audience after making sure he has put the shop's name over. At 30p a throw in commission, with more than 700 passengers as potential customers, the money adds up. Others sell their own 'parchment-look' maps to each port, antique-looking charts that they buy wholesale from the publishers.

Jewellery is big business on cruises. Jewels of the World, a store in San Juan, is one of the world's largest jewellers and caters largely for passengers off cruise ships. Free buses run from the pier and there are free rum drinks as well. The cruise directors earn substantial commissions, making San Juan one of their favourite ports. If a cruise director wishes to dissuade his passengers from spending money in a port where his commission is small or unsatisfactory, it is easy to put them off. He simply says in his pre-arrival lecture in the Caribbean: 'This is a really beautiful island but they are not too keen on Americans and Europeans in the town. It's quite natural, given their history. But it's a real pity.'

Night tours to shows ashore commonly pay £1 a head, with £40 incentive money for every seventy-five heads. Since most passengers will be game for a run ashore at least once in a cruise, a director on a boat with 700 passengers stands to clear over £1,000 from this. Neither are the passengers being cheated. The pina colada may be pre-mixed in great plastic containers the afternoon before the cruise ships sail in, and the floor show may be a bit wooden, but night tours often offer excellent value and the director earns his commission.

The cruise director is not the only person to line his pocket, although he is the one that the American Internal Revenue Service is currently most interested in. The IRS has complained that directors working on popular cruise ships from Florida, which attract many British and European passengers, are declaring incomes of less than £10,000 a year. This may be what the cruise lines are paying them, says the IRS, but their salaries are multiplied many times by commissions and perks that have become part of the job. Some directors clear £75,000 a year and several are thought to be making more than £125,000 a year.

Given the turnover in passenger spending, this is not surprising. Over and above the actual cost of the cruise, the passengers on a typical cruise in the Mediterranean or West Indies will shell out £150 each on drink, tours, duty free, curios, clothes, bingo and so forth. On a 700-berth ship, that comes to £105,000 every ten days.

'The disposal of that sort of cash attracts some very skilful operators,' says a director. 'It should be obvious to the passengers, but it isn't. They think a cruise is a holiday, not a business. To them a business is a serious thing – an office, a bank, a shop, a shoe factory. But a cruise ship is business, and very big business indeed.'*

* Worldwide cruising was estimated by *Newsweek* as a $20 billion a year market in 1979. Boosted by TV programmes like 'The Love Boat' sea-soap opera in the US, it was expected to grow by a further thirty-five per cent by 1983. The capital requirement is very considerable. With custom-built cruise liners costing £40 million each, Royal Caribbean Lines recently cut their *Song of Norway* in half, put another piece in the middle, and joined it all up again. This increased passenger capacity from 880 to 1,196 and, at a cost of £7 million, saved several times that on a new vessel.
The running costs are also high. The 67,000 ton *QE2* was costing £65,000 a *day* to keep at sea in 1979. A quarter of this went on fuel, a quarter on labour costs, and the rest on port charges, running expenses, advertising, administration at sea and ashore, and depreciation.
John Lancaster Smith of the Passenger Shipping Association reckons that there is a 2½ to 5 per cent profit to be made on an initial investment, and that the investment will only show a profit after twenty years, compared with four to five years for a hotel. Maybe, in a bad year, but if it were generally true no investor would enthuse on cruise lines.

Who's looking for what?

The passengers on cruise liners are renowned for snobbishness. The word 'posh' itself came from liners, being the shipping clerk's abbreviation for Port Out Starboard Home on reservations to British India. Before air conditioning, it was cooler to have a portside cabin sailing South through the Red Sea, and starboard on the return.

'The worst are the ones who go nautical,' says a British steward. 'The man gets himself a yachting cap from Captain Watts and shouts *bon voyage* to the people on the quay instead of the other way round. The woman gets a watch coat from Simpsons and a Hermes scarf with anchors all over it, and they keep talking about eight bells and where the wind's coming from. Of course, the wind always comes from the front on a moving liner, unless its blowing a gale, in which case your nautical types are the first to take to their beds. Or bunks as they call them.

'They are great ones for the Captain's Table. Frankly, most cruise Captains are crushing bores. If they weren't when they started, a few months playing Neptune at the head of the table makes them that way. But people will spend a small fortune bribing their way on to the table. They aren't there for the conversation, you must understand. They are there to be seen.'

It seems that people's social sensibilities are heightened at sea.

'They snap their fingers at you, and shout, and complain at the slightest thing,' says the steward. 'They do things they wouldn't dare do ashore. Mousy little men demand clean tablecloths and spinsters send back their boiled eggs. People on cruise ships behave as if the Empire was at its height and they were at the height of the Empire.

'If they pulled half those stunts in a restaurant ashore, you'd throttle them. But we don't mind because they tip as if the sun hadn't set on the Empire. Bad tippers are rare amongst cruise regulars. The word would soon get round and anyway they all suffer from *folie de grandeur* to some extent and it comes out in tips.'

It comes out in other ways, too, to the delight of the jewel thieves who ply the cruising lanes.

'Most lines still have a ball with black tie and evening dress, and the ladies bring all their rocks with them,' says a security man.

'I had one woman, who came equipped with two diamond rings, a diamond and amethyst necklace, a white and gold sapphire bracelet, a watch set in diamonds and sapphires, an emerald brooch, pearl and diamond earrings. She looked like a jeweller's front window.

'Thieves get plenty of opportunity, because people drink a lot on cruises and get high and make mistakes like going into the wrong cabin or not locking the doors. This lady forgot to lock her cabin when she went to sleep. Actually, I think she was hoping someone might join her – she was a divorcee. She lost the lot. I searched the whole ship, but its hopelessly easy to hide the stuff.'

Sexual sensibilities also appear to be heightened on cruises. Shipboard romance is an old tradition but there are now Swinging Singles cruises from the US that rely on nothing else. This is despite the fact that women are more attracted to cruising and so single men are often in short supply. 'When the ship goes down, they should put the single men in the lifeboat ahead of the women and children,' said a woman on a Caribbean liner. 'They are the most valuable people aboard.'

The junior officers on a European ship operating from Port Everglades put in an official complaint to the line: 'We are regarded as sexual objects by the women passengers. This attitude is encouraged by company advertising, which has photographs of officers dancing and drinking with passengers, and by the senior officers who consider it part of our duty to fraternize with passengers.'

There is, the line chairman remarked as he altered the advertising, junior officers being in short supply, no pleasing everyone on a cruise.

There may be no point in complaining either. The captain of a ship has the right to put passengers ashore if he believes that their behaviour is affecting the proper running of his vessel. Thus Captain Santorini of the Italian world cruise ship *Galileo Galilei* put a British couple and a German ashore at a Mexican port.

He claimed that the passengers had paraded with banners through the ship's ballroom and dining room and campaigned for a mass hunger strike. The liner had been delayed through taking an injured seaman off another ship and the Captain had been forced to cancel a stop in Acapulco. The passengers had objected to this.

The Captain said: 'There was trouble and I forced them to leave. A captain sometimes has to make harsh decisions for the sake of his ship and his other passengers.' The passengers were put ashore from a barge in Acapulco.

Cruising is very much a question of what the passenger pays for. For fifty thousand dollars, he gets an outer stateroom, amidships, on a high deck on a 120-day world trip that circles the globe from Southampton to Southampton via Lisbon, the Canaries, St Helena, Cape Town, Mauritius, Ceylon, Penang, Bali, Darwen, Fiji, Samoa, Easter Island, Panama, Port-au-Prince, Miami and Bermuda. The menu changes every day and the cabaret every week.

Or, for $149, he could have gone cruising to nowhere on the 723-foot liner *America* from New York. Launched in 1939, the *America* was the flagship of the United States Line, the New World's largest, fastest and best liner. When the jets took over the Transatlantic market, the *America* was sold to a Greek line for world cruising.* The Greeks sold her on to Venture Cruise Lines Inc., who refurbished her. In the summer of 1978, 960 passengers turned up on a pier at New York City for a 'Cruise to Nowhere', a non-stop party on a floating hotel.

Venture Cruise advertised it as 'complete and luxurious as any cruise costing two or three times the price'. The *America* had bars, a disco and a casino with blackjack, roulette and slot machines. It had two pools, as well,

* *Time* magazine, 17 July 1976.

though one was empty for two days and the other could only be reached by climbing over piles of garbage and dirty laundry.

She was also overbooked. There were 150 more passengers than available cabins, and some of the cabins were half-painted, and the beds and showers were already occupied by cockroaches. The less fortunate passengers bunked down on deck next to their luggage.

The passengers began to mutiny as the stately liner left harbour. They drew up a petition to the state attorney general requesting refunds. One of the ship's owners, Leonard Lansburgh, tried to pacify them with free drinks. A drunk took a swing at a woman purser who screamed into the PA system: 'Emergency! Emergency!' The crew, including Greeks, Jamaicans and Koreans, had difficulty in speaking to each other as well as to the passengers. But eventually they hit on a common protest, too. The *maître d'* fled from his dining room, saying: 'I'm going to stay and get killed by people?'

Then the passengers set up a chant: 'We want to get off! Give us rooms, or let us off!' The ship reversed course and was back in New York less than twelve hours after leaving. More than 250 passengers jumped ship and were taken by tugboat to Staten Island.

The remaining 700 passengers resumed the cruise. When the ship put back into New York after two days at sea, she was met by public health officials who awarded her only thirty-two points out of a possible hundred. The ship's management promised to make repairs and the inspectors let her sail again that afternoon.

Filled with 641 new passengers bound for Nova Scotia, the *America* ran into a storm off New England. The twenty-foot waves and fifty m.p.h. winds forced the captain to cancel a call at Martha's Vineyard. Fresh water pipes broke and portholes began to leak. The plumbing went wrong as hundreds of passengers abandoned ship and flew home.

'At least,' said one, 'it did not sink.'

4 THE DAMAGE

Morals

Tourists bring great prosperity to resorts and ships. The take in Benidorm reaches £83,000 an hour, almost round the clock, at the height of the season. The investment in a Swiss ski resort like Gstaad exceeds £700 million. Tourism tripled foreign exchange earnings in the Seychelles over four years. The *Song of America*, launched for Royal Caribbean Cruise Lines in 1981, with a passenger lounge encircling the funnel 130 feet above the sea, is costing her owners £68 million but can generate £10 million a year profit. A minor fire on the 69,000 ton *Norway*, converted from the liner *France* at a cost of £45 million, cost £500,000 for one short cancelled cruise. That is what the 1,900 passengers would have spent in her 460-foot shopping street, fourteen bars and discos, and elsewhere.

But tourists bring more than cash, cheques and credit cards with them. They bring pollution. Partly, it is physical. Their sewage and sun-tan oil gives a sheen to the sea. Their feet wear out the stone floors of ancient buildings. Their cars jam old streets and exhaust fumes hang in smog.

They also bring moral pollution. Sex is a significant part of world tourism. In Ibiza, it is controlled by Argentine Italians. In Mexico, it is an item of national importance. Sixty per cent of Mexico's tourist revenue is raised in the red light districts of Tijuana, Cuidad Juarez, Nuevo Laredo and Matamoros. These areas, 'boys towns' to Americans and 'zones of tolerance' to Mexicans, are worth $1.8 billion a year.

Japanese sex tours to Thailand bring in $500 million a year. In London, it is reckoned that prostitutes and 'hostesses' take £1 million a week in foreign currency during the summer.

Mrs Roseta Simpson was convicted of organizing prostitution in London in 1981. Her girls, masseuses with names like Kitten, Angel, Mandy and Lady Jane, were equipped with bleepers so that they could attend clients round the clock. Amongst the leading hotels visited by the Simpson girls were the Savoy, the Churchill, the Waldorf, the Britannia and the Hyde Park.

A fair part of the income of Nevada comes from prostitution. It is the only State with legal brothels, and has thirty-five of them. The two big brothels for the tourists, Sheri's Ranch and Betty's Coyote Springs Ranch, are sixty miles north-east of Las Vegas. They are considerable places. Sheri's has a swimming pool, a long bar, billiard room and a private aircraft landing strip conveniently equipped for night landings. An air taxi service flies direct from Las Vegas's McCarren Field to the 4,000 foot runway.

So respectable is prostitution in Nevada that a group of British banks put up $25 million to buy the Mustang Ranch near Reno. This claims to be 'the world's largest whorehouse', employing sixty girls on a shift system: 'business is so quick that they don't have a chance to sit down, unless they lie down'. It rates four stars in the Bachelor's Guide to the Brothels of Nevada, itself claimed to be the 'Michelin of sex tours'.

This may do little harm in the empty desert air of Nevada, but tourism has had a corrosive effect elsewhere. Local resentment of Japanese tours has reached dangerous levels in Thailand and South Korea, with violent demonstrations against 'prostitution tourism'. The Filippino Foreign Ministry had to formally ask Tokyo to stop Japanese package tours to the Philippines 'for the purpose of sexual relations'.

The Philippines show that a country which offers a hint of promiscuity to the first pioneer tourists will swiftly be swamped and corrupted as the word gets round.

Spartacus is an international travel guide for male homosexuals. The editor, John D. Stamford, wrote an editorial called 'The Rape of the Third World' in the 1980 edition. He said that the original welcome of the Filippinos for homosexuals had been so poisoned by easy money, drugs and broken promises of a new life in the West for willing boys, that a dozen homosexual visitors had been murdered in the previous year. Others were mugged and robbed.

The guide now warns visitors to keep clear of the Philippines unless they are discreet.

Like many tourist stampedes, this one started after a glowing description appeared in a guide book. Stamford had described the Philippines in the 1976 edition of *Spartacus* as a place 'where friendly, smiling, happy people gave of themselves for the pleasure of their foreign guests'.

A flood of homosexuals arrived from Germany, Japan, France, Scandinavia and America. Pimps and a 'call-boy' system became established, and there was drug trafficking in discos and bars. Stamford said: 'I have personally seen some twenty delightful young men reduced to derelict wrecks of humanity within one year by selfish tourists.

'Little wonder that those fortunate enough to live in the few unspoiled gay paradises in the world write to *Spartacus* pleading with us to keep the tourists away.'

Agencies in Holland and Germany run sex tours to Thailand, and Kuoni run 'Night Life Specials' from Britain. The Kuoni tour goes to the Grace Hotel in Bangkok. 'The hotel has the reputation as the "hottest place in town",' says Kuoni. 'Especially the back coffee shop which seems to be the meeting place of all the night owls in town. The problem is that we never know whether people go for their reasonably priced meals or the friendly company! Definitely *not* for families – but bachelors seem to rate it very highly.'

The left luggage area of Bangkok airport is crowded with golf clubs left by Japanese tourists who have told their wives that they are on golfing holidays. The Tourist Organization of Thailand has asked Western travel agents to stop selling sex tours, in order to clean up Bangkok's image.

With close on three million foreign tourists a year, many of whom have come mainly to visit the bars and massage parlours, the business is too big to stop. Tourism is Thailand's third highest source of foreign exchange. Police and politicians are involved. The body is big business in Bangkok: one massage parlour, the Mona Lisa, cost £2 million to build. It has 216 private rooms and 400 masseuses, and claims to be the largest in the world.

Tourist behaviour can outrage the locals. The Greek Government was obliged to assign armed policemen to protect West German nudists at the Salandi Beach resort in the south of the country. Led by Greek Orthodox bishops, a thousand villagers were determined to destroy Greece's first official nudist camp.

They held prayer meetings on the beach, chanting 'Nudism is the invention of the Devil' and 'Take your orgies back to Germany.' The National Tourist Office backed the nudists and accused the bishops of being 'religious fanatics.' It seems a curious attack to make on a bishop, but the tourist office backed it up with police patrols.*

The Greeks have also been upset by homosexual holidays. Stay Gay Holidays describes a stay in Mykonos: 'Let us help you reach your holiday climax. At night a mixture of the outrageous prevails. Nudist beaches famed for their permissiveness. Enjoy the bazooki in gay abandon. Small boy souvenir sellers whose innocent smiles hide a remarkable talent for bargaining. Muscular attendants compete to massage customers.'

It is inevitable that sex tours like these should involve disease. STD, subscriber trunk dialling to some, is sexually

---

* Nude bathing was commonplace at the beginning of Queen Victoria's reign. As late as 1874, another man of the cloth, the Wiltshire vicar Francis Kilvert, wrote angrily: 'At Shanklin, Isle of Wight, one has to adopt the detestable habit of bathing in drawers. If ladies don't like to see men naked, why don't they keep away from the sight?' He noted that he could still bathe in the buff at Weston-super-Mare.

transmitted diseases to doctors. It has been intimately connected with travel since Columbus' crew contracted
syphilis in the New World. It has been estimated that forty
per cent of syphilis in Britain is caught abroad. Forty per
cent of the men involved are in 'itinerant occupations',
airline pilots, sailors, lorry drivers and salesmen.* A substantial percentage of the remainder are tourists.

Holiday resorts have a high incidence of venereal disease
because of the promiscuity that flourishes in them.

'You get three million people a year passing through a
place like Benidorm,' says a venereologist. 'A fair number
of those sleep with each other. You need only a small
reservoir of infection at the beginning of the season and,
by its end, the growth has been tremendous. It has been
exported back to Britain, Sweden, half Europe.'

The Seychelles are notorious. 'The venereal disease rate
in the Seychelles is high,' wrote Douglas Alexander.† 'It
has been described as rampant and ferocious, which is not
surprising in view of the promiscuity. One observer has
quoted a medical services report as saying that nearly every
male in the islands averages four to five gonorrhea infections in a lifetime.'

Hawaii has not recovered from Captain Cook. 'No other
women I ever met were less reserved with no other view
than to make a rapid surrender of their persons,' wrote
the circumnavigator. They were rewarded with STD. In
Bangkok, a medical survey of massage parlours revealed
that more than half the girls had gonorrhoea. Other areas

---

* I am obliged to admit that foreign correspondents should be
  included in this category. An incident with a colleague
  produced the neatest description of STD I have heard. We
  were in Danang, in the then South Vietnam, when he came
  down with a bug transmitted to him some days earlier in the
  Happy Hotel in Bangkok. Seeking aid on a Red Cross
  hospital ship, he was turned away by a nurse. 'We are here
  to deal with war wounded,' she said. 'Not pleasure
  wounded.'
† *Holiday in the Seychelles.*

considered by experts to be of 'exceptional risk' include the Philippines, Singapore, Malaysia, Thailand, Fiji, Madagascar, Nigeria, Ghana, Gambia, Haiti, the Dominican Republic, Jamaica, Grenada, Nicaragua, Guatemala, Guyana, Colombia and north east Brazil.

Mutated strains of the disease are immune to many drugs. An epidemic in Liverpool in 1976 took two years before it was brought under control. 'It came from West Africa, but it is traditional for a seaport to have outbreaks like this,' says a venereologist. 'We know who and what we are dealing with and we can warn seamen and prostitutes. It's when you get holidaymakers going back to a suburb that there are problems. There was a nasty strain from Morocco that created havoc around Dorking.'

Traditional pleasure grounds can cope with mass tourism. There is little that could shock Capri. 'A place where new perversions are daily discovered, and new words coined to describe them,' wrote Tacitus, and that was under the Romans. Modern Paris has difficulty in establishing the gender of its prostitutes. A police check in the Bois de Boulogne in 1980 failed to reveal a woman. The belles were all beaux, the majority of them Brazilian transvestites. Though this has led to a number of bad jokes about the boys from Brazil and gay Paree, it will not undermine the French Republic.

Other countries are more at risk. Areas of Fiji where tourists go are subject to prostitution and petty crime that is not found elsewhere. The murder rate in Hawaii has increased fivefold in the past ten years, with tourists often the victims. Large areas of beachfront are no longer considered safe.*

* Tourism fell in 1980 for the first time since 1949, after growing at an average of fifteen per cent a year for a decade and a half. Crime was largely to blame. Murders were up sixty-seven per cent in two years, robberies up twenty-three

Tourists are blamed for destroying the Hawaiians' sense of themselves. 'It's ridiculous,' says a former President of the Hawaiian Visitors Bureau. 'Since real cultural events do not always take place on schedule, we invented pseudo-events for the tour operators who must have a Dance of the Vestal Virgins precisely at 10 a.m. every Wednesday.'

David Babeau, a game warden, spoke of new dishonesty amongst men in the Serengeti game reserve. 'The heart of the problem is the poverty of my African brothers and the terrible wealth of the tourists,' he said. 'African drivers are constantly being tipped by tourists to break the rules of our park and to chase the animals. What can you do? Our people are poor, it is easy for them to be corrupted.'

It is possible for locals to get their own back on tourists. Warriors of the Okapa tribe discovered they had not won the singing and dancing section of a tourist-inspired arts festival in New Guinea. They responded by firing their bows into the audience of tourists.

More generally, the locals submit to it. The first sign of mass tourism is usually a decline in local agriculture. The farmers become property speculators. In the Swiss Alpine village of Kippel, land prices went up from $200 to $186,000 an acre when a new ski resort was started. The labourers work in the building industry, their wives as chambermaids in the hotels. A survey of the Spanish resort of Fuenterratia showed that the traditional idea of *vecindad*, the importance of being good neighbours, withered as the resort grew.

---

per cent, and purse snatches and muggings more than doubled.

The Honolulu prosecuting attorney, Charles Marsland, said: 'What was once the paradise of the Pacific is now a jungle prowled by thieves, pimps, prostitutes, robbers, rapists and murderers.' Over-rapid growth had left areas like Kalakaua Avenue, the once handsome promenade on the ocean at Waikiki, littered with stalls selling Filippino woodcarvings, paper leis and aloha shirts.

The town had enjoyed social cohesion. It split it into two classes, in open conflict. The farmers, shopkeepers and particularly lawyers prospered. Some farmers, who had barely scratched a living before, became dollar millionaires overnight as their land was built on. The lawyers, who fixed the contracts with the hotel developers over drinks in the town's new country club, moved up from small minis to Mercedes.

The small fishermen, labourers and farmers with land in the wrong place found themselves squeezed by inflation. They were strangers in their own town, priced out and driven out by swarms of foreigners.* There was a sharp decline in moral standards.

Many people do things on holiday they would not dream of at home. A British couple arrested for making love in the main street of a Greek village at mid-day were asked if they would do the same thing back in Lancashire. 'Good heavens, no,' they said. 'What do you think we are?'

The divorce rate amongst the big colony of British expatriates on the Costa del Sol in Spain is four times higher than in Britain itself. A travel company, Earthwatch Research Expedition, report that the four men who went on one trip to China all came back and got divorced.† On another trip to China, two members of a group, both in their sixties, got married.

---

* Particularly the British, by no means everyone's favourite tourists. British holidaymakers came bottom of a poll amongst girls in Majorca. They classified the British as poor, loud, smelling of beer, badly dressed, and interested only in drinking and football. The Germans came top, as well-dressed, attentive and generous, giving them a romantic evening out with dinner and wine. Also well placed were all Scandinavians and the French and Belgians.
† History does not relate what happened on this trip. It might have been Chinese houris who were responsible. 'We do not have prostitutes in China,' said the Vice-President. 'But we do have girls who make love for money.'

Some countries are virtually run by tourism and this has led to resentment, rioting and attacks on tourists. During a conference on Caribbean tourism, a Hilton manager said: 'Without Hilton, most of these islands would just dry up and blow away.' Curt Strand, who succeeded Conrad Hilton in charge of the giant group, claimed that most developing countries would prefer a Hilton to hospitals, schools or sewers. 'They say we are newly independent and we want some of it now. It'll take 100 years before we have enough sewers.'

Edgar Rice Burroughs Inc., which was interested in setting up Tarzan villages in Africa, considered taking over an African country. 'We've been talking to the Rothschild bank in Paris,' said a company spokesman.* 'There are a number of very small African countries which have absolutely nothing. No economy, no nothing and the thought is to merchandise the whole country. Take it over. Change the name and just take the resort ideas on a national scale, so the entire country is run as a beautiful place.'

Air Tarzan was to be formed, and planes with zebra-striped tails would jet tourists to a 'land of beautiful girls in the various Lost, Hidden and Forbidden Cities, the barely obtainable Utopia once only reached by arduous swinging through the jungle'.

The company had Gambia in mind. Fortunately, perhaps, for Gambia British Caledonian got there before Edgar Rice Burroughs Inc. Nevertheless, Gambia became tourist dominated and this lay behind an attempted coup in 1981.

You're welcome. Really?

This dependence can lead to a deep and sometimes active loathing of tourists. Resentment has flared into physical attacks in St Croix, Jamaica, the Philippines, Curacao, Trinidad and Tobago, Guyana and France. In Bermuda,

* *Down the programmed rabbit-hole*, by Anthony Haden-Guest.

a population of 53,000 residents plays host to more than half a million tourists a year. Sometimes it no longer feels like playing host, and troops have been airlifted to Hamilton to protect tourists and hotels from rioters.

Frustration is fed by the poor working hours and career prospects in the tourist industry. Two-thirds of the labour force must work at weekends or at night. Sixty-four per cent of experienced staff do not get beyond the level of 'operative'. Seventy-two per cent of those surveyed by the British Hotel and Catering Industry Training Board had not improved their status since they first joined the industry.

The density of tourists also causes trouble in places like the Caribbean island of St Martin, where the 7,000 people who live on the Dutch half of the island 'welcome' 130,000 visitors a year. The densest area, in terms of tourist nights per square mile per year, is Monaco at 1,040,000. Five other places have more than 100,000 tourist nights a year to the square mile: London with 140,000, and Bermuda, Singapore, Malta and Hong Kong.*

Governments have had to launch campaigns to prevent their citizens from verbally or physically attacking these sources of foreign exchange. The Jamaicans had a 'Be Nice Programme'. Tanzania attempted to persuade visitors to call waiters 'Rafiki' or 'friend' instead of 'boy'.

The English have become increasingly hostile to tourists as their numbers grow. In 1977, London was full to overflowing, with tourists camped out in church halls and tents.† There was a native backlash. Locals bought badges

---

* If you really want to get away from it all, try Mali. This African country has the least tourist density on record, at 0.05 of a tourist night in each square mile a year.

† London first went beyond saturation point on 18 July 1977. Even the hotel touts, who normally flourish in such circumstances, could not cope. Said one at Victoria Station: 'The demand is so great it is like being the last man in a machine gun post watching millions of Chinese coming over the hills.'

that read: 'I am not a tourist'. It was suggested that patriots should deliberately give strangers the wrong instructions, if asked directions in the street, so as 'to frighten them off'.* Playwright John Osborne referred to tourists as 'offal'. A group of Kensington residents started a 'Friends of Calais' society, the idea being that foreigners should be encouraged to stay there.

A retired Colonel living off Knightsbridge complained: 'It's worse than an invasion. The place is crawling with thieving Arabs, stinking rich Americans and noisy Germans.' He was roundly applauded at a local meeting, although he had it wrong. Arabs figure well down the shoplifting lists, which are headed by Iranians and Colombians. The Americans spend less than Germans, Scandinavians and Gulf Arabs. The tourists most likely to be in trouble with the police for rowdiness are Australians.

Tourists were accused of coming to Britain for free medicine and health treatment, for unemployment benefit, to have babies on the Health Service and to get free repatriation home. Cases of all these have, in fact, run at less than 2,000 a year out of a total of thirteen million tourists.

The Burlington Arcade Association now gives gold medals with a wide red ribbon to people who are particularly polite to foreign tourists. A member of the Association tours London incognito talking to taxi drivers, hotel doormen, and so on. The head beadle at the Burlington Arcade itself, Robert Bruce, said: 'Eastern Mediterranean people tend to be the most difficult. I mean Greece, Spain and towards Suez. They cannot explain themselves. They think we should be able to read their minds.' Well, have a better sense of geography, perhaps.

Few Governments try to cut down tourist numbers. The

---

* Nothing new in this. Thackeray, in 1860, got so tired with being asked what statues were whom in London that he resorted to saying that they were all of the Duke of Wellington.

industry is worth too much, even in poor countries where a large slice of the income goes straight out of the country to pay for the imports that keep the tourist happy. A University of West Indies study showed that thirty-nine per cent of Jamaica's earnings from tourism were immediately spent abroad on food and drink, foreign hotel developers' profits and overseas airlines.

The West Germans paid out $21 billion on foreign holidays in 1980, the Americans $10 billion, the British $6.5 billion, the French $6 billion, the Japanese $4.5 billion. Incoming tourists spent £4.1 billion in Britain in 1981, worth more to the country than cars, trucks, ships and aircraft combined.

Spain gets over a third of her foreign exchange from tourism. A Soviet statistician worked out that the average profit from one foreign (capitalist) tourist in Russia was equal to nine tons of coal or oil or two tons of grain.

Yet the tensions created by an industry, which has altered the physical appearance and behaviour of countries more than any other since the war, are immense. The Madrid paper *ABC* says that tourists are 'turning Spain into an alien land where foreign languages are spoken, foreign currency is accepted and Spaniards are discriminated against'. In Jamaica, armed guards patrol hotels to protect the tourist.* In the US Virgin Islands, where one-third of the workforce is dependent on tourism and which registered one of the highest crime rates in the Caribbean

* The Society of American Travel Writers finds Britain to be the friendliest country towards tourists, followed by Canada, Australia, Japan and Mexico. The most hostile countries are France, Russia, Iran and Jamaica.

    That is not the same as the British being the friendliest tourists. They are still thought to suffer from the advice given to them in a 1908 tourist handbook: 'His Majesty the King Emperor is personified in every Englishman abroad and orders must be given in a suitably imperious tone. Shout if necessary. God is your authority.'

in 1980, a senator talks of the 'senseless killing, raping and humiliation of mostly white tourists'.

A heavy price has been paid by the resorts for their expansion.

The haven of parasites

The resorts extract a toll in return.

Every great tourist attraction has a service street behind it. This is where those who feed off the tourists relax and eat, the hustlers, waiters, whores and souvenir men. There are wholesalers for the goods sold to the tourists a few yards away, the postcards, key rings, hamburgers and rolls of film. There are short-time hotels where the hookers take their customers, and all-night clubs where the chefs and barmen meet after the tourists have packed it in for the night.

The rue de Ponthieu services the Champs Elysées in Paris. It runs parallel to Europe's busiest tourist avenue, immediately behind the imposing facade of airline offices, cinemas, boutiques and pavement cafés. The other side of the Champs Elysées is a respectable void of embassies, banks and fashion houses. Only the few girls plying their trade in the hotels of the Avenue George V remind one of the stewpots close by.

It is an upstairs, downstairs world. The punters are out front on the Champs Elysées, spending, trying to cut a figure. The hustlers are in the rue de Ponthieu, scheming, drinking, before making their sorties to attend on the tourists.

Each passage that connects the two has its own scene: horoscopes in one, secondhand records and tapes in another, whores in a third. So does each café. Snatch thieves go to one. They sell the cameras, leather jackets and shopping bags they have just lifted from the Champs Elysées. Pickpockets frequent another. They emerge from the Metro underground station, from the buses and off the street and sort out their hauls. They keep the cash from the handbags and wallets, but sell the traveller's cheques, credit cards and passports on to the specialists who regularly visit the cafe.

The beggars congregate in one bar. It is by no means the cheapest on the street. The beggars make up a big group, and the most successful of them can hope for £15,000 a year. Champagne is the common way of celebrating a good day's business.

The king of the beggars is a Spaniard who is listed on his papers as Manuel Araujo, but who is known on the street as Shakespeare. He rises at 11.30 each morning and takes a stroll down the Champs Elysées looking for day-old copies of the *New York Times* and the London *Times* in the wastebins. When he has found them, he takes them to a cleaner's shop in the rue de Ponthieu and carefully irons them so that they look fresh and new.

He could well afford to buy them. 'I don't as a matter of principle,' he says. 'A beggar is a very economical person. He hates waste. So I scour the dustbins for my newspapers. Every morning, I get a little glow of satisfaction when I find them.

'If I don't find either of them, which is rare, but which can happen, then I don't work that day.'

He breakfasts on orange juice, coffee and croissant in the cafe and chats to his fellow beggars about the state of business. He is particularly interested to check how many English-speaking tourists there are in town, for they are his stock-in-trade.

He starts work at two. 'People never give you money before they've got some lunch and a couple of beers in them. So there's no point in being an early bird,' he says. His working clothes are a replica of Charlie Chaplin's tramp. He has boots, which he keeps highly polished – 'it proves I am a decent, respectable man at heart'. His black serge trousers are too short for him, and are kept up by a pair of red braces. 'That makes me look vulnerable, like a kid. The women like that.' He wears a black jacket, a cast-off from a hotel receptionist down the street, and a bowler hat. 'You don't see many bowlers these days,' he says. 'So that's my way of getting attention.' The effect is helped by a large black beard and granny glasses, which make him look a good fifteen years older than thirty-eight.

'It's important to look old in this game. People won't give money to a young guy. They think he ought to have a job, or get unemployment benefit from the State, not from them. With an old man, they feel sorry.'

His pitch is simple. He attracts a tourist's attention by quoting Shakespeare. It is always the funeral speech from Julius Caesar, 'Friends, Romans, Countrymen . . .' That is because it is the only bit of Shakespeare he knows, though nobody would guess that from the learned passion he puts into it. It was taught to him by an Englishman who was down on his luck in Barcelona. 'I rewarded him with a bowl of soup. It's the best bargain I've ever struck. I've lived off it ever since.'

When he has finished the funeral speech, he makes his pitch. 'Sir,' he says in heavily accented English. 'I am a foreigner, but there are only two things that give me pleasure and both are in the English language. Shakespeare and *The Times*.'

He produces his copy of yesterday's *Times* from under his arm. He selects the New York or the London paper according to his guess of his subject's nationality.

He looks at the paper fondly. 'There is only one trouble with *The Times*. Shakespeare is free. It is in my head and in my soul. But *The Times* costs money. Would you loan me the money so I can get today's edition? Just seven francs, and it would give me such pleasure.'

'Shakespeare's' knowledge of English is very patchy and he is not capable of reading a paragraph in either the New York or London *Times*. But he speaks the phrases he knows with an air of great authority and education. More often than not, he gets his 65p. In a good hour, when the tourists are out in strength, he can make fifteen successful pitches.

'You get the wise guys who say, sure, I'll get you a

Times. And they go to the newspaper kiosk next to where I stand and buy me one. That's no problem, because the vendor gives me five francs when I take it back.'

Another beggar, Manfred Schwager, works a similar version of this, the telephone ploy. 'I say it's my mother's birthday back in Germany, and I always phone her, but today I haven't enough money. You get people who say yes, I'll pay for the phone call but I'm going to dial it for you and listen. You wouldn't think you'd get people who go to that amount of bother, but you do.

'Well, that's fine by me, because Mum likes the odd phone call from time to time.'

Schwager says that clothes are an important part of begging. 'First, your own clothes matter. You mustn't be dirty. People don't like that. You've got to be threadbare but obviously striving to keep up appearances.

'And other people's clothes matter. You can tell a lot from that, whether someone is worth approaching or not. If it's a really sharp dresser, natty, up to the minute, forget it. People like that are garbage, all they are is clothes. People who are obviously in their best clothes, dressed up for a big evening out, are very difficult. They are having a big occasion, and they hadn't planned a beggar entering into things.

'If someone is wearing good everyday clothes, someone who always dresses well, then the odds are that he'll give. Couples are always best. The women want to be impressed. The poor can be very generous. They've been there before.

'As the beggar, you've got to come on strong. After all, you're at work — and the public is not.'

Schwager reckons the Champs Elysées to be Europe's most profitable street at present. 'Leicester Square used to get the money askers, the gangsters and the bitches, the prostitutes, from the Continent. Not any more. There's no money there.

'The Ramblas in Barcelona is still good and the Damrak in Amsterdam. I've worked all these places. And Germany is fine, the Ku-dam in Berlin, the Kaiserstrasse in Frankfurt, the Konigsallee in Dusseldorf. But a telephone man can't operate in his own country. I mean, the most I could get to phone my poor old Mum from inside Germany would be 20p or so. But from Paris I can easily ask 75p.'

Buskers are another group. Most of them are English. They meet in a café that does a brisk trade in businessmen's lunches but that changes character, and staff, in the evenings. They divide out their takings, amongst shouts of: 'Oi, you've been dipping', an accusation of taking money out of the hat.

They play the theatre and cinema queues and pavement cafés. Colin Miller has been on the road from Shepherd's Bush for twelve years. He has married and has two children and a comfortable flat off the rue de Ponthieu. He has his own trio, two on guitars and one on a washtub base. 'It's fairly steady in a place like the Champs Elysées. You reckon to take around £80 a night. The resorts are the biggest gambles. I opened up the ski resorts. Nobody had thought of busking ski queues before. It was genius. All skiers seem to do is queue for lifts so the market potential was fantastic.

'We went to Zermatt. I felt a real fool, I can tell you, hanging around in my Texan boots and Afghan woolly and prayer beads halfway up the Gornergrat. But the money rolled in. We took £350 one day. And then the word went round. Every busker who'd hung up his mouth organ for the winter came out of hibernation and made for Switzerland.

'You couldn't have heard an avalanche for all the skiffle-boards and accordions and guitars. The skiers got fed up and so did the authorities. They booted us all out.'

Busking is an international business. Miller has flown his trio out to Fremantle in Australia when he heard of rich pickings on the grapevine. He had a good three months before the competition grew too numerous. He played Miami Beach during the boom summer for British tourists of 1980. 'They liked a little bit of home,' he says.

'Tourists aren't always the best customers. I've done Greek islands where we didn't make a penny off the tourists, but the locals kept us going. You've got to work pretty hard with tourists, and give them what they want. With locals, you can just be yourself.'

Across the street from the buskers, the con men and tricksters and midnight car park men have their cafe. There are Italian breakdown specialists. They drive out to the Porte de l'Italie, where the German, British and Belgian tourists come through Paris on their way back from the sun. The con men flag down a car with tourist plates.

They explain that they have broken down before they can make it into the centre of Paris, where a bank draft awaits them. But luckily they represent a big firm of leather manufacturers from Milan. The car boot is full of highest quality leather jackets, one of which is bound to fit the tourist.

'I'll give it away to you for £45. No, I can get a tow into town for £35. You can have it for that.'

On close examination, the jacket turns out to be made of imitation leather.

A Spaniard named José Fernandez runs the midnight car park at the bottom of the rue de Ponthieu, where it meets the elegant Avenue Matignon and its fashionable night clubs. After the traffic wardens have gone off duty, he claims that he has the parking concession. He explains to foreigners that his charges are 50p an hour. Since this is said before they park, the drivers have no excuse for not paying up when they return.

Some specialize in the counterfeit currency ploy. They accost tourists as they walk away from a restaurant. Producing 'identification' as plainclothes detectives, they claim that the bill was paid with forged notes. As the tourists protest, the detectives become sympathetic. They agree that the tourists must have accepted the notes in good faith. They point out that, if the affair goes to superintendent level, the couple are likely to be stuck in town for some time whilst the facts are established.

The best thing will be for the couple to pay again, in foreign currency. The detectives will undertake to return the money to the restaurant and nothing more will be said. Indeed, they will write out an 'official' receipt for the amount. They pay twenty per cent of the haul to the waiter who tipped them off about a potentially gullible couple, and who gave them details of the bill.

At its smart end, the rue de Ponthieu boasts a Regines, one of the world's better nightclub chains. Other clubs are pick-up bars, with striptease thrown in. The Japanese are reckoned the best customers now that the Iranians have had their revolution and have run short of money. A small group of men who call themselves 'agents' exists to lure them into the clubs. Commissions paid are high, and when the Japanese are out in force the agents become the street's high spenders.

'If the Japanese come in numbers, four or more, then you can get them. They'll go for the chicks,' says an agent. 'On their own, they are too shy, too nervous. And you've got to make sure that there are Oriental chicks in the club. They won't go for them. They'll prefer the blacks and white girls. But it makes them feel at home. It leads them on.'

The girls on the Champs Elysées itself, who will bring their customers back to the hotels of assignation in the rue de Ponthieu, will start at 500 francs. But there are other girls, the hasbeens, the chambermaids after pocket money, who service the denizens of the street itself for fifty francs.

The Champs Elysées girls often work in pairs. Whilst the customer is busy with one girl, the other picks his pockets.

From their own cafés, bars and sections of pavement, the groups join up in an all night club after 2 a.m. when the tourists have gone. The club is still full at six a.m. when the dustcarts and the more honest of the street's citizens begin to turn up: the bakers, the glaziers to mend windows broken in brawls the night before, the electricians to mend the ovens and roasters in the fast-food joints, the security men to empty the pinball machines, the chemist to dispense cures for hangovers and other social diseases acquired during the night.

And the priest settles down to listen to the confessions.

The need for confessionals is not restricted to Paris.

'The more tourists there are, the more rubbish drifts in to prey on them,' says Commander C. V. Hewett, head of the Metropolitan Police C Division in London. 'There are more hotel thieves, more prostitutes, more clip-joints, more dips, more bent photographers, more unlicensed traders selling hot dogs that make you sick, more rogues, more gamers.'

The biggest group are the pickpockets. The 'wires', the top international pickpockets, follow the tourist season. They arrive in London in early spring, moving on to Paris and Switzerland until the end of June. They make day trips to fashionable sporting events with their rich crowds: the Monaco Grand Prix, the Derby, Wimbledon.

They work the wealthy resorts in July and August, Marbella, St Tropez, Nice, and then fly to the US. Starting in New York in September, they cover the Autumn race meetings in New England and the Christmas shoppers on the East Coast. Their winter season opens in Miami in the New Year. February sees many of them in Rio for Carnival, before they return to Europe via the Caribbean.

They are predominantly Latin American, Colombian and Brazilian, with Spaniards and Italians. Bob Arno is a Swedish expert on pickpocketing who makes a good living demonstrating the art in cabaret shows. He reckons that a top wire can make $2,000 a day when he is working. Few risk more than three days at a time in the same location.

Arno estimates that there are only twenty-five or so top 'wires', staying in the best hotels, well-dressed and prosperous. Some are graduates of training schools in Bogota paying off their tuition by remitting a proportion of their earnings to the organizers in the Colombian capital. They are taught to be 'pit workers', skilful enough to steal from inside pockets.

A good wire runs his own 'jug troup' which specializes in working outside banks. An 'inside man' loitering in the bank indicates how much cash has been drawn by the 'score', the intended victim, and which pocket it is in. The wire, also known as the pit worker or 'cannon', bumps against the victim in the street. He steals the 'leather', the wallet, as he apologizes. He immediately passes it to a 'runner', who makes off with it, so that the wire is clean if he is caught.

A third arm is used for the sophisticated 'Paris dip'. An artificial arm, with a plastic hand holding a newspaper, fills one jacket sleeve. This leaves the wire with one real arm free to dip into the handbag of a woman asked for directions. Wires who steal only from women are known as 'moll bussers'.

The 'Caracas bump' is simple. Two urchins bend down suddenly in front of the score, as the third lifts his wallet as he bumps into them. 'You may think kids are sweet and innocent,' says Arno. 'Don't. There may not be any more "kidsmen" like Fagin in London training children to steal. There are plenty in South America and the Far East. Italy has child gangs run by adults.'

Pickpockets in the beach resorts use attractive, scantily dressed girls as their 'fluffs' or partners. The pickpocket gets to work as the fluff distracts or 'suckers' the victim's attention.

Those who use artificial devices are looked down on in the trade, but are none the less effective. 'The Arabs have no real dexterity,' says Arno. 'But they do some beautiful razor work on hip pockets in bars.' Acid sprays cut round pockets in Japan and Europe. 'Coners' are at the cheap end of the market, dropping ice cream on their victims' feet to get an easy psychological and physical advantage whilst apologetically mopping it up.

'There are obvious defences against pickpockets,' says Arno. 'Never put a wallet in a hip pocket. Fold your arms in a crowd. Be wary of people with raincoats or jackets over their arms. A wire uses a coat to cover the pocket he is working on.

'But the traveller's best defence is to have pace in his face. If he looks alert and aggressive, the pickpocket will leave well alone.'

There are thieves who do not go to the bother of picking pockets. In Japan, children at railway stations use sharp hooks on their fingers to cut watch and camera straps. In Hong Kong, wet fingers relieve tourists of rings as they are helped aboard sampans and junks. The wetness lubricates the ring as it is slid off.

In Italy, pillion riders on motorbikes snatch handbags and cases, using the speed of the machine to break the owner's grip. Another Italian job is to slash the tyres of a tourist's car as it stops at traffic lights. The owner gets out to change the tyre, and his car is robbed as he does this.

Thus Londoners Chris and Jane Durham were robbed of £200 and their credit cards after their hire car suffered a slow puncture on an autostrada outside Milan. 'We had been very careful, it being Italy,' says Jane Durham. 'But we were relaxed in the car. How can you get robbed on a motorway? So we both got out to look at the puncture, and a boy just swooped out of nowhere, grabbed our money off the back seat, jumped into a waiting car and was gone. Apparently we must have been given a slow puncture at a toll booth. When we dropped the car back with Avis we were warned of the puncture robbers, but it was a bit late by then.'

Three Italians were imprisoned for anaesthetizing and then robbing passengers on the Rome to Paris Palatine express. They sprayed an anaesthetic through the ventilators of sleeping compartments. With the passengers soundly asleep, they were able to rifle luggage and clothes at leisure.

Hotels are most at risk from thieves, often amongst their own guests. Merritt Kanner, senior vice-president of Rocky

Pomerance Associates, a Miami-based security consultancy agency, outlined one hotel manager's day: 'At 8 a.m. thieves stole a $2,000 statue from the lobby. At 10 a.m. a guest reported a stolen car. At 3 p.m. thieves came back again and stole a piano.

'One guest in three takes something, towels, glasses, ashtrays. Other guests carry out furniture, tear off wallpaper, rip off pictures that are bolted to the wall.' Kanner estimates that the industry in America loses $1 billion a year through theft, with another $30 million lost through unpaid bills and stolen credit cards and traveller's cheques.

Taxi drivers also prey on tourists. They rig their meters or break them in many countries. They dream up exchange rates, take detours and levy illegal extras for luggage.

Taxi touts are a problem even in London, which, together with Hong Kong and Singapore, has one of the few excellent taxi services of any major tourist destination.

Bill Offner of the Stork Room says that he loses customers because he refuses to pay exorbitant commissions to taxi drivers. Offner claims that drivers come into his club and warn him: 'If you don't pay, I don't drop my passengers.' The driver then goes back to his cab, says the club is full and suggests another where he will get his commission.

'I got into a cab one night and asked to be taken to the Stork Room,' says Offner. 'My own club. The driver said, "Didn't you know, Sir, it's closed." '

Police are worried by the 'club touts', the minority of drivers who make their living out of commissions. They cruise what the cab officer at Scotland Yard calls the 'Royal Circle', Great Windmill Street, Brewer Street, Rupert Street and Shaftesbury Avenue in Soho.

They look for likely groups of men, and refuse to stop for other fares. The rewards are high, with £6 commissions paid by many clubs, and earnings of up to £300 a night.

The practice is most widespread in Bangkok, and is growing in the Mediterranean countries. It has finally arrived in Britain, notably in London. One hotel advertises: 'Commission paid on guest's departure, £1.25 per person per night.' A more generous West End club pays £4 commission per head and invites drivers to 'meet the lovely door ladies'.

The manager of a Bayswater hotel, told the magazine *Private Eye*: 'Most hotels pay commission. We run a taxi club. The drivers get £3 for everyone they bring here. We give each driver a club card which we mark up, and after every ten visits he also gets a bottle of Scotch.'

It can be better than that for the driver. A luxury restaurant gives taxi drivers a voucher for every two people taken to the restaurant. For the first fifteen vouchers collected, the driver gets a free dinner for two. When they collect 150 vouchers, they get an additional prize of a weekend for two in Paris.

Those who do not pay commission can get in trouble. When a club owner ran an advertisement stating that he did not pay commissions drivers threatened to put him out of business. He reckoned that his business dropped by thirty per cent as a result.

Trash

A young Thai-Chinese sculptor called Yas has a flair for ancient Khmer art. His work is so good that Thailand's leading art historian, Piriya Krairiksh, a consultant to the National Museum, has trouble distinguishing it from the eleventh-century originals. The tourists, who pay eleventh-century prices for it, cannot judge any difference.

An ex-rock group bass guitarist, Yas worked in an antique store in Bangkok making the bases for fakes brought in by dealers. 'I thought I could make better ones,' he said.* So he could. He uses sandstone blocks from north east Thailand, which is similar to the stone found at the Angkor temples where the original sculptors worked. He breaks the head from the body, as happens to many of the old sculptures, heats the stone with a hair dryer and then buries it in earth for a fortnight to give the effect of age.

He puts his signature, discreetly, on his best works. 'If they are perfect, I always sign my name somewhere,' he says with an artist's pride. 'That way I know which are mine.' He then sells them to dealers for $1,000 or so. The dealers pass the copies on to refugees, who say they are loot from a crumbling Cambodian temple. Tourists pay up to $15,000 for their 'ancient' sculptures.

The Thais are also active in the cheaper end of the tourist-based faking industry. They make English horse brasses, selling them to British tourist shops and antique stalls for 80p each. Marked 'genuine olde English', the brasses are sold from £7 each.

There are not enough genuine curios to satisfy the demand. Were all the horse brasses sold in England the real thing, no horse could have moved for the weight of

* *Time*, 7 December 1981.

metal it was carrying. A faking industry has grown up to ensure supply. The Rumanians have made 'Persian' carpets since the Ayatollah-troubled Iranians became unable to do so themselves. Italian woodcarvers make the wooden elephants, fly switches and 'tribal' masks that the Masai in Kenya are reluctant to continue making.

Anatolian ceramic pieces flood on to the tourist market in Turkey. They are excellent figures, beautifully made, and they reflect great credit on the artist-forgers who churn them out in distant Pisa, Italy. Egyptian dealers import scarabs by the boxful from Italy. A scarab with crude hieroglyphics will be bought for a few cents and sold for a few dollars, but a carefully made fake can sell for $50 upwards.

In London, watercolourists are paid 80p a time to colour prints, which are often themselves reproductions of originals. Putting colour on a black and white print cut from an old book can add £50 to its price. Much of the tribal jewellery sold by American Indians is manufactured under contract in Hong Kong.

Street salesmen use finesse. They offer expensive but genuine Persian rugs, Spanish lace, Moroccan leatherwork or Italian carvings. They turn down every offer with disgust and turn to go. Then, looking hurt, they agree to the tourist's figure. They hand over the article, which is now a machine-made copy of the original.

There are ways to check on some of the methods used by modern fakers. Horse brasses will have an artificial green patina. The result of chemicals rather than age, it will bite deep into the metal. A fingernail or a little metal polish removes the patina from an original brass, but not from a fake.

The same holds true for many metal sculptures, the 'period' bronzes sold by antique shops in tourist centres. Little can be told from the form and style of the piece, since a genuinely period cast may have been used. However, bronze oxidizes as it ages and the patina on a fake should be resistant to a fingernail scraping the surface.

Some Italian forgers are skilful enough to reproduce the false patina used by their Renaissance forbears to make 'Roman' antiques. It is then difficult to tell age without laboratory tests.

Forgery has a long tradition in Italy. Michelangelo faked a Sleeping Cupid for Lorenzo de Medici by burying it in dung for three months. He then sold it as being 1,500 years old. Men and boys now pore over dentist's drills in the backstreets of Pisa, Florence, Rome and Naples. They make catacomb lamps, cult vessels, vases with erotic scenes. These are aged with dust and soot, and slightly damaged as if they have just been dug up from a field.

Wax figures are antiqued with a scent spray, which covers them with diluted turpentine, and dust. Bronze figures, Roman coins, Renaissance swords are buried in dung or acid-steeped earth for a few months. A microscope must then be used to detect the forced ageing, or the marks of a power drill on marble and alabaster.

Padua is the centre for fake Roman coins and medals.* Parma specializes in Renaissance silverware. It also does a lively trade in English Georgian silver.

The sales patter can indicate a fake. With exaggerated secrecy, the dealer claims that the piece has been dug up illegally or has wandered from a museum. This is common in Pompeii, where the sale of fakes may exceed £2 million a year, and in Turkey and Greece.

Print faking is widespread, particularly in Paris, Rome and London. The last is notorious for the modern hand-colouring of monochrome woodcuts, engravings and atlases. Prints were coloured immediately after printing and the paint stayed on the surface of the paper. The pulp prevented it from soaking deeper. Paper becomes porous with age and modern hand-colouring will show through

---

* This was the case 500 years ago, when the painter Marmita gave up painting and 'devoted himself entirely to the making of medals in the ancient fashion'. The Paduans are skilful at it by now.

to the back of the sheet. Prints where the paint has soaked well into the paper are suspicious.

Medieval woodcuts, county maps, views of the Tower of London and Buckingham Palace are easily reproduced. A photograph is taken and transferred to a zinc plate, which is retouched by hand to give added definition and clarity. This is then printed on paper.

Fakers add spots of mould and perforate the paper with minute holes to simulate woodworm. Aged in the sun, a £1 reproduction bought commercially can become a £50 original off the Portobello Road or on the Left Bank. The fakes can be spotted because the sun ages the paper uniformly, to the same bland colour, where old paper will have shades and highlights.

With copperplate engraving, the forger transfers an original print to a copper sheet with a sensitized coating. The result will either lack depth or, if etched deep to compensate for this, will not have delicacy of line.

The subject matter provides important clues. Generations of tourists have wanted old maps of England, scenes of St Paul's, prints of coaching inns and fox hunting, portraits of Nelson and Wellington, and anything by Hogarth and Rowlandson. In the stalls along the Left Bank, they want Notre Dame, châteaux, Louis XIV and Napoleon.

The odds of finding a genuine print of an attractive subject are remote, unless the tourist spends a considerable amount of money at a well-established and expensive dealer. 'At least half the prints of St Paul's, the old London Bridge and that sort of thing are faked in some way,' says a dealer. 'At best, it will be old paper and new ink. If tourists went for, say, Chichester Cathedral and Sir Robert Peel, they could get some excellent work at a good price.'

'But they don't. They want something that the dimmest of their friends will recognize as coming from London when they hang it on the wall. London gets twelve million visitors a year. Do they really think that our ancestors were so obsessed with St Paul's, or the French with Notre

Dame, that they left behind enough prints to keep that number of people happy?'

Antique furniture is also irresistible to tourists, and dealers like the Frenchman André Mailfert kept them happy. He took daily delivery of some ten wooden beams from old demolished houses over a twenty-two-year period. He turned them into an estimated 70,000 antiques which were sold to visitors to Orleans. More Sheraton furniture has gone to the US and Germany from Britain than Sheraton could have made in several lifetimes.

Cheaper items, easy to ship home, are most at risk: wine coolers, seamen's chests, linen-presses, card tables and butler's tables.

Wood is artificially aged in drying kilns. The rule of thumb is that a century of appearance is added to it every two days. Diluted acid, which evaporates in the kiln, helps the ageing process. The wood is scoured with a machine and stains are put on it with potassium permanganate. The piece is then stained overall with nut oil and darkened with polish. Patterns and decorations are routed out by machine and hand finished. Plastic tortoiseshell is used for inlay.

The forgers finish their antiques by hanging them in the smoke of a wood fire.

'It gives the piece a woody smell that convinces the buyer it is old,' says a British antique dealer. 'And the worm holes will be there, too. Any old piece will have some worm. All that stuff about fakers blasting their work with shotguns is nonsense. It would be easy to probe for the pellets. Augurs leave holes that are too neat and too straight.

'The fakers just stick the piece in a pile of infected logs and in a couple of months it will have as many genuine wormholes as anything two centuries old.'

The fakers often damage their work and crudely repair it. They scour it with a Brillo pad, drop candle grease on it and spill ink in the drawers.

Wear is a good indicator of a genuine piece. The feet of

chairs will have wear and cuts if they have been dragged across floors, and the stretchers across the front will be worn where people have rested their feet on them. The edges of tables will have scratches and should be rounded with use.

Anything hinged, like a butler's tray, will have heavy wear on the surfaces that hinge together. Drawers should be worn through being opened and shut, and the bottoms will often split as the wood shrinks.

'The best fakers are aware of the details,' says the dealer. 'Take mirrors. There will be less shine on the wood at the bottom than at the top, because the bottom will have been dusted more. The good faker knows that and takes it into account. He'll buy hand-wrought nails and old-looking keyholes and handles from Birmingham, where they still make them. So the buyer can still be caught out, although at least he'll get a better class of fake.'

Authorized reproductions of china and porcelain are ideal for fakers. The modern trade mark is substituted by an earlier mark, and the result is an article that is made by the firm he says made it. Only the date is different.

Profits are high. A faker could buy two dozen Wedgwood cream jugs, reproduced by the manufacturers to their original 1790 design. The reproductions cost £25 each. The base with the modern mark is taken off with a disc grinder. The surface is filled with paste. The faker paints in the manufacturer's mark for 1790. The base is still porous so that the paint soaks in, giving it the blurred look of age.

The faker polishes the surface and coats it with glaze. He cracks the glaze slightly by squeezing the jug gently in a vice. He breaks the handle and repairs it. The tourist notices this and bargains the price down to £225.

Thus £600 worth of Wedgwood reproductions, the sort that can be bought by post from advertisements, are now worth £5,400.

The results can be good enough to fool experts. A French Sèvres vase bought by the Victoria and Albert Museum transpired to have been faked from a vase produced innocently by the very British Coalport manufacturer. Sèvres is widely faked because the mark was not applied under glaze until after 1897. Painted trade marks on copies are bleached out with fluoric acid.

Glass is antiqued by roughening the exterior with acid. Metallic oxides are added to give the yellowness of age, or dyes are brushed on to produce a shimmer. Lapis lazuli ornaments may have a thin outer skin of the brilliant blue silicate stuck over stone. J. Pierpoint Morgan, one of the richest men of his age, bought two 'high Renaissance' columns of lapis lazuli as a tourist in Paris. He put them on both sides of his drawing room fire when he returned to New York. Come winter, he lit the fire and they exploded. The heat evaporated the glue that bonded the lapis lazuli to the stone.

Forgers are active in clay and ceramics, and nowhere more so than in Central and South America. Inca, Aztec and pre-Columbian utensils, gods, bowls and sacrificial vessels are made and often designed by villagers. A few days later, they are heading from the shops in the big resorts for the US and Europe in tourists' luggage.

Hong Kong and Singapore shops sell 'early Chinese' figures in clay and coloured glaze. T'ang period is a speciality, dating the figures between AD 618 and 907. These are currently being made by South Koreans working for Japanese exporters in a Tokyo suburb. Japan also has workshops that make African hand-woven textiles for sale in Nairobi, Indian ponchos for the tourist markets in Peru, and old lace for souvenir shops in Spain and the Canaries. These tend to be stiffer and heavier than the originals, and the machining shows up in the regular patterns.

Regularity is also a clue to carpets. Pakistan produces cheap but well-designed copies of Persian rugs, a market which Rumania has also entered. Forgers buy copies of original rugs and 'mercerise' them, a commercial process which gives lustre and shine. For the first few months of use, it looks as if it is made of the silk it is sold as. The

£40 Karachi rug becomes £500 worth of silken Khashan, a magic carpet indeed.

A real Oriental handmade rug has a fringe which is part of the final knots in the rug itself. A machine-made rug has a fringe which is sewn on separately. A real silk thread will glow when a match is put to it, where synthetic thread shrivels up. But few people set light to a carpet before buying it, or check the fringe.

Ivory is difficult to age, although its smooth, coloured varnish can be copied. Deer and cattle bone – and fossilized mammoth bone – are used for the elephants, chess sets, dragons and figures sold in India, Hong Kong and Europe.

Cairo is a leading centre for imported fakes. 'You can get German-made scarabs, Italian alabaster, Swedish wood-carvings, Japanese damask, Yugoslav glass paintings and Birmingham-Bedouin coffee pots,' says an archaeologist. 'And the Cairenes are experts at the just-dug-it-up-in-the-desert and the fell-off-the-back-of-a-museum ploys. But these fakes keep a lot of people and a lot of craftsmanship alive. It's not wholly bad.'

Dirt

Moral pollution has co-existed with tourism since the latter began. At Covent Garden, in 1714, a German tourist named Johann Schellendorf was tempted to part with a sum of money to a young lady in return for services which she did not render. At a crucial moment, with the tourist in a state of undress, a man claiming to be the girl's husband burst into the room. Mr Schellendorf fled but sued. Identical cases were being heard at Marlborough Street court 268 years later, to tourists picked up in the same street. In most cases little lasting harm is done to pride or pocket.

Physical pollution, dirt, is on a great scale and may inflict permanent damage. Some of it is a new phenomenon, such as the polluting of seas, and the destruction of coastlines. People talk of a coast, or a village or an area of beauty as being 'ruined'. They do not mean this literally. They mean that it has become so congested, so tatty, so full with the wrong sort of people, that they no longer want to go there. 'Ruin' may be correct, however, for some areas, in the sense that they may not recover fully from the onslaught of tourism.

The tourist does not see himself as part of this, of course, as one in the gigantic swarm of 100 million locusts who ravage the Mediterranean each year. Still less, if he sets off to a new and rapidly expanding resort like Sri Lanka, does he see himself as the advance guard, the scout for the ensuing plague. As an individual, dirt means a bad meal and a pain in the stomach.

Montezuma's Revenge, Paella Belly, or what you will

Cleanliness lags well behind Godliness in the tourist business, and as we have seen Godliness itself does not rate high. David Allamand, Westminster City Council's chief public health inspector, has said: 'I know many chic, fashionable and expensive restaurants where the kitchens are so filthy that I would not eat there if you paid me.'

Dirt goes right across the board. In the supposedly spotless US, Baltimore health commissioner John DeHoff created a gold star award for clean restaurants. He spent seven months searching for a place that would score high on clean cooking equipment, good food and the absence of vermin and dust. DeHoff then sighed: 'Nobody qualifies for the award.'

In France, eighty-one eclairs were examined in a laboratory in 1979, and forty-five, more than half, failed to meet health regulations. Of 6,171 ice creams examined in France, 2,424 were classified as of poor standard and 443 were found to be dangerous. Prosecutions in food processing in the UK went up thirteen per cent in 1980, whilst cases of food poisoning increased from 10,800 in 1977 to 15,200 in 1979. Hair, nuts and bolts, rat meat and bits of razor blade were all found in food: 'Its a true horror story,' said environmental health officer William Thomas in 1981.

Poor hygiene was not restricted to Chinese restaurants or to backstreet bistros in the Continental resorts.

The four-star Park Lane Hotel was fined £4,795 in 1977. Health officer Peter Kemp said that he had found dead cockroaches in the kitchen, and that most of the food preparation area had grease and slime deposits on the walls, floors and ceilings. To round things off, he also found flies, 'a slimy trail of slugs' and 'a rotting chicken carcass causing a strong stench'.

Perhaps this was not surprising, since the food group of the Association of Environmental Health Officers reveals that ninety per cent of London's hotels and restaurants have cockroaches or mice or both.

Fortnum and Mason, one of the best known food stores in the world, received three summonses under the Food and Drugs Act. The companies themselves claim that cleanliness is impossible in big tourist cities. A lawyer for one of them said: 'The entire Leicester Square area is infected with rodents. They are particularly fond of the Piccadilly Tube Line, probably because of the warmth. Railway staff tell me that after the station closes the platforms are full of mice, who come out of their hiding places. Then they go to the many restaurants in the area to eat, including my client's.'

Sounds like a jolly night out.

It is not just capitals that have problems. So do places like Bognor Regis. The Butlins camp at Bognor was fined £1,940 after the district council claimed that conditions were like a Victorian workhouse. Crockery and cooking equipment was found encrusted with stale food, kitchen walls had pieces of cucumber and tea bags sticking to them, extractor filters and hoods were clogged with grease and floors and walls were filthy.

A big name like Butlins is no guarantee of hygiene. The London Eating Houses Group operated seventy-four restaurants in the South of England under names like Aberdeen Steak Houses, Texas Pancake Houses, American Hamburger and Pizza Pizza. It had to give an undertaking to the Office of Fair Trading to obey hygiene regulations, or face prison sentences and an unlimited fine. The group was convicted ten times in six years.

Lack of hygiene is not confined to buildings. It can pursue the luckless traveller aboard his train. British Rail's catering subsidiary has been fined £2,000 for Inter-City offences.

Two health inspectors travelled on the Glasgow–Euston express from Carlisle to Penrith and Preston. They found that kitchen pans, shelves and the oven range were coated with grease, that the surface of the buffet sill was ingrained with dirt, that the fridges were dirty, stained and rusty and that there was no soap or towel in the washbasin. The train also had aboard 12 lbs of steak, 2¾ lbs of plaice and 1¼ lbs of tomatoes that were unfit for human consumption.

Going to sea is no escape. Less than a dozen of the 270 British and foreign ships checked in Britain's major ports in one year measured up to the minimum hygiene requirements of restaurants ashore. Standards were said to be lower on British cruise ships than on foreign ones.

Brian Goode, Southampton's principal port health inspector, said that if the galleys of two of the British ships he inspected had been kitchens in restaurants ashore, he would have closed them. Ten per cent of passenger ships are verminous.

Poor hygiene partly reflects the poor wages paid to catering staff. They are traditionally amongst the lowest paid groups in all the major tourist countries. Hotel workers in London get only sixty-seven per cent of the average wage in the capital. In France, Britain and the US, many are illegal immigrants without proper work permits, frightened of being found out, willing to work for less than the legal minimum. They may have a poor command of English or French, and no idea of their rights. In Spain and Italy, they will come from the poorest farming areas of the South.

Easy to exploit, it is understandable that some of them are not too concerned with the niceties of hygiene. Their employers do nothing to encourage them in terms of working conditions.

The heat in kitchens is intense. Some men work with just underpants under their aprons, sweating profusely. Hired by the week, and subject to instant sacking, they start by peeling potatoes, chopping onions, making salads and sweets as the floor turns into a skating rink of food, water and olive oil.

The Hotel and Catering Workers' Union published a guide to the hazards, called Risks à la Carte in 1978. Food poisoning is up by a quarter in five years. Of 300 hotel kitchens inspected in 1980 only three were found to have adequate cleaning procedures. There is an average of six restaurant fires every twenty-four hours. Kitchen employees face burns, scalds, cuts, loss of fingers, hands and eyes, and food poisoining. Cockroach infestations are growing, particularly in cafe and restaurant kitchens. At one establishment: 'It is like a whole cockroach city in the staff rooms in the basement. They tour round sometimes, like any human being. One day they will raid us.'

Tourists often charitably put down their stomach upsets to a change of climate or of cuisine. It's the heat or food they are not used to that gives them that touch of the summertime runs. Seldom is it so. It is the dirt their stomachs are unused to.

Buying hot dogs, hamburgers or ice cream from barrows has been described as 'Mexican roulette'. Not that Mexico is markedly worse than other big tourist areas in this, only that it has been more noticed to lead to the Aztec two-step.

Beach and street stalls are required by most European hygiene regulations to carry a first-aid kit, a towel, soap, a nailbrush, hot water and a washbasin. The vendor should wear a washable coverall. If he is selling sausages or hamburgers, he should have a closeable lid and he should keep the meat either above 145 degrees or below 50 degrees F. He is not allowed to smoke or to spit.

Most stalls have nothing to wash with, let alone in. The vendors often wear jeans and T-shirts. A bucketful of spare hamburgers and hot dogs is kept inside the stall to top up from during the day. The inside of the stall is hot because of the gas stove used to heat the burgers. An average temperature is an illegal 110 degrees F, neither hot nor cold enough to stop poisons breeding, but an ideal temperature for their growth.

One vendor off Oxford Street in London was seen preparing his stall. He peeled the onions in water collected from a building site, handled the meat with dirty fingers, picked up dropped rolls and urinated into the gutter.

Outside Europe, a bad stomach upset can almost be guaranteed for any visitor foolish enough to buy anything from a stall, unless it is a bottle of a well-known proprietory soft drink like Coca Cola or 7-Up.

In Turkey, flies swarm on the schwarma stalls like bees round the hive. The water for ices and lemonade in Denpasar, Bali is taken from a stream that acts as a sewer. The meat for hamburgers in Bangkok comes from dead water buffalo, well spiced to disguise the age. Fish stalls in Mombasa sell suspect fish from Taiwanese and Japanese trawlers with refrigeration problems.

Totally pure food is impossible even in a hygiene-conscious place like the US, where it is known as 'zero contamination'. The Food and Drug Administration has what it calls 'filth toleration levels'. Thus the accepted filth limit for herbs and spices is: 'Two parts rat excreta, or fifteen milligrams of other animal excreta in each of two samples from one lot; up to four whole dead insects; up to forty-nine mites of winged insects; up to five per cent seeds and roots burrowed up by insects; up to five per cent mould visible to the naked eye; from 0.5 to two per cent extraneous matter, such as stones, dirt, wire and string.'

The water supply is a prime cause of infection. Modern travellers think it naïve to ask the old question: 'Is the water safe to drink?' Often it is not, and this can apply in a country with the reputation for cleanliness of Switzerland.

As clean as a Swiss village
A healthy image is vital to the tourist trade.* An epidemic with deaths is the worst thing that can befall a resort. The Swiss are acutely aware of this: their fortunes were

* British resorts used to vie with each other for the lowest death-rate. Torquay advertised heavily its claim to be England's healthiest town in Victorian days. As the resorts began to attract the retired, their death-rate went well above the national average. Sunshine figures took their place as a source of rivalry.

founded on the healthiness of their climate and they run a substantial business in sanitoria. The Swiss will lie and twist as much as any banana republic when this image comes under threat.

The ski resort of Zermatt snuggles at the head of a valley beneath the Matterhorn. No cars are allowed to disturb the calm of its streets. Instead, there is the muffled thud of horses' hooves and the hiss of sled runners. New hotels blend in with the atmosphere of a mountain village, although displays of diamonds and high fashion show through the carefully hand-hewn wooden windows. Zermatt is no longer a poverty-ridden peasant backwater. Land can fetch £300,000 an acre. Doctors charge £500 for setting a leg. A Scotch in a disco costs £5.

Tourists are its lifeblood and at the height of one skiing season they started falling sick. The first infections were noted on 18 February, 1963. The town's water supply was not checked and the sick tourists were simply shipped home, suffering from an unspecified fever.

There were further large-scale infections between 1 and 5 March. The town's water supply was not chlorinated. No precautions were taken until 10 March, when the filter of the water supply was cleaned. When a health officer was finally called in on 11 March, he found the filter was satisfactory and, unaware of the failure to chlorinate, he declared the water safe.

Not until 14 March did the authorities drop the pretence that the sickness sweeping the resort was tummy trouble. It was typhoid. Cases were appearing at the rate of forty a day. The super-rich municipality took little action to help the visitors it lived off. It merely sent out a circular to hotels that contained 'useful commentary and information' but took no positive action. It warned hoteliers against talking to the Press and added, falsely, that 'contamination by drinking water can be ruled out'.

'That was all we had to go on,' said a hotelier. 'We received it on the morning of 15 March, the day of international ski races with over 15,000 tourists in Zermatt and every hotel packed. You would never think there was a dangerous situation from reading this harmless-looking circular and we advised clients accordingly.'

By then, so many sick had appeared that the local school was turned into a field hospital. On 17 March, the municipality implied that the typhoid had been imported from abroad and that it had not been caused by its own water supply. It said that the measures taken 'are deemed sufficient and do not justify new ones'.

There were no placards, no warnings on the radio or television, and no vaccinations.

The international ski races were not cancelled. 'There were entries from Britain, France, Germany, Italy, Finland, America, Austria and Switzerland,' said M. Cachin, head of the Zermatt tourist office. 'Zermatt was fully booked. There was no sense in cancelling since everybody was already here.'

This dismal, greedy municipality crossed its fingers and hoped it would go away – the typhoid, that is, not the tourists and their money. After more than 750 tourists had fallen prey to the disease, it was found that the source of typhoid was the town water supply. The disease was then brought under control.

Pollution

At sea

Dirt does not simply affect restaurants and fresh water. Tourist-induced pollution fouls the sea and coastlines.

'You don't swim off the Costa Brava,' an English tourist wrote to *The Times*. 'You merely go through the motions.' In the South of France, xenophobia is said to be more common than sunburn as the brochure image 'disappears under a mound of litter, foully served food and paralysed traffic. Tourists now represent little more than arrogant squatters,' part of an occupying force which deserves to be fleeced for its own stupidity.

By Italian Health Ministry standards, every one of the 6,000 registered beaches in Italy has been dangerously polluted at some time. Many have bacteria counts five times higher than the limit. In Greece, parliamentary deputy Anastassios Peponis says: 'Look at the Plaka area of Athens. It used to be something special, something Greek – real Greek cafés and restaurants, art galleries, artisans' shops. Now it is a bad imitation of Times Square and Soho with neon lights and foreign signs, people yelling at the foreigners to come into their shops. During the summer, Greeks can't bear to go there.'

The Mediterranean, the world's largest tourist area by far, is becoming a disaster area. It accounts for a third of all world tourist receipts. The growth rates are phenomenal. Tourists are up 500 per cent in Yugoslavia over the last fifteen years, 690 per cent in Tunisia, 400 per cent in Turkey. The increase in the Greek islands is almost 1,000 per cent. Mr Peponis describes the popular island of Mykonos as: 'a catastrophe, discos and restaurants, foreign boutiques, foreign music, foreigners buying land'.

In the South of France, tourists outnumber locals by thirty to one in some areas and locals have slashed car and caravan tyres in protest. Some of the beaches are clogged with 12,000 bodies to the square kilometre. At Argeles-sur-mer, the camping capital of the world, there were 220,000 campers in 1981, crowding sites with an official capacity of 35,000. At St Tropez, police said many tourists were just throwing down a blanket, stripping off and 'living in their own crap for a month'.

Tourism is too big to be restricted. But it may poison itself, for there is a limit to what the Mediterranean can take. Twenty years ago, half the visitors to Spain spent some time in the interior of the country, looking at its cities and culture. Now eighty-nine per cent of visitors never leave the coast. Many, indeed, never quit their hotel and its beach except to take the airport bus.

The Mediterranean is both small and fragile. It is less than a thirtieth the size of the Atlantic, and must deal with a coastal population of 120 million that almost doubles in the summer. Its tides are neglible. Only the narrow Straits of Gibraltar prevent it from becoming a desert, for its rivers provide less than half the water it loses through evaporation. Without the Straits, it would lose a metre a year.

It is known to French ecologists as the Great Sewer. Commander Jacques Cousteau has told the United Nations: 'If things continue as they are, only sickness-carrying bacteria will survive in the Mediterranean. The dimensions of the disaster which could face us in a few decades are difficult to grasp.' Cousteau reckons the Mediterranean's vitality has declined by thirty per cent since 1960. Lord Ritchie Calder has called it a 'delayed action epidemic bomb'.

It takes the untreated microbes, parasites, bacteria and viruses of millions. Only one in ten of the towns from Gibraltar to the Ebro in Spain has any sewage treatment plant. Nine million people live between Catalonia and the Gulf of Genoa, a figure that rises five times in summer, and eighty-five per cent of their sewage is discharged into the sea straight off the beaches. In the forty miles from Cannes to Menton there are 175 open drains discharging untreated sewage into a tideless sea.

In Italy, only 7.2 per cent of coastal towns have treatment plants. The Yugoslav coast only has one proper treatment plant for a summer population of two million. Greece treats three per cent of its sewage. The Bay of Smyrna in Turkey is hardly able to support fish because of the lack of oxygen through pollution. Viral hepatitis and typhoid affect the Lebanese coast.

The colon bacilli is a good gauge of pollution. This hardy, sewage-born bug causes the upsets holidaymakers round the Mediterranean know so well. The World Health Authority considers that water with more than 20,000 colon bacilli to the litre is 'highly polluted'.

Large swathes of the Mediterranean are suspect. Levels of over 23,000 have been recorded at le Grau-du-Roi in France, in Barcelona, Marseilles and Tel Aviv. Beirut and Trieste have 30,000 and 38,000 has been recorded in the Bay of Naples. The record of three million is held by the salt lake of Berre, just north of Marseilles airport. 'That is getting near the level where you could walk on the water,' says an observer.

High levels of streptococcus have been found in popular resorts such as Port Grimaud, Monte Carlo and Cassis. The Costa Brava is particularly badly polluted. A survey there showed that fifteen per cent of swimmers had stomach upsets compared with three per cent of non-swimmers. 'It isn't what you eat in Spain that does most of the damage,' says a doctor. 'It's what you swallow when you swim.'

Other bad areas include the French coast from Narbonne to Beziers and from Marseilles to Toulon; the Gulf of Genoa; the Tyrrhenian Sea from Naples to Palermo and the northern Adriatic. Resorts like Menton disinfect their beaches several times a week, discreetly, at dawn. The beach at Hyeres has had to be closed to swimmers.

A WHO report states baldly: 'It is no exaggeration to say that the Mediterranean, an almost closed sea, has the best and maximum conditions for contact between men and the pathogenic agents responsible for epidemic and contagious diseases.' Thus the typhoid rate in relatively clean Britain is 0.4 per 100,000. In France, it is 17.5, in Greece 43.6, in Italy 48.2 and in Spain 53.3.

Industry does not help. The great rivers, the Ebro, Rhône and Po, dump tons of mercury, lead, cadmium and arsenic into the sea from inland plants. There are 'red holes' where chemicals have killed off all marine life. One between Bandol and Cassis is more than a mile wide. The Provençal basin may be deserted by fish and closed to swimmers by the end of the century if nothing is done.

Around 350,000 tons of oil gets into the Mediterranean each year, from coastal refineries, spillages and tankers cleaning their tanks. The UN Food and Agricultural Organization says that: 'The majority of beaches and harbours in the Western Mediterranean are moderately to strongly sullied with tar.'

The worst affected beaches are round Barcelona, Tarragona, Valencia, Castellon and Cartagena in Spain; Sete, Berre-Lavera and Marseilles in France; Naples, Bari, Brindisi, Venice and the Gulf of Genoa in Italy; Rijeka, Bakar and Koper in Yugoslavia; Piraeus and Salonika in Greece; Izmit, Smyrna and Mersin in Turkey; Tartas and Baniyas in Syria; Beirut; Haifa and Ashkelon in Israel; Rizerta and La Skhira in Tunisia.

Fifteen years ago, it was very rare for a Mediterranean fish to have more than 0.5mg of mercury per kilo. Now, the International Review of Medical Oceanography reveals that seventeen sorts of fish have average levels above that. Swordfish average 2.96mg, ray 2.61, crab 1.8, rouget 1.44, tuna 1.20 and lobster 1.04. Tuna in the Mediterranean are three times as contaminated as those in the Atlantic.

Fish are starting to disappear. Catches in the Mediterranean increased steadily to 1.2 million tons a year in 1965, and have been decreasing as steadily since. Refrigerated trucks carry seafood for the tourists down from the West of Scotland and the Channel and Atlantic coasts. There are virtually no shellfish or fish off Barcelona, Marseilles, Genoa, Venice, Trieste, Split, the Kishon estuary in Israel, Beirut, Bizerta and Tunis.

An industrial report says: 'The future of Mediterranean fishing lies in the Atlantic. The boats will have to pass Gibraltar to find the fish.' What fish is left can be dangerous to eat. A quarter of the typhoid cases in Italy come from shellfish. Doctors in the South of France confirm that half the patients who see them in the summer have got sick either through eating seafood or swimming.

British beaches benefit from strong tides. They are generally cleaner than the Mediterranean, though there are plenty of black spots. Most big coastal towns pipe untreated sewage into the sea. A list published by the Coastal Anti-Pollution League in 1980 revealed that 190 out of 633 beaches suffer from sewage pollution. More than half the sewage outfalls round the coast dump crude sewage on to the beach or into shallow water.

New Brighton is reckoned to be Britain's most polluted resort. It gets Liverpool and Bootle sewage that floats down the Mersey. It is estimated that 494 million litres a day float into Liverpool Bay. The main outfall at Blackpool discharges less than 200 yards from the low water mark.

Seascale, Heysham, Crosby, Brighton-le-Sands, Waterloo and Grange-over-Sands are other beaches in the North West with serious sewage problems.

Common Market regulations set bacteriological limits for popular beaches. A survey of 330 Welsh beaches in 1978 found that 190 complied with the directive, and the Welsh water authority said that it would cost £200 million to bring the main beaches up to standard.

Blackpool has a tourist population of half a million in high summer. Yet the resort was excluded from the list of twenty-five beaches in Britain where 'swimming is traditionally practised by a number of bathers' and which will be brought up to the Eurobeach standard. It would have cost £25 million to get Blackpool included.*

Swimmers feel that the salt in the sea gets rid of contamination. They will swim in a polluted sea where they would not go near a similarly fouled lake. At a conference in Brighton in October 1980, V. J. Cabello of the American Environmental Protection Agency said that surveys of 30,000 bathers and non-bathers on beaches in New York and Boston showed that swimmers had significantly higher cases of vomiting, diarrhoea, fever and stomach ache.

The link between health and the bacteria count in the water is strong. There were eight cases per 1,000 swimmers of gastrointestinal disease among swimmers when the sea had ten enterococci per 100ml. When bacteria levels rose to 100 per 100ml, cases rose to thirty. At 1,000 bacteria per 100ml, a level often recorded in the Mediterranean, there were fifty cases of sickness for each thousand who ventured into the water.

On land

Damage is caused ashore as well as on the beaches. Tourists are literally wearing out some buildings. When Thomas à Becket lay dying on it in the twelfth-century, the floor of the nave of Canterbury Cathedral was five inches thick. The stone is now less than one inch thick, and will have to be replaced. Two million people a year go past the altar steps, and their feet have worn the stone down by an inch in the past fifteen years.

Visitors are no longer allowed to stand in the inner circle of Stonehenge. Children are forbidden to climb on the fallen stones. Visitors have worn down the grass and kicked gravel against the pillars, chiselling away the soft bluestone. More deterioration has been caused in the last few years than over the previous five thousand. Turf is being relaid and rubber walkways are replacing the gravel.

* *New Scientist* 16 July 1981.

The weight of feet is also causing serious problems in Venice, Notre Dame, the Acropolis, the Aztec pyramids, Pompeii and the Tower of London. The tiled floor of the Chapter House at Westminster Abbey is wearing out. A corps of six marshalls tries to deal with the congestion round the Royal Tombs and the Henry VII chapel. Tourists steal the toes from statues. The numbers involved are great: 2,500,000 visit the Tower each year.

Breath causes damage elsewhere. The exhalations of the crowds are giving Botticelli's 'Birth of Venus' a sort of eczema. This has also attacked the paleolithic paintings in the Lascaux caves in France, which are being closed to the public.

Athens is a notable casualty of the tourist boom. It is not simply the Acropolis that is crumbling under the impact of fumes and feet. The city itself is losing its character and becoming one of the most congested cities in the world. Only three per cent of it is covered with trees, parks or squares. Of the 700,000 cars in Greece, 400,000 are in Athens and its population is swelling as, attracted by the boom, people swarm in from the countryside.

'Athens is in the process of destruction,' says Evangelos Kouloubis, president of the Technical Chamber of Greece. 'There are serious doubts as to whether the city can survive. In a few years we may have to abandon Athens, which we are not eager to do.'

Athens now has a record twenty-seven per cent of the Greek population, and a yellow fog of fumes hanging permanently over it. The country had 400,000 tourists in 1960. Twenty years later, the figure was above six million. The receipts were running at $1.7 billion a year, making it difficult for any government to cut back on the traffic.

The big shift in population to the coast, of both the permanent and the passing through, is general round the Mediterranean. Present numbers will double to 200 million by the end of the century if the present growth is sustained. It well may be, since the average age of those living on the Mediterranean is less than twenty.

As a rule of thumb, a quarter of a coastline must remain unspoiled if the whole is to survive. There are just thirty kilometres of undeveloped coast out of 240 km left on the Côte d'Azur, which has a density of 280 people to the square kilometre compared with an average of 100 in the rest of France. In a five-year burst to 1980, twenty-two per cent of the coast of the Alpes-Maritimes was developed.

Not only the coast is being developed. So is the 'infralitoral', the area just offshore. Monaco has traditionally poured concrete into reclamation schemes to get a bit more surface area to develop. It has now built on three-quarters of its 210 acres of infralitoral. Nice has used up a quarter.

The principal is to put the maximum number of people into the closest contact with the sea. That involves wide roads, car parks that are used for two months of the year, hotels built right on the beach, digging back into the mountains. What is not built up is camped on.

The South of France now gets six million campers a summer. A parliamentary commission of inquiry predicts that this will lead to 'either a catastrophic epidemic or a flare-up of tempers'. In Herault, only a fifth of the campsites have septic tanks of any sort, and only three per cent have a month's storage capacity. No matter for the owners. The commission found that: 'There are few closures of camping sites and, in the majority of cases, a site deemed unfit for sanitary reasons will not be proclaimed such until two or three months after the inspection, which is to say after the summer season has ended.'

The string of Spanish Costas, the Brava, Dorada, Blanca, del Sol, stretches for more than 1,000 miles from the French border. Most of it is built up. It has been said that the area around Benidorm should be called the 'Costa Concrete'. Even the Spanish Ministry of Tourism is worried by the dirt, noise, cheap hotels, paella joints, marinas, villa estates, golf courses, coach parks, car hire agencies, bars, pedalo shacks, airports, souvenir stalls, stage set villages, apartment blocks. 'A barrier of cement which has broken down the line of our coast, the scenery ruined by man's own erosion,' it said.

A Minister, Sanchez Bella, went further: 'Little by little, the coastline is being covered by a cement wall threatening to deprive us of a view of the sea. The disorder in the construction of installations to receive the masses constitutes an unstable factor in the environment.

'The tourist invasion threatens the biological balance of the region. The zones affected by the degradation are losing their capacity to attract and are ceasing to be supply centres for the tourist market.'

In 1960, Plaza de Aro had 500 peasants and fishermen, three small pensions and five holiday cottages. Its summer population is now 125,000. Benidorm was a fishing village in 1958. The Puchadas family, father Alfonso and sons Antonio and Jaime, have done well out of it. They bought around five million square metres of land, including most of the Helada mountain, for 'peanuts' in 1950. 'A master plan for Benidorm? I don't believe in uniformity,' said Jaime Puchada. 'We go as high as we like so long as the plot is large enough. Eight thousand square metres, for instance, if we want to put up twenty-six storeys.'

Benidorm now can take 250,000 visitors. As late as 1975, the Benidorm fire department consisted of fire chief Fernando Quesado and seven men, three of whom were on duty at any one time. Fire aids for this huge resort ran to one engine and a Land Rover and trailer with assorted pumps.

The speed of development is extraordinary. In 1975, Larnaca in Cyprus had six hotels and a few restaurants catering mainly for locals. By 1980, at least sixty-one hotels, night clubs and restaurants had been built or were under construction.

Not only concrete has bitten into the maquis, scrub pines and forests that border the sea. So have cattle and goats, from Spain to Lebanon. There are 135 million sheep and over fifty million goats, fifteen per cent of the world total, on the Mediterranean. The problem of preserving vegetation and soil is acute enough for Tunisia and Israel to have banned goats in many areas.

The only great forests left are in Corsica and Sardinia. Of the scrubby woods along the coasts in France, Spain and Italy, an average of 90,000 acres is lost to fire every year. Some fires are caused by lightning, but most by tourists. The lack of trees and the heavy demand for water has led to high salinity in tourist areas. The water table is lowered by the constant demands of tourism, for baths, showers, swimming pools, hotel and villa lawn sprinklers, gardens. The remaining water gets salty. Malta is a classic case of a tourist country where no river flows any more, and where the water shortage is a major election issue.

Those Mediterranean winds, the mistral, bora, vordorac, chergui, sirocco, shlouq, khamsin, no longer bring the smell of the maquis, the shrubs and the mimosa, or the noise of crickets. They carry the scent of sun-tan oil and the sound of a disco.

What tourism cannot achieve, industry abets. The stone of Venice is attacked by fumes, the marble deteriorates under the attack of nitrates, sulphur and hydrocarbons. UNESCO says that the city is losing the detail of six per cent of its sculptures each year.

The oxygen content in the lagoon is half that of the rest of the Adriatic. Fish have abandoned forty-five kilometres of canals. Floods come. The Venetians abandon their ground floors and, at the rate of 3,000 a year, their city also.

Never mind. There is a plan to take down the statues of St Mark's, and to put plaster replicas in their place. That way, the tourists will keep coming to the bitter end.

Conclusion

The Club Méditerranée, asked if there is a limit to its expansion, says: 'None whatsoever.' It is probably right. Tourism is impervious to recession, natural disaster, war and politics. Record numbers of impoverished Britons escaped to the sun in the winter of 1981. A hurricane affected Haitian tourist receipts not a jot, and ski resorts in the western US survived a winter without snow. Tourists arrived in the Seychelles in 1981 within days of the emergency evacuation of others who had been caught up in a bungled invasion.

Rip-offs, strikes and hardship have little discernible effect on the industry. A Sussex woman booked a trip to France at Christmas, 1981. On waking, she discovered that her false teeth were frozen in a glass of water by her bed. The electricity supply had failed and she thawed them out over a coal fire. Her car skidded into a ditch on her way to catch the Newhaven ferry. Pulled out, she arrived in Newhaven to discover that the sailing had been cancelled.

Undaunted, she set off again the next day.

People want holidays, and they come back for more. It is where they go that will change. The Club Méditerranée's Gilbert Trigano talks of three great 'tourist lakes' into which the surrounding population of holidaymakers drains: the Mediterranean, the Caribbean and the China Sea. All are close to the industrial reservoirs of tourism, Northern Europe, North America and Japan and Australasia.

The China Sea, which Trigano pushes to include islands like Mauritius and Tahiti, is the least developed and is thus set for the most rapid expansion. As the Japanese, and Hong Kong and Singapore Chinese get the holiday habit, some China Seas Benidorms are on the cards.

Europeans will travel more beyond the Mediterranean. A non-Mediterranean, non-European destination for Britain's seven million package tourists appeared for the first time in the top ten list in 1981. North America entered at fourth, behind Spain, Greece and Italy, and ahead of France, Malta, Yugoslavia, Portugal, Austria and Tunisia.*

The industry is already one of the world's ten most important, in terms both of employment and revenue, and will become more crucial. In the US, domestic travel and tourism were worth $140 billion in 1980. The knock-on effect is considerable. The $5.5 billion spent by foreign tourists that year generated a further $17 billion in economic activity.

Some think that holidays by the year 2000 will consist of electronic sightseeing, or 'autogawping'. Without leaving home, the tourist will switch on a multi-lensed system of cameras which will back-project pictures on the four walls of the room. This will give him the impression of strolling through the Parthenon or surfing in Hawaii.

Unlikely. More, much more of the same is the most feasible order of the days to come. Crowds up the Amazon, three card tricks in China, ersatz camel stew joints in the Gobi and, above all, more Murphy.

It is Murphy who writes the Laws that always have, and may for eternity continue to dog the tourist. The man at the head of the short queue in the bureau de change is converting Guatemalan quetzals. The room with the best view is above the disco. The resort at the end of the rainbow was discovered by Fred's Fly-Drive tours last year.

That does not change.

---

* No American resort made the top ten, however. This read: Corfu, Benidorm, Magaluf on Majorca, Paris, San Antonio on Ibiza, Lloret on the Costa Brava, Palma Nova on Majorca, Salou on the Costa Dorada, Crete and Puerto de la Cruz on Tenerife.

Index

Brian Moynahan
Airport International £1.75

A new edition of the sensational book that takes the lid off the world of international air travel. How smugglers operate, and how they're caught . . . when and how luggage is pilfered . . . how air traffic control really works . . . how airports cope with a crash landing . . . which are the dangerous airports that pilots try to avoid . . . your chances of survival in an air crash.

Arthur Eperon
Encore Traveller's France £2.95

A guide to six more routes across France, for a motoring holiday without motorways. These six new routes explore areas not covered by *Traveller's France* and suggest some different ways of getting to the South. There are new maps and all the information you'll need on places to eat, drink, stay and see.

Margaret Allen
The Money Book £2.95

Work out your income properly; fill in your tax return; make the best use of your bank; buy a freezer, a house or a car; decide on an allowance for your children; understand a company annual report; make a will; get a divorce; invest in unit trusts, or buy by mail order . . . A fully revised and updated edition of this essential handbook.

'The most comprehensive book about money'
MANCHESTER EVENING NEWS

Barty Phillips
The Bargain Book £1.95

There are a thousand-and-one ways to pay less if you know where to go and how to go about it. Packed with shrewd advice and lots of addresses, from clothing to camping equipment, insurance to incense, rugmaking to records, here's the handbook for everyone who loves a bargain.

Simon Hoggart
On the House £1.50

Merry tales from the Mother of Parliaments by Westminster's wickedest columnist . . . Sir Keith Joseph pursued by a punk of dissenting views; George Brown inviting the papal nuncio to dance; the surprising video-viewing habits of Tony Benn; plus everything you always wanted to know about John Nott, the defence minister. . .the finest wit and wisdom from the celebrated *Punch* column.

'Some of his tales are incredible, but most are hilariously plausible. Even if Mr Hoggart's stories are not true, they should be'

OBSERVER

Fritz Spiegl
Dead Funny £1.50

'Beneath this sod lies another' – the long-awaited second book of Grave Humour from the ever-watchful Spiegl, who, during the years of success of his first collection of the funnier side of tombstones, *A Small Book of Grave Humour*, has continued to collect mirthful *mementos mori* and has now put together a second book which promises to be every bit as popular as the first.

Fiction

☐	**Options**	Freda Bright	£1.50p
☐	**The Thirty-nine Steps**	John Buchan	£1.50p
☐	**Secret of Blackoaks**	Ashley Carter	£1.50p
☐	**Winged Victory**	Barbara Cartland	95p
☐	**The Sittaford Mystery**	Agatha Christie	£1.00p
☐	**Dupe**	Liza Cody	£1.25p
☐	**Lovers and Gamblers**	Jackie Collins	£2.25p
☐	**Sphinx**	Robin Cook	£1.25p
☐	**Ragtime**	E. L. Doctorow	£1.50p
☐	**Rebecca**	Daphne du Maurier	£1.75p
☐	**Flashman**	George Macdonald Fraser	£1.50p
☐	**The Moneychangers**	Arthur Hailey	£1.95p
☐	**Secrets**	Unity Hall	£1.50p
☐	**Simon the Coldheart**	Georgette Heyer	95p
☐	**The Eagle Has Landed**	Jack Higgins	£1.75p
☐	**The Master Sniper**	Stephen Hunter	£1.50p
☐	**Smiley's People**	John le Carré	£1.95p
☐	**To Kill a Mockingbird**	Harper Lee	£1.75p
☐	**The Empty Hours**	Ed McBain	£1.25p
☐	**Gone with the Wind**	Margaret Mitchell	£2.95p
☐	**The Totem**	Tony Morrell	£1.25p
☐	**Platinum Logic**	Tony Parsons	£1.75p
☐	**Wilt**	Tom Sharpe	£1.50p
☐	**Rage of Angels**	Sidney Sheldon	£1.75p
☐	**The Unborn**	David Shobin	£1.50p
☐	**A Town Like Alice**	Nevile Shute	£1.75p
☐	**A Falcon Flies**	Wilbur Smith	£1.95p
☐	**The Deep Well at Noon**	Jessica Stirling	£1.95p
☐	**The Ironmaster**	Jean Stubbs	£1.75p
☐	**The Music Makers**	E. V. Thompson	£1.50p

Non-fiction

☐	**Extraterrestrial Civilizations**	Isaac Asimov	£1.50p
☐	**Pregnancy**	Gordon Bourne	£2.95p
☐	**Out of Practice**	Rob Buckman	95p
☐	**The 35mm Photographer's Handbook**	Julian Calder and John Garrett	£5.95p
☐	**Travellers' Britain**	Arthur Eperon	£2.95p
☐	**Travellers' Italy**		£2.50p
☐	**The Complete Calorie Counter**	Eileen Fowler	70p

☐	**The Diary of Anne Frank**	Anne Frank	£1.25p
☐	**Linda Goodman's Sun Signs**	Linda Goodman	£1.95p
☐	**Mountbatten**	Richard Hough	£2.50p
☐	**How to be a Gifted Parent**	David Lewis	£1.95p
☐	**Symptoms**	Sigmund Stephen Miller	£2.50p
☐	**Book of Worries**	Robert Morley	£1.50p
☐	**The Hangover Handbook**	David Outerbridge	£1.25p
☐	**The Alternative Holiday Catalogue**	edited by Harriet Peacock	£1.95p
☐	**The Pan Book of Card Games**	Hubert Phillips	£1.75p
☐	**Food for All the Family**	Magnus Pyke	£1.50p
☐	**Everything Your Doctor Would Tell You If He Had the Time**	Claire Rayner	£4.95p
☐	**Just Off for the Weekend**	John Slater	£2.50p
☐	**An Unfinished History of the World**	Hugh Thomas	£3.95p
☐	**The Third Wave**	Alvin Toffler	£1.95p
☐	**The Flier's Handbook**		£5.95p

All these books are available at your local bookshop or newsagent, or can be ordered direct from the publisher. Indicate the number of copies required and fill in the form below

6

....

Name._____
(Block letters please)

Address._____

_____

Send to Pan Books (CS Department), Cavaye Place, London SW10 9PG
Please enclose remittance to the value of the cover price plus:
35p for the first book plus 15p per copy for each additional book ordered
to a maximum charge of £1.25 to cover postage and packing
Applicable only in the UK

While every effort is made to keep prices low, it is sometimes
necessary to increase prices at short notice. Pan Books reserve
the right to show on covers and charge new retail prices which
may differ from those advertised in the text or elsewhere